You Are Your Child's First Teacher

You Are Your Child's First Teacher

Encouraging Your Child's
Natural Development
from Birth to Age Six

THIRD EDITION

Rahima Baldwin Dancy

TEN SPEED PRESS
Berkeley

All rights reserved. Published in the United States by
Ten Speed Press, an imprint of the Crown Publishing Group,
a division of Random House, Inc., New York.
www.crownpublishing.com
www.tenspeed.com

Originally published in the United States in somewhat different form by
Celestial Arts, Berkeley, CA, in 1989 and 2000.

Ten Speed Press and the Ten Speed Press colophon are registered
trademarks of Random House, Inc.

Library of Congress Cataloging in Publication
Baldwin Dancy, Rahima.
  You are your child's first teacher : encouraging your child's natural
development from birth to age six / by Rahima Baldwin Dancy. — 3rd ed.
      p. cm.
  Includes bibliographical references and index.
1. Child rearing. 2. Parenting. 3. Early childhood education—
Parent participation. I. Title.
  HQ769.B31244 2011
  649'.1—dc23
                              2012007445

ISBN: 978-1-60774-302-6
eISBN: 978-1-60774-303-3

Printed in the United States of America

Design by Chloe Rawlins

10 9 8 7 6 5 4 3

Third Edition

CONTENTS

PREFACE TO THE REVISED EDITION

What can parents do with and for their children from birth to age six that will enhance their development without having negative effects at a later age? How can we help our children develop the skills needed for life in a world that is changing at a dizzying rate? These and other questions led me to an in-depth exploration of early childhood and parenting that resulted in the writing of this book.

When I began to study Waldorf education in 1980, I was a young mother overwhelmed by family life and relieved to find that what I was learning about child development and the work of Rudolf Steiner had immediate application in my home life. I was excited to share with others what I was discovering, just as I had with birth and midwifery. I wrote the first edition of this book in 1989 to form a bridge between Steiner's insights and all those parents like myself who were looking for a coherent understanding of the developing child that resonated with their values.

After the publication of the first edition, I returned to practicing midwifery by cofounding The Birth Center in Dearborn, Michigan, where we served parents from forty-three different countries over nine years. Following that, I completed a master's degree in gerontology and organizational change while caring for my mother and mother-in-law in my home for six years. Then, in 2008, I returned to a focus on early childhood by opening Rainbow Bridge LifeWays Program in Boulder, Colorado, together with my daughter, Faith Baldwin Collins.

So, as I complete this revision, I am again immersed in the world of one- to five-year-olds and their parents—and find that most parents today are as clueless as I was when my children were young. But how could it be otherwise when the forces working against childhood have only strengthened in the intervening years? These forces include the push toward teaching academics in preschool, high-stakes testing that has eliminated self-directed play in kindergarten, the continuing isolation of mothers and a lack of support for mothering, the obesity epidemic, and young children's increasing screen time, to name but a few of them. Countering these influences is the increased ease of finding information, support, and resources for creating a home life that meets the real needs of children and parents alike. I am encouraged that since the original publication of this book, there has been a proliferation of Waldorf schools, LifeWays centers and in-home programs, books, online stores, and blogs supporting this understanding of child development and parenting.

For me, one of the unexpected pleasures of having adult children is getting their feedback about what they remember from when they were young, what worked for them, and what didn't. From this vantage point and contemplating how we all got to where we are today, I am filled anew with gratitude for having been led to the insights of Rudolf Steiner. Like many of you, I can say, "I wish I had come across them sooner," and I tell new parents, "I made every mistake in the book—that's why I wrote the book!" It is my wish for you that the insights and practical suggestions described in this book will help you develop your own conscious ethic of parenting and will enrich your personal and home lives as much as they did mine.

I feel strongly that we don't need another authority or set of rules by which to raise children, and I remind parents that Steiner himself never had any children. But if we can enlarge our understanding of child and adult development to encompass the whole human being—body, mind, emotions, and spirit—then we will be better equipped to make our own decisions based on a combination of cognitive and intuitive knowledge.

As a midwife, I came to see myself as a guardian of normal birth, providing a tremendous amount of support but intervening only as needed. This comes from a fundamental respect for women and their ability to birth normally. Now I see myself as a guardian of normal childhood, speaking up for a new common sense about raising children, one that helps children be children while enabling us to recognize our important role as parents and first teachers. Our task is to understand the child's development and to allow that new knowledge to strengthen our intuition about our own children and grandchildren. Through this we may come to see the value in the simple things we do, as well as the spiritual in even the most mundane.

Wishing you and your growing family all the blessings!

Rahima Baldwin Dancy
Boulder, Colorado, 2012

ACKNOWLEDGMENTS

Both this book and my ongoing work as a parent and early childhood educator take their greatest inspiration from the work of Rudolf Steiner, an Austrian philosopher and educator who founded the first Waldorf school in Stuttgart, Germany, in 1919. Steiner's understanding of child development and his reverence for life have enabled me to be with young children in ways that complement the natural unfolding of their capacities. I also owe a debt of gratitude to the late Werner Glas, who served for many years as codirector of the Waldorf Institute, for inspiring me to undertake the task of making the wisdom of Rudolf Steiner more accessible to parents so they can apply it in their home life.

I would also like to acknowledge the work of Burton White, founder of the Center for Parent Education in Newton, Massachusetts. While director of the Harvard Preschool Project and the Brookline Early Education Project, he observed mothers in their homes to see what parenting practices were being used on siblings of "wonderful children" rather than starting from some theoretical or laboratory base. His observations and conclusions about the first three years of life strongly support many of the principles set down by Rudolf Steiner a half century earlier. His book *The First Three Years of Life* and his New Parents as Teachers project, which was so successful in Missouri, have encouraged me in writing this book and developing ways of working with parents and children during these vital years.

The research and work of Jane Healy on developmental neuropsychology and the effects of computers on brain development and education have also been of tremendous help to me. It is wonderful to have someone completely outside the Waldorf movement provide a synopsis of the current research that ends up being so supportive of the indications of Rudolf Steiner. It is satisfying to find, so many years later, that Steiner's insights—far from being dated or anachronistic—are, in fact, on the leading edge of developmentally appropriate education. Healy's books, such as *Your Child's Growing Mind: Brain Development and Learning from Birth to Adolescence,* provide parents with the latest information on developmentally appropriate learning. She is also an authority on how to guide our children in the digital revolution, writing *Failure to Connect: How Computers Affect Our Children's Minds—for Better and Worse.*

I would like to thank my own grown children and stepchildren, Leif, Seth, Faith, and Jasmine, for leading me on this path through parenting and for providing me with so many opportunities for growth!

My husband, Agaf Dancy, also deserves hugs and kisses for his ongoing support at Rainbow Bridge and for his editorial skills. Thanks also to Katherine Czapp, Susan Howard, Wahhab Baldwin, Mary Lynn Channer, Ann Pratt, Joan Almon, Barbara Stern, and others who read and commented on the original manuscript. Special thanks also to Judith Johnstone, the late David Hinds, Lisa Westmoreland, and Lisa Regul at Celestial Arts and Ten Speed Press for their help in making and keeping this book available to parents.

CHAPTER 1

You Are Your Child's First Teacher

A UNIQUE OPPORTUNITY

The years between birth and age six are a time of growth and learning that is unparalleled in later life. The formative power of children's experiences during these years has been recognized by thinkers and educators throughout history and may seem obvious today. It certainly is to marketers, who deluge parents with ways to make their child smarter and more mature faster. Of course, all parents want what is best for their child, but how can they sort through all the theories and products on the market and make their own best decisions? Throughout this book we will consider two elements that are vital to this process: understanding child development and creating a home life that provides what your child needs while still being sustainable for you as the mother or father.

Since the 1990s, brain research has refocused attention on how critical the first three years are, not only for the development of intelligence but also for building the social and emotional foundations for everything that comes later. Viewing images of the brain reinforces what parents and psychologists have long known. For example, the special edition of *Newsweek* titled "Your Child from Birth to Three" reported, "New technology, such as positron emission tomography (PET) imaging of the brain, has provided hard data on the importance of these years. Simple activities, like cuddling and rocking a baby, stimulate growth. The long-term effect of inadequate nurturing can be devastating. In profoundly deprived children—for example, orphans left to languish in an institutional nursery—critical areas of the brain remain undeveloped."[1]

The renewed interest in the first three years has its modern roots in the 1960s and 1970s. While many researchers at that time were focusing on Head Start and other programs for at-risk children, Burton White and his associates at Harvard undertook a thirteen-year study of how children develop in the first six years of life. White states:

> In our studies we were not only impressed by what some children could achieve in the first years, but also by the fact that a child's own family seemed so obviously central to the outcome. Indeed, we came to believe that the more informal education that families provide for their children makes more of an impact on a child's total education than the formal educational system. If a family does its job well, the professional can then provide effective training. If not, there may be little a professional can do to save a child from mediocrity. This grim assessment is the direct conclusion from the findings of thousands of programs for remedial education, such as the Head Start and Follow Through projects.[2]

In the Brookline Early Education Project, White continued his studies by focusing on the question of what helps children develop into "wonderful" people. First he found "great" six-year-olds—children who were not only intelligent and well developed but also well balanced and a pleasure to be with. To try to determine what parental factors and experiences in the early years had helped make them that way, he involved their families in the study when a new baby was expected so he could observe the ways these parents interacted with their children from birth to three. White's work is especially interesting because he truly observed and learned from mothers and babies in their own homes, and he was concerned with the children's overall balance, not just their intellectual development.

White discovered that most families get their children through the first six to eight months of life reasonably well in terms of overall development. Unless a child was part of the small percentage of children who are born with a significant handicap or acquire one within the first year, there was little measurable difference in development among babies in their first eight months. But White and others have shown the period that begins at eight months and ends at three years is uniquely important in the development of a human being. White feels that perhaps not more than 10 percent of American families get their children through the ages of eight to thirty-six months as well educated and developed as they might be.[3] He also observed that "raising a bright three-year-old is much easier than raising a pleasant unspoiled three-year-old."[4]

Another educator who recognized the importance of the early years in the development of the human being was Rudolf Steiner. Steiner, a scientist and visionary as well as an educator, founded the first Waldorf school in Stuttgart, Germany, in 1919. Albert Steffen, who attended many of Steiner's lectures, reports, "Many times in his writings Dr. Steiner has shown that it is in the earliest years of childhood that things happen which are the deciding factors in later life. Whatever is done well or ill to a child in its earliest age will reappear in the grown person as faculties or failings, health or disease. On this account we should feel it our duty at the outset to gain an understanding of the whole course of life."[5]

PARENTS' DILEMMA TODAY

All parents want to do what is best for their children, to give them the best possible start in life. But what is best? Many parents feel that they ought to be doing more with their eight-month-old. But what? Or parents want to spend "quality time" with their child but find it boring to sit and do puzzles together. That we are plagued with so many questions, doubts, and guilt about how to raise our children is the result of living in a time of tremendous changes. Our culture no longer provides a strong and unified message about how children should be raised. In addition, most of us live far away from our own parents or extended family, the people who traditionally provided wisdom, help, and continuity in rearing children. The art of mothering has been replaced by the science of parenting, yet many parents have come to question the values their own parents embraced in such practices as bottle-feeding every four hours and letting the child "cry it out." And many parents today want to stay home longer with their children, reacting against their own experience of having been in child care from an early age, but they are at a loss as to what to do or wonder why being home with a young child can be so difficult.

It is appropriate that we question everything, that we bring issues to our consciousness so that we can go on to create something whole and nourishing. For example, by questioning modern practices of technological intervention in birth, we discovered that there is no such thing as "natural childbirth." All childbirth is influenced by the culture in which it takes place. It is not possible to simply do it "naturally"; rather, we have to reeducate ourselves and try to bring our minds, bodies, and feelings into a new harmony, a new integration that will allow us to birth as complete human beings, with body, mind, and emotions working together.

The same is true of parenting. It is appropriate that we question what we are doing and that we discuss our attitudes and intentions with one another—but not in front of the children! It is beneficial for children to think we know what we are doing, even if we aren't so sure ourselves. They don't need to be involved in the intricacies of adult considerations and thought processes. Rather, they need to feel that mother and father are united in what they are doing.

Being in a state of questioning or not knowing can be very beneficial, but it can also be frustrating because children don't wait until we have it all figured out! They demand constant interaction and require that we make decisions that will influence them in both the present and the future. Just as babies don't wait until the world and our lives are in perfect order before they are born, children don't wait until we are perfect parents. Indeed, we will be better off if we can give up the idea of perfection in parenting. Parenting is a process of mutual growth, during which parents and children grow on different levels through their interactions and through the elements they bring into one another's lives.

As new parents, many of us find ourselves in a real quandary about what to do in various situations. And we often find we have no way of foreseeing the effects of our actions on our children—especially the first child! Should we encourage our child to express all of his emotions and perhaps end up as a little tyrant, or yell at him and risk producing a repressed and resentful adult? Neither alternative is very inviting. Should we start teaching our nine-month-old to read or swim? If our two-year-old loves smartphone apps, does that mean they're good for her? Does our three-year-old need to be computer literate in order to get ahead in today's world? We don't seem to have any way of judging and therefore find ourselves at the mercy of whatever notion comes along. We need to listen to our own inner knowing. And we need to acquire knowledge about how the young child develops so we can make informed choices with confidence and receptivity. Most new parents have no knowledge of child development, and we haven't even been around children since we grew up. Many of us have forgotten what children are like and find ourselves on the path of parenting without any knowledge of the landscape.

CULTURAL DILEMMAS

We need to begin to see the child in a new way, one that takes into account physical, emotional, and mental development, as well as the less tangible spiritual dimensions of the human being. Once we begin to perceive the whole child and how he or she unfolds, then our choices will begin to have coherence. No longer wanting a cookbook of "how to's," we will trust our own decisions, based on our understanding of the developing child and our observation of the resultant flowering of our own children.

But we need to realize that there are many cultural forces working against seeing the child in such a way and responding with what really supports our children's development. First of all, we need to recognize that childhood is being squeezed out as a valuable phase in itself as legislators, academicians, and marketers bring academics and clothing styles to ever-younger recipients. Our society tends to regard children as little adults, so we are encouraged to reason with them as if they were grown-ups and to teach them with techniques appropriate for much older children. Despite years of studies by Piaget and neurophysiologists, educational politicians determine curricula and textbooks seemingly without any regard to the way children actually think and learn, pushing curricula earlier and earlier and teaching to the test.

Our culture also regards children—and human beings in general—as machines. People liken the human brain to a computer instead of reinforcing that the power of computers—to process data, not to think—is a product of the human brain and involves a very simple "on-off" process occurring at remarkably high speeds. The computer culture so permeates our values that popular articles on brain research refer, time and time again, to children being "hard-wired from birth" for certain capacities or tendencies.[6] We also see the mechanized model in the sphere of medicine, in which worn-out parts are replaced as they would be at the auto repair shop. And it permeates the materialistic psychology of behaviorism, in which the individuality of a person's soul and destiny are reduced to a complex series of conditioned responses.

We also need to recognize that our society values intellectual development above all else and tends to ignore other aspects of development, both for their own value and for the impact they have on learning. The No Child Left Behind act has reinforced the impetus to introduce elementary-school curriculum earlier and earlier, so that kindergartners are now doing what used to be taught in first grade. The fact that many children are now failing kindergarten while functional illiteracy continues to rise in this country has only led to starting "reading readiness" with four-year-olds in an increasing number of school systems. The fact that there is a difference between kindergartners and first graders—that is, that there is a major developmental change that goes on around age six or seven—is being ignored as parents and educators continue to "hot house" preschoolers into academic channels.

This disregard for the natural development of children has resulted in what David Elkind calls "miseducation," or practices that put preschoolers at risk and have no real benefit. His newest book, *The Power of Play*, complements his earlier titles (*The Hurried Child* and *Miseducation: Preschoolers at Risk*) in detailing the forces in our culture that are jeopardizing the healthy development of our children.

We have lost touch with natural processes in child development, convinced that we have to "do something" rather than allowing the child's own inner processes to unfold. Pediatricians try to reassure parents that each child has his own timetable for achieving milestones such as walking, but educators do not reassure parents or try to maintain the self-esteem of a child who does not learn to read until age seven or eight. Rather, he is labeled "learning disabled" in kindergarten and put into remedial classes, in which the basics are drilled to the point where he loses out on the richness and excitement of learning.

Rudolf Steiner had tremendous confidence in the natural processes of development and reminded us that "That which is asleep will awaken."[7] That doesn't mean we do nothing; rather, it means that the things we do need to be consonant with the child's own developmental stages as they unfold. It is unhealthy to skip stages or to rush the child through various phases. Although it is sometimes possible to do so, just because something can be done doesn't mean that it should be done! Again, we need an understanding of the development of the human being to be able to judge what is in harmony with a child's development and what violates it.

One of the best discussions of how children develop and ways to respond by creating a sustainable home life is *Simplicity Parenting* by Kim John Payne. Payne delivers on the promise of the subtitle ("Using the Extraordinary Power of Less to Raise Calmer, Happier, and More Secure Kids") by developing the case for simplifying children's—and one's own—life on four all-encompassing levels: environment, rhythm, schedules, and filtering out the adult world. If you don't read any other book, this is the one that will take you from early childhood through adolescence.

LACK OF SUPPORT FOR MOTHERING

Compounding the dilemmas faced by parents today is the changing nature of family life. An increasing number of women find themselves single mothers, forced to juggle one or more jobs in order to make ends meet. Many other women today enter marriage and motherhood later in life, having already completed undergraduate or graduate degrees or after having had careers for several years. Today's economic situation often requires incomes from both parents to pay high mortgages and maintain the lifestyles to which people have become accustomed—and not many people want to sacrifice financial comfort for their children.

But even without economic necessity, some women prefer to work for relatively low wages and pay for child care rather than be home day after day with their child or children. Why has it become so difficult for many women to be with children? The answer lies partly in the changing nature of our society. In rural yesteryear, life for women centered around survival tasks that took most of the day—gardening and canning, washing and ironing, baking and cooking, sewing, chopping wood, or other farm chores. The children tagged along, helping their parents as soon as they were able, but life never centered around them.

To expect a thirty-seven-year-old PhD candidate or a woman who has had an exciting career to be fulfilled spending her days in an apartment with a two-year-old is unrealistic. In the nuclear or subnuclear family, far too much energy gets focused on the child because he or she is the most interesting subject around (try getting excited about waxing the kitchen floor!), but after a time many mothers find themselves getting cabin fever. It becomes increasingly difficult, both emotionally and intellectually, to be home day after day with this child. This is due, in part, to a lack of the perceived value of mothering, but also because children's demand for attention expands to use up whatever might be available.

The wide variations in modern daily life were emphasized when I was a midwife offering home birth and delivery at an urban birth center in Dearborn, Michigan. I got to know families from all walks of life. Some were recent immigrants who were still trapped in "biology as destiny"; although these women were exhausted by having babies every year, their husbands wouldn't let them use birth control. But there were also American women who were having their sixth or seventh babies, or more. They felt that children were the jewels in their crown; not only were they having a lot of them, but they were often homeschooling them as well. They didn't feel as if they were sacrificing themselves but seemed genuinely fulfilled in their roles as wives and mothers. For the most part, these women seemed to have a strong religious faith that infused all areas of their lives. Most were Mormons, practicing Catholics, or fundamentalist Christians who were supported by a worldview that still valued these roles and activities.

Women today who lack such a coherent framework often find themselves trying to balance many conflicting forces. Many women don't want to feel as if they are sacrificing their own individuality to their marriage or their children, but they don't know how to balance this impulse with the often contradictory pulls of family and work outside the home. The women's movement in this country helped women develop their individuality and continues to fight for their right to be equal with men in the workforce. At the same time, however, it disparaged women's place within the family and neglected family issues. (This has not been the case with the women's movement in developing countries, which has helped women primarily by strengthening the family and women's and girls' positions in it.)

When I was in my early twenties, I found myself a feminist outside the main women's movement. Despite having been laughed out of a newly opened feminist bookstore in 1972 for asking for a book on pregnancy, I knew that women's reclaiming of their bodies, health, and birth had to be key feminist issues! Women slightly younger than myself, who entered into careers right after college, were told that they could "have it all." But many found they were pursuing a career and still doing the majority of the housework and tasks relating to raising the children, despite the men's movement and greater participation and support by many husbands and fathers. Over the years a realization arose that it might be healthier to "have it all sequentially," and the current generation of new mothers seems much more interested in "phasing" and demanding changes in the workplace. They not only watched what their mothers went through trying to juggle family and full-on careers, but many also experienced the stress and disappointment as children of having parents who were too busy for family life. This change is also being reflected in some areas of feminist thinking, as when Betty Freidan advocated moving beyond gender issues to issues such as parenting, day care, and quality of life for all members of the family.[8]

Although it is my own conviction that support for mothering is a feminist issue, neither present society nor the feminist movement supports stay-at-home mothers. Mothering, like so much of "women's work," is both invisible and undervalued by our culture. Strong economic forces are still working against mothering, just as they did during World War II. At that time society needed women to enter the workforce in droves. This goal was supported by the medical community's dictum that breastfeeding should be replaced with the modern, scientific practice of formula feeding. When women were not as bonded to their babies and not tied to feeding them, they were more willing to enter the factories. Similarly today, bottle-feeding, widespread use of epidural anesthesia, and other routine obstetrical practices work against maternal-infant attachment, enabling many women to blithely plan during pregnancy to return to work at six weeks postpartum (although some are shocked by the unanticipated strength of their feelings when it comes time to put their infants in full-time child care).

But sometimes returning to work is an economic necessity. Unlike countries in Europe, the United States does not offer extended paid maternity leave. In Denmark, for example, a woman is given six months of maternity leave and can apply for another six to twelve months with benefits at 70 percent of the initial six-month period. This is a far cry from the six weeks of paid or unpaid leave an American woman receives—if her job even provides that much! A survey of executives reported in *Fortune* found that concern about their children was the biggest problem facing both men and women executives—perhaps with good reason.[9]

Fortunately, our society is finally considering how it can support families by promoting quality child care and by exploring measures such as flextime and on-site child care. There aren't enough good solutions yet, but at least the questions are being asked. At the grassroots level, the rise of the Internet has resulted in a number of support groups for stay-at-home mothers (and dads). Whether a mother finds it the most wonderful thing in the world to stay home with the children, whether she is struggling to make a go of it, or whether she is trying to juggle a work schedule with a child's needs when he is sick, she needs to get more support for her mothering.

CHILDREN ARE NOT TINY ADULTS!

One key to avoiding many problems that accompany parenting today is to have an understanding of children's development. If we can understand the nature of the young child as it unfolds, we will be able to meet the child's real needs for balanced development of mind, body, and emotions.

Although children are obviously very different from grown-ups, our culture tends to treat them as privileged but miniature adults and to rush them through childhood. Many problems arise when we fail to realize how different a three-year-old is from a nine-year-old, a teenager, or an adult. That sounds obvious, but many parents take all their children to the same movie in an effort to be fair, or they reason with their five-year-old as if his ease with words ought to translate into control of his actions in the future.

The hurried-child syndrome is apparent in all spheres of activity today. It is obvious that children's bodies are not yet physically mature, yet we try to speed up babies' development with walkers and baby gymnastics. Marketing to "tweens" (eight- to twelve-year-olds) has pushed Barbie and Bratz dolls and designer jeans down to even younger children, contributing to an ever younger entry into the teenage world of makeup, clothes, and dieting.

It is also obvious that children are not the same as adults emotionally. A young child can smile through his tears when given the simplest distraction. The basically happy four-year-old stands in sharp contrast to the brooding adolescent. How does the one turn into the other? It is clear that the emotional inner life only gradually develops the complexity and texture with which we are familiar as adults. Yet many parents try to develop their children's emotions and their awareness of emotions by naming, expressing, and even practicing emotions with them. We also tend to expose young children to situations that are far too powerful for them emotionally; notice the unhappy children in the theater at the next movie you attend!

It is obvious that children do not reason as adults do. They are able to come up with amazing statements, both about how the world works and about how something they shouldn't have done managed to happen. Logical thought and problem-solving ability are slow to develop. Very young toddlers lack "object permanence" and will look for an object where they have repeatedly found it hidden rather than in the place where they have seen you put it. Children younger than age six lack the ability for what Piaget calls "concrete operational thinking." Rational thinking does not develop until age ten or eleven, as observed in Piaget's studies. So it has long been documented that the ability to reason and to think logically is a gradually unfolding power that children grow into. As adults we have forgotten what it was like to live in a nonlinear, nonsequential world. We expect to be able to reason with our children as soon as they are verbal. We reason with them about everything from their behavior and its consequences to why the sea is salty—and, indeed, some five-year-olds show a great ability to conduct such conversations with their parents, but they have learned it through imitating that type of conversation. Young children do not yet think rationally, and reason has little impact on changing their behavior.

Similarly, we offer lengthy scientific explanations as answers to children's questions when a direct experience of something similar or an image that can live and work in their imagination would be much more satisfying to them. Providing rational explanations is like giving a hungry child stones instead of bread. Elkind points out that when young children ask questions like "Why does the sun shine?" they are really asking about purpose rather than mechanics. As a result, they are much more nourished by an answer such as "To keep us warm and to make the grass and the flowers grow" than a lecture on thermodynamics.[10]

THE CHILD'S CHANGING CONSCIOUSNESS

Differences in physical, emotional, and mental capacities between children of various ages and adults are easy to recognize, though they are often ignored. Differences in consciousness are equally apparent when we observe children's growing awareness of themselves and their surroundings. An infant, for example, has what can be called "participatory consciousness," with no differentiated sense of self and other. Between the second and third years, however, a major change in consciousness occurs with the development of memory and the first saying of the word "I." This change is the reason most people can't remember very much before the age of three. Most young children are fairly dreamy, living in a stream-of-consciousness state that follows whatever comes into awareness without adult concern about intentionality and task completion. If you send a four-year-old to get ready for bed by himself, you can expect to find him playing with the toothpaste or the water when you join him. Young children have a completely different orientation to time and space. They live in the present, without adult perceptions of the past and future. This is why they find waiting so hard and don't understand "ten minutes" or "three days" when told they must wait that long.

The achieving of adult consciousness is a gradual process. It does not happen at birth or age eight or even age fifteen. The preschool child, elementary-aged child, adolescent, and adult are all very different; they perceive the world differently, and they think, learn, and feel differently. We can call the gradual process of achieving adult consciousness "incarnating," which literally means "coming into the body" or into earthly life. This incarnating process is an important one, for if it does not occur the person remains childlike, not fully able to seize hold of life on this earth. This process unfolds according to its own natural order and time and should not be either rushed or hindered.

If we recognize that the process of incarnation is a gradual one, we will interact with and teach children differently at different ages. For example, the preschool-aged child is centered in the will and in the limbs, in movement. The tremendous growth of the first seven years is accompanied by nearly constant movement as muscles and bones grow and coordination is gradually achieved. During these years the child learns primarily through repetition and movement and by imitating everything around her. Sitting still for long periods is unhealthy if not impossible for the young child, who desires to experience everything through her body.

The elementary-school-aged child is still growing physically, but his "center of gravity" is shifting to the feeling sphere. As the emotions mature between the ages of seven and fourteen, the child learns with the greatest enthusiasm when a picture is given of what life was like in ancient Greece or on the American frontier. Artistic or imaginative presentations have the greatest appeal and make school topics easy to learn and remember. Instead of being centered in the movement of the limbs, as was the young child, the child between seven and fourteen is centered in the "rhythmic system" of breathing and the heartbeat. This means that music, which always involves rhythm and often involves the breath (as in singing or playing a wooden recorder), is especially important for the child in the middle years. The breath and heart are also associated with emotions, which we can see in the way our breathing and heartbeat change when we are excited or afraid.

Not until puberty is the child really centered in the head, as he exercises his newfound capacities to analyze and criticize the world. Certainly major changes are still going on in the body with the maturing of the sexual organs, and the adolescent's emotions can also seem overwhelming at times. But the exciting new elements are now rational and abstract thinking, which now need to be engaged by subjects such as the proofs of analytical geometry or the laws of physics. Similarly, an ability to see causes and patterns emerges for the first time, so that courses such as "Trends in Western Civilization" are also vital to the high-school student. It is during these years that independent judgment begins to be born.

With the gradual maturing of the body, emotions, and thinking, the vehicle is ready for the person to assume the responsibilities of adult life. The traditional age of twenty-one as the age of majority coincides with Rudolf Steiner's perception that the will (movement, imitation) dominates development between birth and the age of seven, the feelings between ages seven and fourteen, and the thinking from ages fourteen to twenty-one. At age twenty-one the body, emotions, and thinking are ready for further stages of adult development.

Steiner was one of the first to share this understanding of the separate development of the threefold human being, consisting of thinking, feeling, and willing. If we are truly to understand the growing child, we must understand how these three aspects shift in dominance and how they influence the child's consciousness during different stages of development.

THE ROLE OF THE CHILD'S INDIVIDUALITY

Steiner also discussed the incarnating process in terms of who or what is ready to be responsible at age twenty-one (not that twenty-one-year-olds always behave responsibly!). Once the body, emotions, and thinking have reached a certain level of maturity, what Steiner calls the "ego" can live out its own biography without guidance from the parents. Steiner does not use the term "ego" as Freud did but instead uses it to mean our unique individuality, or what he also calls the "I." He perceived the human being as having an individuality that is capable of breaking the bounds of stimulus-response mechanisms and manifesting the unpredictable: free behavior and the possibility of fulfilling a particular destiny on earth.[11] This individuality has been variously described and named by the great religions and by psychology as the self, I, ego, spirit, observer, or consciousness. By whatever name, it is this presence that is felt so strongly in the newborn child, evoking feelings of awe and wonder in all but the most jaded adults.

Rudolf Steiner speaks of this presence as the spirit, or I, of the human being and asserts that it is involved in a continuing process of incarnating (coming into the physical body) that is only in its beginning stages at birth. The spirit at birth is, in a sense, larger than the physical body and loosely connected with it, and gradually, over the course of development to maturity, becomes more and more the master of (and slave to) the body. Perhaps you have had the experience of walking into a room where a newborn is sleeping and wondering how the room can feel so filled by such a tiny creature sleeping over in the corner. This individuality is present from before birth, which explains the feeling many parents have around the time of conception of a child wanting to come to them or the perception that a pregnant woman has that this second baby is certainly going to be different from the first. Perhaps the glow that we experience around a pregnant woman is really the being of the child that we are vaguely sensing.[12]

Steiner believes that the child is a knowing, spiritual being. Whether or not you have ever thought of children (or yourself) in this way, you have no doubt had the feeling that your children are their own people, not copies of their siblings or extensions of you. Often it is not until parents have more than one child that they experience how different children can be. They seem to bring their uniqueness with them when they arrive, and we have to adjust our parenting accordingly. Perhaps you have had a sense of your own individuality at important moments of decision when you needed to be "true to yourself."

Even if the language of this discussion doesn't match your vocabulary, the phenomena of the incarnating process are still observable: the progressive mastery of physical processes as they come under the young child's control and the simultaneous narrowing and focusing of the child's initially diffuse consciousness. These phenomena will be explored further in chapter 3.

HOW CHILDREN LEARN IN THE FIRST SEVEN YEARS

The child between birth and age seven experiences the world primarily through her body. The senses are completely open, without filters or buffers, beginning at the moment of birth. The newborn continues to experience each sensation with her entire body and being. This is easy to see in the infant, who is all hunger or the pain in her stomach, or all the blissful sensations of nursing that cause her eyes to roll back and her toes to curl. The three-year-old, as well, is much more open to impressions of the world coming through the senses than is an adult. We can even observe that children's eyes stay open longer between blinking than do an adult's.

Two things are happening through sense impressions from birth through age seven. The child is both learning about the world and being shaped by the impressions she takes in, just as a sculptor might work with clay. This phenomenon does not occur very often with adults, who are less open and responsive to the environment than young children, but we can see a similar phenomenon in the molding of the features that the elements of light and weather etch into the face of a seaman or farmer.

This "sculpting" effect of impressions on a young child's developing organs, which was pointed out by Rudolf Steiner in the early 1900s, was not meant to be taken metaphorically. Current research has demonstrated that this is physically true for the young child's brain, which is still forming, not just growing larger. According to an article in *Newsweek*, "'Only 15 years ago,' reports the Families and Work Institute in the just-released study 'Rethinking the Brain,' 'neuroscientists assumed that by the time babies are born, the structures of their brains [had been] genetically determined.' But by last year researchers knew that was wrong. Instead, early childhood experiences exert a dramatic and precise impact, physically determining how the neural circuits of the brain are wired."[13]

The second thing the child is doing through sense impressions is learning about the world. Through the body the baby learns about near and far, attainable and unobtainable, as when she learns that a spoon can be grasped but the flowers on the table remain out of reach. As she begins to learn the names of things, memory, language, and thinking develop so she can give expression to her own and the world's emerging complexity. When the child reaches age three and beyond, what is taken in with the senses is also transformed and comes out again in the creative play and imagination of the young child.

The child's major task in the first year of life is taking control of the body. Sitting, crawling, and walking are quickly followed by running, jumping, climbing, and other feats of dexterity as fine and gross motor coordination increase. Everything is done for the first time—using a shovel, sitting on a seesaw, cutting with a scissors—and then it is done over and over again. The child loves to move and to imitate, learning through doing something with someone else or after seeing it done. And the young child loves repetition, hearing the same story over and over or playing the same circle game, no matter how simple or boring it may seem to an adult.

The young child is also learning about the world emotionally, learning the fundamental lessons about trust and attachment, and later lessons about sharing and consequences. It has long been known that babies and young children in institutions where they are denied the love of a primary caregiver suffer "failure to thrive syndrome" and can die, even though their physical needs are being met. Now PET scans of the brains of orphans who have been institutionalized since shortly after birth show that the temporal lobes, which regulate emotions and receive input from the senses, are nearly quiescent.[14] Such children suffer emotional and cognitive problems resulting not only from a lack of stimulation but also from a lack of love and bonding.

The baby *is* love. Bonding is less a process of babies learning to love their parents—because children will love even parents who abuse them— than of parents establishing the connection that will enable them to make room in their busy lives for another being who needs attention twenty-four hours a day! Children enter the world with a great deal of love and trust. They are not yet able to perceive good and bad, but they take everything as good and appropriate to absorb and unconsciously imitate.

OUR TASK AS FIRST TEACHERS

One of our primary tasks as our children's first teachers is to provide them with impressions of the world that are appropriate for them to take in and copy. This means guarding and protecting them from sensory overload in a world of urban frenzy, and surrounding them with experiences that teach them about the world in a gentle way by letting them do things directly themselves and later act them out in their play.

We also need to strive to model appropriate behavior—that our emotions are under control with our children, that we don't spank them while admonishing, "Don't hit!" and so forth. Our actions speak louder than our words with the young child, who cannot help but imitate. Through us, children learn whether or not their initial love and trust in the world were well founded.

Another of our main tasks is to understand our children's physical, emotional, and mental development so we can guard it and let it unfold without hindrance. No one would want to stop a child from walking, but it is also something that we don't have to worry about teaching the child. The child will walk when she is ready, as a natural expression of the mastery of her own body—the development of balance and the achievement of verticality in the face of gravity that has kept her horizontal for so many months. There *is* a task for us—to guard, to protect, to understand, to share, and to enjoy with the child the unfolding of his or her abilities. We can do things to enhance abilities by providing an example and allowing the young child to express them freely from out of his own being. We can also note discrepancies in development and areas at risk and take gentle steps to help ensure balance. But with the young child much more is achieved indirectly through example and imitation than head-on through lessons.

No matter what our family situation or lifestyle, we as parents are our children's first teachers. The importance of what they learn in the home and through their relationship with us cannot be underestimated. By understanding how children develop and some things we can do to help their balanced and healthy growth—physically, mentally, emotionally, and spiritually—we will not only help our children but also increase our own enjoyment and growth as parents.

TRUSTING OURSELVES

Sometimes we parents can become overwhelmed when we contemplate the momentous nature of the task before us. Contradictory advice from books and friends can leave us feeling frustrated or annoyed. Becoming painfully aware of the times we fall short of our own ideals can be downright discouraging!

As a first-time mother, I fell into most of the pitfalls of mothering today. Although I had prepared myself for labor and delivery, and my first child's birth went smoothly enough, parenting (and boys) were a gigantic mystery to me. Fortunately, children are resilient, and my son developed into a fine man despite my confusion and shortcomings. But I've realized through the years that much frustration and grief can be avoided by keeping in mind a few basic principles.

1. *We need to accept who we are and build up the support we need.* Today there are many more possibilities for balancing home and work than in the past. Not working outside the home when your children are young, managing a home business, working flexible hours, having your mate be a stay-at-home parent, living communally, inviting grandma to live with you, going back to work when the baby is six weeks or six months old—all of these approaches have their difficulties and rewards. No matter what you do, you will find you need and deserve support.

   The real difficulty comes when we are doing something that we don't want to be doing. For example, if we must work when we want to be home, or if we are staying home when it is driving us crazy, then our parenting will tend to be influenced by guilt, resentment, and a whole range of other negative emotions. We need to make our best choices at each moment. We can't always have what we feel would be ideal, but we can actively do the best with the options as we see them.

   In my own life, I ran Informed Homebirth out of my home and my husband and I lived with other adults and children when our children were young, so I had the support to be a midwife and to write *Special Delivery* without excessively disturbing the children's lives. This situation brought other complications along with it, but I am grateful for the parenting support I received.

2. *We need fathers to be actively involved with children.* Fathers need support for their fathering, not for babysitting while the children's mother steps out for a few hours. When both parents assume responsibility for care of the children, everyone benefits—especially the children. The different styles in parenting and their importance have been wonderfully explored in the book *Mothering and Fathering: The Gender Differences in Child Rearing* by Tine Thevenin. As a professor of psychiatry at Yale aptly stated, "Even when they are the primary caregivers, fathers do not mother."[15]

   In addition to developing their own nurturing aspect and becoming more active with the children, fathers need to support mothers in their mothering. This support is partly financial, but it is also emotional. Fathers and mothers need to discuss and be in harmony with one another concerning basic issues of discipline and parenting styles. This can include actively supporting the mother with trite but true statements such as, "You heard your mother," or "Don't talk back to your mother," when necessary.

   In single-parent families, support needs to come from a wider circle of friends and social agencies. The parent (most often the mother) not only needs other significant people in the child's life, but she also needs the perspective that another adult can provide on her parenting and her relationship with the child. Perhaps the most important thing a single parent can do is to find or create those connections with other adults that can keep her (or him) from being so single in her parenting. Single parenting is a momentous task and involves special stresses and needs.

3. *We need a true understanding of children and their world.* When we have an understanding of children's real developmental needs, we can respond to them in ways appropriate for their age that can lead to their balanced development. In my own floundering as a first-time mother, I turned to Effective Parenting

courses, but I found they were really geared to the child who was six or older. The instructor said, "Well, try these things with the younger child as well to start building up good habits." But it was clear to me that parenting a two-year-old required something entirely different.

When I began studying Rudolf Steiner's indications for Waldorf education and child development, lights began to go on. For example, I had three children but still hadn't realized that up to the age of six they learn primarily through imitation! It seemed so obvious once I had read it. Why hadn't I thought of that? I found in Steiner many insights of that nature—and many other things that made no sense whatsoever on first reading. But I approached the ideas with an open mind and in a pragmatic way. Could I observe the same things? Did this new approach improve the situation? I found that Steiner's understanding of the developing human being provided me with ways of seeing children that made a difference. When I saw children in those ways, suddenly everything worked: home life became more harmonious; I was able to enjoy young children and relate to them more confidently; I was even able to become an early childhood teacher, something that I never would have foreseen under other circumstances.

4. *We need to trust the natural process of development and not interfere with it.* By understanding a child's physical, mental, and emotional development, we will be able to avoid doing things that are appropriate for a child at one stage of development but can possibly be damaging for a younger child. Just as it is important for children to crawl before they walk (to establish the neurological patterns in the brain), so we need to let children be children and unfold according to their own inner timetable, which always demonstrates both pattern and individual differences. If we see each child as a unique individual, we will be able to do things to enhance their gifts and to work on their weaknesses with a view toward a balanced development of thinking, feeling, and physical abilities.

5. *We need to trust ourselves and our children and to let go of guilt.*
   Because we usually live isolated from young children and other
   families before starting our own, we don't have much knowledge
   about parenting. The discrepancies between expectations and
   reality are often shocking to new parents. I know that when I
   was pregnant for the first time I felt that I would never put my
   child in preschool because no one could possibly do as good a
   job as I would. As a result, I was discouraged when I found the
   two of us constantly at odds at home and so put him in preschool, where he was the model child. At that point it seemed
   that anyone could do a better job than I!

   As mothers we tend to feel that "it's all our fault." Naturally,
   I did things differently with my third child than with my first,
   based on my increased experience as a mother and my increased
   understanding of young children. If I hadn't done things differently, maybe I could be accused of not having grown. But it is
   fruitless to feel guilty for what I did earlier, because I was doing
   the best I could at the time. If we can see parenting as part of
   our own inner growth and development and see our children as
   unique individuals with their own personalities and lives to live,
   we will be less likely to fall into feelings of guilt. The problem
   with guilt, aside from being bad for your health, is that it takes
   you out of the present moment, which is where your child lives
   and where you need to see and act clearly right now.

6. *We need to trust our children as individuals.* We are not the only
   ones participating in our children's development. They also have
   something to say about it, albeit not consciously. If this were not
   so, how could children growing up in the same family be so radically different? Each child is unique, neither merely the sum of
   his or her experiences in the family nor the product of our skill
   as parents. Sometimes it is only when they have a second child
   that parents realize how different children can be and how they
   help create what happens to them.

   You can neither take all the credit nor all the blame for how
   your child turns out. We cannot consciously select the children
   who come to us, which is no doubt a blessing. Our task is to do

our best, and to trust in the best. We need to trust our children to be resilient, to be able to heal, to be terrific people despite our flawed efforts and our most regretted actions. We can, however, strive to help each child's experience (and our own) be as positive and rewarding as it will be varied. This striving can be one of the most important things children learn from us.

7. *We need to value our parenting.* There is a way in which no one can do a better job than you of raising your child. No paid caregivers, however skillful and loving, can feel as much excitement as you do over your baby's every accomplishment. Parents have a unique involvement with their offspring that is nourishing to the child. Taking a child under the age of three out of the home and putting her in an institutional setting is stressful for the child—and many children will have been in several such situations by the time they are three. However, not everyone can stay home with their children in the first three years, and various child care options are discussed in later chapters, including LifeWays, which takes family life as the model by providing relationship-based, mixed-age care in homes or homelike settings.

8. *We need to value our homemaking.* We are our children's first home, which then expands to include life as it unfolds in our physical house or apartment. When we have children, we are creating a home willy-nilly. The more attention, awareness, and creativity we can put into the process, the more home life can become a platform that effectively supports every member of the family, including ourselves. This is the topic we will explore in greater detail in the next chapter.

RECOMMENDED RESOURCES

Parenting and Early Childhood

Beyond the Rainbow Bridge, by Barbara J. Patterson and Pamela Bradley (Michaelmas Press). A Steiner-oriented guide to nurturing our children from birth to age seven, with an excellent section on creating balance.

Heaven on Earth: A Handbook for Parents of Young Children, by Sharifa Oppenheimer (SteinerBooks). A Steiner-oriented discussion of how children learn and ways to create a nurturing environment for them.

The Incarnating Child, by Joan Salter (Hawthorn Press). An excellent Steiner-oriented book covering conception through the age of two by the founder of the Gabriel Baby Centre in Australia. Highly recommended.

LifeWays North America. Nurtures family life and offers an innovative vision of child care that takes the home as the model. Learn about their training programs, workshops, membership, and newsletters at www.lifewaysnorthamerica.org.

Navigating the Terrain of Childhood, by Jack Petrash (Nova Institute Press). Considers the entire scope of childhood to develop "meaningful parenting and heartfelt discipline." One of my favorites.

Simplicity Parenting: Using the Extraordinary Power of Less to Raise Calmer, Happier, and More Secure Kids, by Kim John Payne (Ballantine Books). Drawing from his experience as a psychologist, counselor, and Waldorf teacher, Payne has written one of the best books today for parents.

Waldorf in the Home. CDs and DVDs available at www.waldorfinthe home.org include:

> "Courageous Parenting: Changing Our Families and the World," by Nancy Poer
>
> "Meeting the Needs of Your Growing Child," by Daena Ross
>
> "Navigating the Terrain of Childhood," by Jack Petrash
>
> "Parenting the Millennial Child," by Eugene Schwartz

Mothering, Spirituality, and the Feminine

At the Root of This Longing: Reconciling a Spiritual Hunger and a Feminist Thirst, by Carol Lee Flinders (HarperCollins). Powerfully brings together the strands of feminism and spirituality. Excellent, although I wish her son received more than just a footnote!

Mothering without a Map, by Kathryn Black (Penguin). A powerful book on becoming the mother you long to be. Insightful, emotionally powerful, and practical.

Motherself: A Mythic Analysis of Motherhood, by Kathryn Allen Rabuzzi (Indiana University Press). Considers the monumental transition to being a mother (attaining mother-selfhood) as a heroine's journey in feminine form—very different from the mythic hero's journey.

Waldorf in the Home. The website www.waldorfinthehome.com provides articles and nearly two hundred DVDs and CDs of keynote presentations and workshops by leading Waldorf educators and other presenters, including:

"Becoming Mother," by Regina Sara Ryan

"Honoring Mother Spirit and Our Gifts as Women," by Nancy Poer

"Honoring the Lost Art of Mothering," by Penni Sparks

"Honoring the Spiritual Feminine," by Nancy Poer

"Mother-Lines of the Spirit," by Carol Lee Flinders

The Woman Awake: Feminine Wisdom for Spiritual Life, by Regina Sara Ryan (Hohm Press). Explores twelve aspects of the feminine, all of which can support us in our mothering. Treat yourself by drinking deeply at this well.

CHAPTER 2

Home Life as the Basis for All Learning

Just as you are your child's first teacher, your home is where the most living and learning take place. This is true whether your child is home with you full time or enrolled full or part time in child care, preschool, or kindergarten. It is also true regardless of your standard of living. Whether you are living in a cramped apartment or a palatial home, the challenges of creating a home where you want to be with young children relate more to your inner state and intention than to your bank balance.

What is home life like for you these days, and how can it become a support for you and every other member of the family? What can we do in the face of so many forces today working against home being a sanctuary where family members love to be? These are some of the questions we'll address in this chapter.

Life today isn't supportive of home life. Financial and other demands on our time often make even *being* at home problematic. Yet women and men who choose to stay home with their children are often surprised by how isolated they feel. They might be the only ones home on the block, and a two-year-old is hardly enough stimulation for someone who is used to having a successful career. Just as adults need other adults to provide balance, many children today seem to be calling out for other children to play with. So there is a demand for playgroups and early child care that wasn't as strong in the past. But this doesn't mean you can't provide a home environment that meets your child's needs—and your own—or that it's vital to sign up for preschool before your child is three. (It may be that for work or other considerations you need to start child care or preschool before age three, but you do not need to do so in order to "socialize" your child or for "enrichment.")

For the picture of home life we're about to consider, it doesn't matter if you work outside the home or are a stay-at-home mom or dad. You could be married, in a committed relationship, or a single parent. Regardless of the number of hours you spend at home or the degree of your focus on it, you are involved in creating a home one way or another. My experience is that approaching homemaking with increased awareness can help you reclaim your time at home together so it can nourish rather than drain you.

HOME LIFE IS UNDERVALUED
IN OUR CULTURE

Almost no one wants to be a homemaker today, and understandably so. If you're home with children and cringe when you have to fill in your occupation on a form, try putting "domestic goddess" next time instead of "homemaker" or "housewife" and see if that doesn't feel better.

Even our schools no longer offer classes in "homemaking," instead offering classes in "consumer science." (What does this name change say about our culture's values?)

In part the rejection of homemaking grew out of the realization of the dissatisfaction of many women who were wives and mothers during the 1950s and 1960s—what Betty Friedan in *The Feminine Mystique* called "the problem that has no name."[1] These women were expected to find all their personal fulfillment in using the many new labor-saving devices around the home, volunteering at their children's school, cooking dinner, and then fixing their hair and putting on lipstick to please their husbands when they arrived home from work. When women stopped thinking of themselves as merely "housewives" (that is, doing all that work for *him*), most also gave up on homemaking at the same time.

As society changed and doors opened for more women to enter careers formerly reserved for men, women found themselves working outside the home while still doing almost everything within the home. It didn't take long to realize that vacuuming, doing the dishes, and cooking were not gender-dependent skills, and couples started to negotiate household chores—a task that is still ongoing, even though time spent on housework is more equitably divided today. Creating a home became something that no one really had the time or desire to do. As a result, today we are often left with homes where no one wants to spend any time.

As I mentioned in the previous chapter, it was my hope that the art of mothering would eventually be embraced as a worthy choice by the feminist movement. And, in fact, Betty Friedan did address this and related issues in one of her subsequent books, *The Second Stage*, but they were never taken up by either the mainstream or the feminist minority.[2] The futility of my hopes finally dawned on me when I realized that Hestia, the Greek goddess of the hearth, was the only member of the ancient pantheon that didn't have a face. Of course! She was invisible . . . just like nurturing work. That's when I realized there weren't likely to be any parades honoring mothering or pats on the back for a job well done.

In other words, the change I'm talking about needs to come from within and will most likely continue to be unrecognized or rewarded by society. It involves both men and women recognizing the importance and value of consciously creating a home for body, soul, and spirit—a place where every member of the family feels recognized and valued, a haven from which they can go out into the world and to which they can comfortably return.

WHY IS IT SO DIFFICULT TO BE HOME WITH CHILDREN TODAY?

Many parents of young children are surprised by how difficult it seems to be to stay at home with them. They often report being out the door with their toddler by 7 a.m. to visit a park or to buy a cup of coffee because the child "doesn't want to be at home." When I talk with parents around the country, many say they hate being home because their two-year-old behaves so much better when there are other adults and children around. A number of at-home parents have reported with shock and sadness that, even though their greatest desire was to be at home with their children, "it's not working" or their toddler is "bored" being home with them. What's going on?

One factor is the prevalence today of the nuclear or subnuclear family. It is my belief (and personal experience) that a college-educated adult was never meant to be isolated at home every day with a one-year-old and a three-year-old. Our society doesn't provide enough meaning, value, or support for this vital work. This is why we need to find other families and reach out to the older generation to stand in for the extended family that used to make raising children much more of a shared task.

This isolation was experienced by a friend of mine who wanted to practice attachment parenting, which draws much of its original inspiration from *The Continuum Concept* by Jean Liedloff.[3] My friend was living in a rural village in Mexico, so she carried her baby in a *rebozo*, or shawl, most of the time. By the time the baby was nine months, she was at her wit's end and realized that she had made a mistake only a foreigner could make: yes, the babies in the village were almost always being carried, but it wasn't always by the mother. Sometimes the grandmother had the baby, sometimes the ten-year-old, and sometimes an aunt.

A second factor in the difficulty of being home with young children is our focus on the child instead of on the "work" of homemaking, which has largely disappeared through prepackaged foods and all our labor-saving devices. Modern life simply doesn't support what young children need, which is to see us doing work that involves movement. What they actually see us doing isn't satisfying to them. As a result, they seem to demand more attention, when in fact they are asking to observe us doing "real work" that involves movement and transformation of materials—something they can both share in and then imitate in their play.

Because of the misunderstandings that have grown up around the work of Jean Liedloff and attachment parenting, it is valuable to consider that Liedloff actually meant for the child to be an observer of real work, not the center of attention all the time. Barbara Dewey, a Waldorf homeschooling consultant, reports her own observations and includes Liedloff's comments on this misunderstanding. Dewey writes:

> As I observe these parents, I see that they are devoted parents who have read everything they can possibly read about parenting and are trying desperately to apply ALL of it! They are usually mothers who have given up a meaningful career to stay at home and raise their children, and they feel a need to raise children FULL TIME in order to justify their being home with them. They carry their child around a good portion of the time and interact with the child every waking minute. . . .
>
> In an article in *Mothering*, Winter 1994, Jean Liedloff, author of *The Continuum Concept*, writes of the misinterpretation of her work. What she says is right in line with what Steiner says about the young child. In her book she recommends keeping babies in physical contact all day and night until they crawl, as is done in the Yequana culture, where the parent or caregiver may occasionally play with the child, but most of the time pays attention to something else, not the baby. She says in her article, "Being played with, talked to, or admired all day deprives the babe of this in-arms spectator phase that would feel right to him. Unable to say what he needs, he will act out his discontentment. This is the attention-getting behavior parents interpret as needing more attention when in reality, the child just wants the parent to take charge of adult life, because the child needs to see a life in order to imitate it!"[4]

So what are contemporary Western parents to do when they are at home with their child? We're handicapped by the fact that the "work" we do around the house these days more often involves pushing a button than rhythmically moving. The dishes need washing? We push the button on the dishwasher. The clothes need washing? We push the button on the washing machine. The floor is dirty? We push the button on the vacuum and jab here and there instead of rhythmically sweeping the floor. Because young children are primarily connected to the world through their senses and through movement, they find all these activities incomprehensible. Because rhythmic activity speaks so strongly to children, it is helpful to bring conscious gestures into household tasks such as folding clothes, sweeping floors, and washing the windows, car, or floor. The children will watch, join in to help, or simply take it all in as they go about their play. As busy parents, we need to realize the value of the things we do in the home and do them as conscious activities around and with the young child. This could involve something as simple as peeling an apple for your child down on her little table instead of up on the counter or sitting and knitting a simple rope that will become a well-used toy while she plays on her own.

CONSCIOUSLY CREATING A HOME

Are you beginning to get a feeling for what I'm saying? It might sound as if we're back at the same old place—housework—but there are two differences. The first is that we're doing these activities with awareness and with love. I am reminded of Mother Teresa's suggestion that we do little things with great love. So, when we put a vase with flowers on the table or sweep the kitchen floor, we can try to do it with an awareness of the quality of our movements, with an awareness of their beneficial effect on the young child, and with care. The second difference is that we might do things we wouldn't ordinarily do, such as sweeping, washing place mats outside in a tub, ironing, grinding grain with a hand mill, baking, cleaning cupboards, repairing a toy, sanding wood, and so forth. It may sound quaint, but let me assure you that it beats having a whiny two-year-old or plugging another kid-vid into the DVD player to get her out of your hair.

It's kind of like the Zen saying, "Before enlightenment, chop wood, carry water. After enlightenment, chop wood, carry water." The activities may be the same, but they have been transformed by our awareness and our care. By becoming conscious of our own activities, by regulating our daily lives in a harmonious, rhythmical way, by valuing what we do around our children, we are shaping their will forces and helping their physical bodies develop in as healthy a way as possible. In return, our children give us the gift of slowing down, of becoming aware of our movements and our emotions, and of appreciating the uniqueness of each moment.

Barbara Dewey concludes by presciently describing what might now be called the "slow parenting movement":

> In less materialistic cultures and in our grandparents'
> day, parents had to work most of the time on procuring
> the basics. In those cultures the child naturally got to see
> those activities. As modern parents, we need to go back to
> that way of thinking. In so doing, we will get in touch with
> ourselves, the sources of our food, clothing, and shelter
> and perhaps discover an old art or craft form which really
> inspires us. When you give your child the gift of being
> home with her, she gives you the gift of a life of your own
> pursuits, the wonders of which you wouldn't have dreamed
> in your wildest dreams! Accept that gift and "Get a life!"[5]

FOUR LEVELS OF HOME LIFE

Creating a home life that can be a sanctuary for every member of the family is a key element in conscious parenting. To decide where to start, it is valuable first to take stock of where you are now. What are things like at your house, and what do they suggest about what's going on? What's working and what's not? To do this, we'll be using a lens suggested many years ago in a talk by Bons Voors, a Waldorf educator from the Netherlands and coeditor of the book *Lifeways*.[6]

Building on Bons's example, let's imagine home life as a simple drawing of a house with four levels: physical, rhythmical, emotional/relational, and spiritual. Each level builds upon and is supported by the one below it.

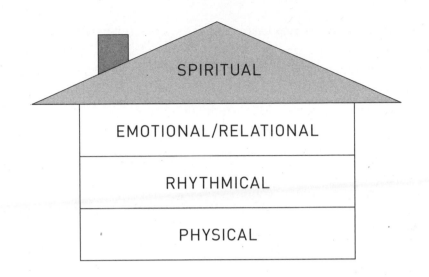

This can be a valuable exercise to do with your partner because it's bound to spark conversation. Your partner might appreciate watching this presentation with you in DVD format, listed at the end of the chapter. But, for now, it may be most useful if you get a piece of paper or a journal and jot down some notes to see what patterns emerge. This is an exercise you can do now and repeat every few years as your children grow older, or whenever you move into a new home.

The Physical Level

The physical environment of your home has a profound effect on both you and your children. Kim John Payne, in *Simplicity Parenting*, builds a strong case about the effect of "too much stuff" in creating stress, emotional upset, and behavior problems in children. He found in working with families from across the financial spectrum that the quality or price of the "stuff" may vary, but the amount was pretty much the same in all households.[7]

Let's take a look with an objective but loving eye at your physical environment. What is the approach to your home like? Do people usually enter through the front or back door? Is there a welcoming gesture, or what would the entry suggest to a visitor from another planet about your family or what is important to you? As you enter, what kind of space greets you?

What might your home reflect about your psychic state? Is the environment relaxed, overly controlled, or out of control? Is your home a constant construction zone, with no home improvement ever quite getting finished? Are you in a minimalist phase, or is there just too much stuff?

What forms the center or central focus of your home? Is it the kitchen or dining room table, where everyone gathers? Or is it the family room, around the entertainment center? Or is the center missing?

Where do your children spend most of their time? What is their relationship to their bedrooms? With young children, "Go play in your room" is often a useless suggestion, because they want to be where you are! If their bedrooms are really only used for sleeping, then does the environment support relaxation and rest? Can you find a path to your child's bed through the clutter? And if there is a big picture of a tyrannosaurus over your son's bed, is this really the image you want him to take into sleep every night?

Do you have any space that is just for you? What a thought! If you don't have an entire room, is there even a nook or an altar—anything that encourages contemplation and remembrance? Or is there any space for artistic activity or movement?

What is the relationship between the inside and outside? When you have young children, having a fenced space and a screen door so your children can go in and out by themselves can be invaluable for your sanity. Is your outside area or yard fenced and kid-friendly? Does it have a sandbox, dirt, or mud that children can dig in? Could you create a small hill or a "hidey-place" behind a bush or clear a path through a small "fairy woods"?

To ponder: What have you learned about your home life from considering its physical aspect? What would an outside observer think was most important to you? What is one area where you might want to make a change? What are the steps that would be involved? If you want to simplify and declutter, don't overlook the book *Simplicity Parenting* as your best friend and companion.

The Rhythmical Level

This is the level where we find the activities of home life, the level that provides a solid foundation and helps everything run more smoothly. When I first started applying awareness to the chaos of raising young children, two things were most helpful to me. One was gaining an understanding of child development so I could stop treating the children like little adults, holding unrealistic expectations, and taking every challenging behavior as a personal affront. The other was learning to apply rhythm to family life. For our family, creating rhythm brought order into the chaos.

Rhythm and ways to introduce rhythm into your home life are so important that they are discussed in detail in chapter 6. Here I simply encourage you to take the pulse of your family's rhythmical life.

First let's look at your daily activities, and then at the weekly and yearly ones. Let's start with meals, because they form such an important part of family life. Do they occur at a usual time at your house? What is the quality of mealtimes? Are they orderly or chaotic? Does everyone sit down together, or are meals more haphazard?

Do your children help with meal preparation, setting the table, or clearing it afterward? Do you start meals with any kind of ritual or blessing? How do meals end? Do you sing a song or blow out a candle, or do the meals just degenerate?

Turning our attention now to bedtimes and sleep, ask yourself what evenings are like at your house. Are there rituals and routines that smooth the transition from dinner to sleep? How do you and your children awaken in the morning? Right now, simply take some notes on what is and isn't working on a typical weekday.

Now let's look at the rhythm of the week. Is there anything you do on a certain day each week? How do weekends differ from weekdays at your house? Do you have any special religious activities, or do you celebrate spirit with a hike in nature or have a day of rest?

Celebrating the cycle of the year through seasonal festivals can help link you to both spirit and nature. What holiday traditions are you establishing with your children, and what do you remember most fondly from celebrations when you were a child? What is your favorite holiday? Your least favorite? How about birthdays?

In summary, based on this preliminary look at the rhythmical life of your family, is there one area where you would be open to making a change? Here's a hint: it's probably an area that isn't working for you right now.

The Emotional/Relational Level

Ask yourself how your children might describe family life if they were grown and looking back on it now. Would they say something like, "Nobody ever talked to one another" or "Mom was always angry" or "They were always on the computer"? To take stock of the emotional tone of your family life, ask yourself how fundamental values like respect, love, and affection are shown. How is conflict dealt with?

Let's consider the relational quality of family life from the inside out, starting with yourself and expanding to your family's relationship with the outside world. Relationships begin with your comfort with yourself and your own inner work. Women can tend to be hypercritical of themselves and their mothering. If children had to have perfect parents before coming to earth, there wouldn't be a population problem! Accepting that no parents are ever perfect, it's really the quality of your striving that communicates to them. We're asked to have patience with our children and their behavior, but we also need to have it with ourselves and our own shortcomings. Taking some time each day—even five minutes—for regular prayer or meditation and a regular time for self-care are also important components of being able to nurture children every day and night.

How is your relationship with your spouse or partner, if you have one? Is there any time for just the two of you? Mothers, are you able to establish and maintain friendships with other women, especially those who have children themselves, or do you unfairly expect your husband to supply all the emotional support you need? If you are a single parent, who is part of the support network for you and your child?

What is your relationship like with your child or children? How would you describe your parenting on the spectrum from laissez-faire through authoritative to authoritarian? Have you and your partner discussed parenting issues and are you in agreement? Any number of circumstances can complicate family dynamics and bring special challenges, such as divorce, coparenting, being a stepparent with a blended family, having a child with special needs, or sibling rivalry.

The final area we'll consider is the relationship between your family and the rest of world. Working outside the home presents the challenges of balancing home and work and managing the reentry transition each workday. Working from home has its own special challenges. How much outside work comes into your home life? Are you happy with the division, or have cell phones, texting, and email made the boundaries too blurred? Do your children know what you and your partner do? Have they ever visited your work, or could they?

What is the relationship between your home and your child's school or preschool? Are the values consonant? Does your child feel as if there is a connection? If you are homeschooling, are you satisfied and supported with how home life and schooling (or "unschooling") fit together? Lastly, do you have social connections with relatives and/or other families? When was the last time you had friends to dinner? Do you feel supported by social connections, or do you wish you had more?

The Spiritual or Values Level

You (and your partner) manifest your values, even if you've never thought about articulating them. Chances are, like most people, life with children has probably "just happened" and surprised you in its complexity. A place to start is by remembering what your hopes and dreams were in having a family. How was it "supposed to be"?

Children are immersed in your values and unconsciously drink them in. It's what you create and what you do, not what you give lip service to or pontificate about, that communicate most strongly to them. What are your values? What guides the choices you are making about where and how you live? Or about the kind of education you choose for your children? What do your children see you doing? I know that every time I pass the Salvation Army bell ringers at Christmas, I give them a donation because I think of my mother giving me a dollar to put in their kettle when we would go Christmas shopping downtown.

Children give you an opportunity to revisit your own childhood and to do things either the same way or differently. If you were physically or emotionally abused as a child, you have the opportunity to let those wounds heal and to do things differently—but please take advantage of the opportunity to get professional help if you need it. If you find yourself having a tough time as a mother, it could be that you were "under-mothered," either through the loss of your mother or through her being physically or emotionally absent when you needed her. An excellent resource for exploring and healing these and related issues is *Mothering without a Map* by Kathryn Black.[8]

Children also give you the opportunity to take another look at religion and your relationship to it. Were you (or your partner) brought up in a religious tradition as a child? Are you still connected to that faith, do you practice a religion different from your parents, or have you drifted away from all religion? What do you want for your children, and why? What things are you certain about? What values are fundamental to your family life, and what values are likely to change as your child matures and is able to make his or her own decisions?

HOME LIFE AS THE CURRICULUM FOR THE YOUNG CHILD

Having considered your home life through these four lenses, it's hard not to want to change everything at once or to give up in despair, depending on your temperament. In either case, I encourage you to start somewhere, anywhere, with a single change. Just as a house isn't built in a day, your home life is a work in progress. It's not a question of "doing it right" or trying to change everything at once. I would encourage you to consider what is your "frontier area," the *one thing* from the above discussion that is calling out to you most strongly. Maybe it's getting out the door on time in the morning, or what to do about the fact that your two boys fight all the time. Hold that question like a hot coal. Let it become a burning question as you read further in this book and explore some of the other resources listed here. If you hold the question, you'll find that inspiration will come to you, followed by practical ideas and a plan. Discuss it with your partner (if you have one), so everyone is on the same page, and then bring the new way of doing things to the children.

If you have gone through the above exercise, you will have made notes on lots of activities involved in nurturing children and creating and maintaining a home. These are what Cynthia Aldinger, the founder of LifeWays North America, calls the "Living Arts." In *Home Away from Home*, she distinguishes four types of Living Arts: domestic activity, nurturing care, creative discovery, and social ability.[9] Can it really be that the simple activities of daily life we've looked at above—doing dishes, making beds, feeding the cat, sorting the laundry—are exactly what your young child needs to grow and develop in a healthy way? There are several ways in which this is true. First, you're modeling "real work," in which your child can share, and which he or she can imitate in play. Second, you're sharing "quality time" without focusing on the child in a narcissistic or hovering way. Third, your child is moving, learning skills, and developing competence. For example, a task like folding the laundry teaches sorting and matching by color, care in folding corners together, and how to put things away; similarly, helping you bake a cake involves measuring, pouring, stirring, being careful, doing something for the family, and impulse control while waiting to lick the bowl.

In addition to LifeWays, with its emphasis on strengthening home life and making home the model in child care settings, there are also a growing number of blogs and websites by parents who are consciously trying to create a nurturing home life for their families and themselves. Some of these parents are homeschooling their children, but others aren't, and it isn't necessary. Among the resources listed at the end of this chapter you'll find the e-zines "Rhythm of the Home" and "The Wonder of Childhood," two of my favorites.

If your family life "kind of just happened" and is much less satisfying than you had hoped, it's not because you're a bad parent! It's because no one ever shared with you the practical steps that can help you create the kind of life you yearn for. Consciously creating a nurturing family life is built, first of all, on understanding the real needs and the developmental stages of young children, which we'll return to in greater depth in the next three chapters. Then we'll spend an entire chapter looking at "Rhythm in Home Life" (chapter 6). Once you understand how to create a rhythmical environment that supports your child's sense of well-being and provides opportunities for self-directed play, you'll find that he or she is much happier and easier to live with. So I hope you'll persevere in your efforts, because the rewards are great!

RECOMMENDED RESOURCES

"Family Matters: Homemaking 101 for Busy Parents," workshop by Rahima Baldwin Dancy in DVD or CD format. Considers in greater detail the four "lenses" described in this chapter. Available at www.waldorfinthehome.org.

Home Away from Home: LifeWays Care of Children and Families, by Cynthia Aldinger and Mary O'Connell (LifeWays). Although written for child care professionals, the resources about creating a home (or a homelike environment) and the "Living Arts" create valuable awareness for parents.

LifeWays North America. Offers workshops and part-time trainings throughout the United States and in Canada for parents and child care professionals. Also offers CDs and DVDs on life as the curriculum, nap time, discipline, and more. At www.lifewaysnorthamerica.org.

Living Passages for the Whole Family: Celebrating Rites of Passage from Birth to Adulthood, by Shea Darian (Gilead Press). Information on creating rites of passage, from birth to adulthood.

Making a Family Home, by Shannon Honeybloom (SteinerBooks). "Creating a home is a process of imbuing our space with soul and spirit, surrounding our family with love, care, comfort."

Mothering without a Map, by Kathryn Black (Penguin). A must-read for navigating the emotional minefields of being a mother.

Radical Homemakers, by Shannon Hayes (Left to Write Press). Stories and inspiration for reclaiming domesticity and sustainability from a consumer culture.

"Rhythm of the Home." An e-zine featuring many articles and resources for conscious homemaking. At www.rhythmofthehome.com.

Sanctuaries of Childhood: Nurturing a Child's Spiritual Life, by Shea Darian (Gilead Press). Considers the sanctuaries of family life, including sleep, nature, music, poetry, stories, and prayer.

Seven Times the Sun: Guiding Your Child Through the Rhythms of the Day, by Shea Darian (Gilead Press). Considers the daily rhythms of waking, eating, playing, working, resting, going to bed, and more—with lots of songs and practical suggestions.

Simplicity Parenting, by Kim John Payne (Ballantine Books). Support for simplifying environments, rhythms, and schedules and for protecting children from the concerns of adult life.

Sophia's Hearth Family Center. A family center combining Waldorf and Pikler/RIE principles for early childhood. Offers workshops and trainings in New Hampshire. At www.sophiashearth.org.

The Spiritual Tasks of the Homemaker, by Manfred Schmidt-Brabant (Temple Lodge). A leading German Waldorf educator (and single father) describes homemaking in its broader context.

"The Wonder of Childhood." A monthly e-zine supporting home life and homeschooling. At www.wonderofchildhood.com.

CHAPTER 3

Birth to Three: Growing Down and Waking Up

We think of children as growing up, but we could also say that they "grow down" in the sense that they seem to gain control of the body from the head downward. First they gain control of the eyes and the neck, then the torso in rolling over, and finally the limbs in crawling and walking.

At the same time, they are changing from sleepy newborns to alert and lively toddlers who run circles around their parents. This change in consciousness from infancy to three years involves waking up, in the sense that the participatory consciousness of the newborn gradually becomes replaced by a strong sense of self (just try opposing the will of a two-year-old!). Before this strong sense of *I* can emerge, the child must first develop language, thinking, and memory.

Penetration of the body, which culminates in walking, is a fundamental task of the baby's first year. Talking is a key task of the second year. And thinking and memory are areas of tremendous development in the third year. All these fundamental milestones of the first three years occur by themselves, according to their own timetable. We need only provide love and nourishment, and refrain from doing things that hamper the child's basic pattern of unfolding.

This chapter presents a picture of the tremendous developmental changes occurring in the child during the first three years. The next two chapters suggest many practical things you can do as your child's first teacher that are consonant with healthy and balanced development.

GROWING INTO THE BODY

Control of the Head

A newborn's head is very large compared to her body, and her limbs are relatively undeveloped appendages, good neither for walking nor for eating as they are with other mammals. The image of "growing down" or penetrating the body also applies to how areas in the brain mature: developmental neuropsychologist Jane Healy reports that because the development of myelin in the spine proceeds from top to bottom, the mouth, eyes, arms, and hands are used adeptly before legs and feet.[1] In the newborn, after the mouth organizes itself around instinctual suckling, the first conscious control begins in the eyes. This is necessary because without a steady visual field, it would not be possible to develop the hand-eye coordination and balance that are necessary for crawling and walking. When a baby is born, her natural focus is about ten inches away—just the distance between a breastfeeding infant and her mother's face. Next the baby learns to follow something with her eyes when it comes into her range of vision, which extends to about twelve inches at two months of age. She may begin to turn her head toward a sound if it comes in one ear more strongly than the other. She begins to be able to hold her head up off the mattress when on her stomach and to turn her head more toward the midline when on her back. But it will be many more months before sufficient head and neck strength will be present for her to sit unassisted.

Around three months she will be able to prop herself up on her forearms with full head and neck control. Consonant with our image of "growing down," we see that control of the upper arms comes before control of the lower arms, control of the wrists before the fingers, of the legs before the feet. During the time from six to fourteen weeks, the muscles in your baby's legs are strengthening by kicking out and being held slightly flexed, but there is no real leg control.

Control of the head also manifests in visual ability, which increases rapidly and is nearly completely under control by three and a half months. Once your baby can focus clearly on nearby objects and create a single image of them, she will discover her hands and stare at them— sometimes for five or ten minutes at a time. Between six and fourteen weeks her hands will no longer be held in a fist most of the time, and she will start bringing her hands together and clasping them. Eye and hand convergence is something only primates and humans have, and it is an important step in the development of intelligence.

You will see eye-hand coordination developing as your two- or three-month-old swipes at an object and later brings it to her mouth. This coordination increases with practice and maturation, so that by six months a baby usually has complete control of the use of her hands.

Reaching is an important developmental skill, one of the major ways that children begin to explore the world and build the foundations of intelligence. Your baby will almost always reach for anything that is nearby and will either bring it to her mouth or look at it, sometimes moving it about or passing it from hand to hand.

Control of the Torso

As the months go by, your baby gains increasing control of her body from the head down. Sometime between two and six months she will probably succeed in turning from her back to her stomach, followed a few weeks later by being able to turn back the other way. The first time is often a surprise—even to the baby—so be careful not to leave her unattended on a changing table or bed where she can flip off! Even a much younger baby can sometimes unexpectedly succeed in turning from back to stomach through powerful leg thrusts, especially if she is angry.

Further control of the muscles of the torso will result in your baby's being able to sit up unassisted, usually between six and eight months of age. This first achievement of an upright posture marks a significant maturing of the muscles.

Once your baby is adept at turning over in both directions and can sit alone, she will try to bring herself from a lying to a sitting position. This new ability is usually accomplished by around eight months of age.

Control of the Legs

All of the movement and kicking your baby does helps strengthen her legs. Sometime around four months of age she will discover that she has feet, because her eyes had been unable to discern them earlier. But she won't be able to use her legs in a controlled fashion. That changes around eight months of age, when she learns to creep and crawl. Some babies are eager to go and may even be frustrated by their inability to get things they want; others are happy to sit and watch the world go by, and they may first crawl four or five months later than the "early" ones. The normal range is tremendous, so don't compare your baby with the neighbor's! Insights into later character traits can sometimes be gained by observing how your child learns to crawl and walk. Simply observe and encourage your baby and trust that she is developing according to her own timetable. If you have questions about how your child is developing, seek answers to them rather than worry!

Physical therapists now tell us how important crawling is in later development. The rhythmical pattern of cross crawling is significant not only for the development of proper physical coordination, but it also affects the development of the brain and how a child learns. Some learning and emotional disabilities are related to a lack of crawling or can be helped by sensory integration or other systems of therapy.[2] For this reason, anything that shortens a baby's time spent crawling (baby walkers, leg splints, or braces) should be avoided during this critical period.

Crawling is followed by the baby's ability to pull herself up while holding onto a table or sofa. The ability to walk while holding onto things is followed by increased balance and coordination and the wonderful first steps alone.

Once your baby can crawl, you will find everything changes! Because crawling is such a momentous change for parents and walking is such a momentous accomplishment for babies, I want to discuss parenting the baby up to the age of eight months before going on to discuss walking.

WHAT IS YOUR BABY LIKE BETWEEN SIX WEEKS AND EIGHT MONTHS OF AGE?

We can say that babies "grow down and wake up," for while they are growing and developing physically, they are also becoming more alert and more interested in the world around them. We have seen how they develop physically; let's explore how they behave as they become more "present" with each passing day.

Your baby will sleep less as the weeks go by and will pay close attention to what is going on around her. Once she discovers her hands, she will use them whenever possible to grasp and explore objects with her eyes and mouth. The tongue and lips are sensitive organs of exploration, and when your baby starts to teethe during this period, counterpressure can sometimes help sore gums. There are many teething rings on the market, some of which can be put in the refrigerator to chill. I especially recommend Hyland's Homeopathic Teething Tablets, which, amazingly, are sold by many major drugstore chains. Being homeopathic, they present no danger of overdose or side effects. It is not unusual for babies to be fussy while they are teething, or even occasionally to have a fever or runny nose.

By three months your baby will probably be smiling regularly at anyone who gets her attention. Three-month-old babies are delightful to be with, and most of our images of babies from television or advertising are of a three-month-old rather than a newborn. We now have much more of a sense that there is a real person present, someone who seems to respond to us. Indeed, a baby does begin to show more special behavior, such as smiling more with her parents or primary caregivers from the fourth month on. But there is still openness and friendliness to all people at this age.

The baby's sense of self and other is slow to emerge, for the consciousness of a newborn is very diffuse. It is as if there is no inner or outer. As we watch the baby slowly distinguish between parents and others, we have the sense that she is more present in her body. It is interesting that you cannot elicit a tickle response from a baby before about fourteen weeks of age. Burton White postulates that tickling depends on the "ticklee" perceiving that another person is producing the stimulation (you can't tickle yourself). He states, "The child younger than about fourteen weeks of age is probably not well enough developed socially to have reached whatever awareness of another is necessary to make the tickle functional."[3]

This is consonant with Steiner's idea of the gradual incarnation of the *I* and the slowly developing consciousness of the self, which is necessary for any perception of "other." Steiner described babies as "sleeping" in their consciousness, "dreaming" in their emotions, and most "awake" in their willing, which manifests in the body. We can see the strength of this willing in the tremendous growth and movement of the body and in the insistence with which a baby demands that her physical needs be met. Try to argue with a crying baby that she's not really hungry and she ought to be able to wait! The force of will behind the physical functions of a baby does not respond to reason or consolation—only to physical activity such as eating, sucking, or rocking.

The next step in the differentiation of others is evident in the common phenomenon known as stranger anxiety. Sometime in the first year, four out of five babies start reacting with hesitation and fear to anyone who is not in the immediate family. This reaction can start as early as six months, and it is not a sign that anything is wrong. Aside from becoming wary of people who aren't familiar, most babies enjoy themselves most of the time during the first year. They are basically happy, curious, and growing throughout this time.

LEARNING TO WALK

During the period from eight to sixteen months of age, most children master their physical body and learn to walk. Note that there can be as much as eight months' difference between early and late walkers.

Children learn to walk through practice and through imitation. It has been found that in the rare cases in which human babies have been reared by animals in the jungles of India that the child never achieves a truly upright posture. There is a strong inner drive in children to stand and to walk, and to be like the people around them. It is something inherent in children and does not require baby gymnastics or mechanical devices to aid its progress. Baby walkers do not lead to early walking; in fact, many physicians now believe that infant walkers may adversely affect muscle development and coordination and lead to a delay in walking.[4] Due to the large number of accidents involving walkers, the Canadian Medical Association has asked the government to ban their sale.[5] Time spent in walkers also takes time away from opportunities to creep and crawl and can affect coordination and balance.

Nor do infant walkers lead to increased social and explorative behaviors, as their proponents say; studies have found no difference in these behaviors for infants in or out of walkers. They may give parents some free time, but not without physical and developmental risks to the baby.[6] There is similar concern about baby bouncers (cloth seats suspended by a spring hung over a doorsill) by many pediatricians because of potential damage to the baby's bones or joints if they are used on hard floors.[7] In general, it's best not to use mechanical aids to produce positions or activities that the child can't attain on her own.

Watching your child learn to walk on her own can sometimes provide insights into character traits, because walking is something the child achieves through her own efforts. Is there a driving will to move, or a great solidity and contentment in sitting? Are falls taken in stride, or are they discouraging? Keep watching and see what your child "tells" you. All you need to do is be there to encourage and share your child's pride in those first steps.

It is valuable to watch the process of learning to walk for what it can tell us of the child's nature and the incarnation process of the *I*. Steiner states, "Walking does not merely mean that the human being ceases to crawl and acquires an upright position. It means that the child attains the equilibrium of its own organism within the cosmos, learns to control its movements and acquires a free orientation."[8] He continues, "And for anyone who is able to observe such a matter in the right way, the most remarkable and most important of life's riddles actually find expression in the manner in which the child progresses from creeping to the upright position, to the placing of the feet, but also in addition to holding the head upright and to the use of arms and legs."[9]

To explain this further, once the baby achieves equilibrium in the upright posture, Steiner observes that the hands and arms are freed to serve the inward life, while the legs serve for bodily movement:

> The liberation of the hands and arms affords the possibility for the soul to find its equilibrium. The function of the legs, the treading, the raising and bending, the harmony between right and left, brings about a relation to what is below us. It has the effect of bringing into the life of body and soul the element of rhythm, of measure, the caesuras of existence. The soul elements which live in the hands and arms become free; this introduces an element of melody, a musical element into the life of the child.[10]

Watching a young child with awareness that more might be going on than meets the eye can make us more open when we are with young children. Even though I can't articulate any great insights I've had, I know that those times of openness and remembrance seem very valuable for me, for my parenting and for the child.

THE SECOND YEAR: MASTERING LANGUAGE

A child's first birthday is as much an anniversary for the mother as for the baby. Exactly one year earlier she was going through labor, and she remembers vividly what she felt holding her baby for the first time. As dramatic as the changes in the baby were in the first year, they will be equally dramatic in the second. By the time a child is two there is much greater distance from the dreamy dependency of infancy and a much greater sense of who this person is in her own right.

Just as mastering the body and learning to walk were the dominant activities of the first year of your baby's life, so mastering language and learning to talk are the major tasks from age one to two. Language development consists both of comprehension, which develops first, and the ability to speak. Learning to talk, like learning to walk, seems to involve both an innate capacity of the brain and a need to encounter models in the environment. Because language comprehension is so fundamental to all later learning and to good social development, it is valuable to consider it in some detail.

Language Comprehension

I hope you have been talking to your baby since her birth as if she were a person worthy of respect. This attention and respect not only increase her sense of self-worth and her loving interaction with you, but also by using proper language rather than baby talk, you are providing a model worthy of imitation.

There are approximately six thousand languages in the world, and your newborn is equally fluent in all of them! But she quickly learns to distinguish between phonemes through staying attuned to whatever sounds the speakers around her are using. By twelve months, an infant's "auditory map" in the brain will have been formed. She will be unable to pick out phonemes that she has not heard thousands of times because no clusters of neurons will have been assigned the job of responding to that sound.

The next step in decoding speech, after recognizing phonemes, is to start recognizing words from the run-together stream of sounds that we register when we hear a language that is foreign to us. Early on babies start to become accustomed to how sounds are used to start syllables in their mother tongue.

Once children start to recognize and play with syllables, they become attuned to metric patterns as well. Peter Jusczyk, a cognitive scientist at Johns Hopkins University, showed that between six and ten months, American babies develop a clear bias for words with first-syllable accents. (The majority of English words, and virtually all the Daddy-baby-birdie diminutives we use with babies, are accented on the first syllable. French words, by contrast, typically have the accent on the last syllable.) His work implies that children less than a year old hear speech not as a blur of sound but as a series of distinct but mostly meaningless words.

The first unmistakable signs of word recognition usually occur around eight months of age. If someone says, "Where's Mommy?" while several people are in the room, a child will turn toward her mother when she really knows that word. That depends, of course, on the mother having referred to herself as "Mommy" or "Mama." If all the child ever hears is her father referring to her mother as "Jenna," she will also call her mother by her first name. There is something to be said for having your child refer to the two of you as "Mommy and Daddy," "Mama and Papa," or some such words because the sounds of these words are appropriate and easy to learn, and because it expresses relationship (parent and child, family).

One of the best things you can do for your child is to talk to her. Talk to her while you are changing her diaper or giving her a bath. She will usually appreciate the attention and, as a knowing being, will appreciate being treated as a person rather than as an object. And you will be helping not only her language development but her brain development as well. And please sing to your child, beginning when you are pregnant and continuing throughout childhood! The melodic quality of language and the emotions expressed through a lullaby or a nursery game are very valuable for your baby's development. Comprehension is not the only part of language, although it tends to be overemphasized by our intellectual adult nature. Nonsense rhymes and action verses such as "To market, to market" become favorites of the toddler and teach the melodic quality of language. This kind of interaction is not only valuable for the developing child, but it can also make parenting tasks go more smoothly. For example, getting into the habit of using songs for activities such as washing her hair or going to bed can melt away the resistance of a willful two-year-old. Many other examples are contained in Shea Darian's book *Seven Times the Sun*.[11]

Because so much depends on the development of language, it is important to watch your child for hearing disorders. If your baby is having frequent ear infections, it is advisable to look for allergies or other possible causes of fluid buildup in the ears. Impaired hearing can impede development in many other areas during these critical years of early childhood, so try to find a diagnosis and plan of treatment that you can support.

As your child comes to understand specific words, she will begin following simple instructions, like waving bye-bye or sitting down. Once your child starts to walk, she will frequently be coming to show you things or ask for assistance. Such times, when her attention is clearly directed toward you, are excellent times to talk about what is at hand and then to act on it. Many parents underestimate what their child can understand at this age. This does not mean that you should explain everything to a one-year-old! It does mean that you should talk intelligently about what is happening in the present—what the child is seeing and doing. Between the first and third birthdays, language comprehension explodes to the point where most children understand most of the words they will use in ordinary conversation for the rest of their lives!

The Ability to Talk

The ability to produce language proceeds much more slowly than the ability to understand it. While your child will show increasing understanding of words before her first birthday, very few children speak before they are one. The reason for this, according to Steiner, is that language development grows out of movement and the ability to walk. Modern neurolinguistic work supports the relationship between learning to walk and grasp, and learning to speak. With this in mind, we can watch not only how our children learn to walk and the quality of their movements, but we can also observe the quality of their speech as it develops over the years and see if there is any discernible relationship between the two. Certainly physical and speech therapists—both conventional ones and those working out of Steiner's indications for "curative education"—can see it. In such curative settings, movement and sound are often used separately and in combination to help overcome developmental difficulties.

A child's vocabulary increases slowly at first, from an average of three words at twelve months to twenty-two words at eighteen months of age. But around a year and a half, children's language abilities explode, so that most start acquiring new words at the phenomenal rate of one every two hours. By their second birthdays, most children have mastered one thousand to two thousand words and have started stringing two words together.[12] How much language is in the child's environment makes a huge difference in how much vocabulary she acquires:

> Studies have shown that the size of a toddler's vocabulary
> and the complexity of her sentences are strongly correlated
> with how much a mother talks to the child; however, only
> "live" language, not television, produces these vocabulary-
> and syntax-boosting effects. Why doesn't all the gabbing
> on TV stimulate language development? Researchers sus-

pect that "language has to be used in relation to ongoing events, or it's just noise."[13]

In other words, language needs to come from a living source and be related to events, emotional contexts, and cause-and-effect relationships in a child's life in order for the synapses to register in meaningful ways that the child will remember. So much for educational TV and preschoolers' language development!

Developmental rates can vary among children by a year or more, and the majority of late talkers are boys. However, there is no evidence that late talkers end up less fluent than early talkers. Where there are speech or other language problems, the pros and cons of early intervention versus waiting until age five to intervene are hotly debated, but the pendulum is swinging toward earlier intervention. In contrast, not hearing what is being said and being slow to develop understanding are both serious conditions, and experts suggest being on the watch for the following red flags:

0–3 months. Does not turn when you speak or repeat sounds such as coos.

4–6 months. Does not respond to "no" or changes in tone of voice, look around for sources of sound like a doorbell, or babble in speech-like sounds such as *p, b,* and *m.*

7–12 months. Does not recognize words for common items, turn when you call her name, imitate speech sounds, or use sounds other than crying to get your attention.

1–2 years. Can't understand difference in meaning (for example, "up" versus "down"), follow two requests ("Please pick up the bottle and give it to me"), string together two or three words, or name common objects.

3–4 years. Does not answer simple "who," "what," and "where" questions. Cannot be understood by people outside the family, use four-word sentences, or pronounce most phonemes correctly. If delays persist until kindergarten, most pediatricians recommend speech therapy.[14]

Dr. Karl König, founder of the Camphill movement for children and adults with special needs, distinguished three levels in speech development, which he called saying, naming, and talking.[15] Saying involves a desire or an emotion that comes out as a one-word sentence, like "Here!" or "Cookie!" Naming involves learning the names of things and the beginnings of the thought processes that link concepts with perceptions and draw relationships between the general ("dog") and the specific ("Fido"). Talking involves dialogue as we are used to it. As the child experiences the world and the way it is expressed in language, with its inherent logic and grammar, she begins to use whole sentences between ages two and three.

Archetypal Images

While the toddler is learning the names of things, a great deal is happening on the preverbal level in the rapt attention with which the child contemplates each object. For example, while an adult or a school-age child will be most interested in what he or she can do with a ball, a young toddler will be most interested in the ball itself—its shape, texture, color, and the fact that it rolls away when it slips out of her hands. Our adult consciousness has lost its connection with what goes on in the dreamy depths of the child's soul, with what is happening behind her dreaming, wondering, or delighted eyes. Daniel Udo de Haes, in his excellent book *The Young Child,* develops a fascinating picture of the unspoken "soul language" by which simple objects speak to the child of qualities in the spiritual world and the nature of the soul's journey to earth. We can get a taste of Udo de Haes's perception in his description of the fascination young children (and adults) have with water:

> Every human soul is aware, consciously or unconsciously,
> of a connection with this watery element. Does not each
> of us long for the clarity which pure water can manifest?
> Does not every soul feel its own ability to stream and flow
> in all directions, to wave and to dash, to seethe and toss
> or to reflect calmly? Ultimately its capacity of rising to
> the heavens and descending again to earth, is brought to
> expression by water. The little child experiences all this
> much more directly and intensely than we do, though less
> consciously, and it is for this reason that he feels his connection with water and plays with it with such abandon.[16]

In a similar way, Udo de Haes explains children's delight in drawing houses or making houses out of the sofa pillows as arising from a reawakening of something within the child's own soul when it encounters "houses" on earth. He states, "Descending to earth, the soul bears within it the task of helping to build the 'house' that it would have to live in during the life that was about to begin; for the task that it was assigned was to help in forming its body. We should therefore not be surprised at the joy with which the child builds a little house, thus symbolically fulfilling the task of building his body."[17]

In *The Young Child*, Udo de Haes develops a very enlivening (and not at all sentimental) picture of the inner life of the young child, which I have found valuable to hold as a possibility when I watch a toddler contemplating an object. Jesus said, "Unless you change and become like little children, you will never enter the kingdom of heaven" (Matthew 18:3). What is the world like for a little child? This is a question worth holding by anyone who cares for young children. And to the extent that their wonder in the world around them can become real to us as well, the rediscovery of this aspect within ourselves can, without our noticing it, be a help to the young child who is exploring his own world of experiences.

Because of the fascination the young child has with simple objects and the resonance within the soul that such objects awaken, Udo de Haes recommends archetypal toys such as a ball, a bowl, a cup (with sand or water to pour), a little wooden house, a box with hinged lid, or a small wagon.

The fact that the objects of nature and the simple objects of human life speak to the inner life of the child, reminding him of truths from the spiritual world, is echoed by the seventeenth-century English poet Thomas Traherne:

WONDER

How like an Angel came I down!
    How Bright are all Things here!
When first among his Works I did appear
    O how their Glory did me Crown
The World resembled his Eternitie
    In which my Soul did Walk;
And every Thing that I did see,
    Did with me talk.

THE EMERGENCE OF THINKING

Just as walking and talking can be seen as the major tasks of the first and second years of life, so thinking is a major accomplishment of the time from ages two to three. But thinking in its most rudimentary forms can be seen as early as the first year when the baby pushes an obstacle aside in order to grasp an object. Piaget describes this problem-solving behavior, with an element of intentionality, as one of the first signs of intelligence.

This early, practical or sensorimotor intelligence isn't replaced by reflecting on ideas until around the age of two. Prior to that time children tend to use trial and error for problem solving. As they turn two, you will increasingly see them pause and think about various alternatives or about the action they are going to do before doing it.

Thinking emerges between ages two and three, after the child has learned to speak. Many people will suppose that one has to think in order to speak, but remember that speech develops as a result of imitation and of feelings and is connected with movement. The first words are interjections, and Steiner says, "When the child says 'Mama' or 'Papa,' it expresses feelings towards Mama and Papa, not any sort of concept or thought. Thinking is first developed from speech."[18]

According to Steiner, logical thinking develops out of the experience of the logic inherent in the grammar of spoken language (grammar tells us who hit whom, whether it occurred in the past or is going to happen, and so forth). Between the ages of two and three years, the child's use of sentences takes off exponentially and includes the rules for tense and for number (plurals). How does a young child learn this? When I read that Steiner said it was an innate gift that the higher hierarchies (that is, angelic beings) provided before birth, I was at a loss for how to present this. But now researchers agree with Steiner that children are somehow born with these abilities. When they talk about the infant's brain being "hardwired" to seek out—and even invent, if necessary—the grammatical rules in language and the logical thinking that follows, isn't that a materialistic way of saying the same thing? Here is a report from the *Los Angeles Times*:

> Babies struggling to turn babble into polished patter use
> a previously undiscovered instinct for rules to master the

building blocks of language, scientists at New York University announced Thursday.

The new insight is persuasive evidence that the ability to think in terms of formulas and rules is not just something that must be learned through school, as some scholars have argued, but is also a fundamental characteristic of every human mind, several language experts said. . . .

The research, published today in *Science,* broadens the understanding of what may be built into every human being at birth, from a rudimentary knowledge of shapes and numbers to a well-stocked intellectual tool kit for learning the complexities of human speech.[19]

Unless a child has a hereditary condition known as specific language impairment, most children are so primed for grammatical rules that they will invent them if necessary, taking whatever rules they find and sharpening and extending them. For example, hearing adults who take up American Sign Language to share it with their deaf children tend to make all kinds of grammatical errors; however, their children still become fluent. But if deaf children are raised without any language, they grow deaf to grammar and are unable to pick it up later, as has been shown in cases in which hearing was restored in adulthood.[20]

Whether you consider that language is a gift from the hierarchies or from the mechanics who create the wiring in the brain, it must still have models in order to develop. So talk to and with your child a lot! Most people would guess that we have language because we can think, but it appears more accurate to say that we are able to think because we have language. According to Rudolf Steiner, the ability to think, reason, and problem solve grows out of language. It is the order in language and the brain's ability to comprehend it that form the basis for later thinking.

However exciting it may be to see your child start to show signs of thinking, this doesn't mean you should start providing lengthy explanations of things or reasoning with her. The young child is still centered around the body and the will and is not governed by thought and reflection. Imitation and example are still the keys for working with a child before the age of seven, as we will see in subsequent chapters.

The Development of Memory

The development of thinking depends on the process of language formation and the maturing of memory. Steiner points out how the development of the child's memory echoes the historical development of humanity. The first type of memory is localized or place memory, which involves recalling something when the child is in the same environment or receives similar sensory cues. For example, she may only visit grandma's house every few months, but she immediately remembers where the toy cupboard and the cookie jar are when she walks in the door. Historically, this kind of early memory is represented by monuments, cairns, monoliths, and other markers that remind people of the events that occurred at that location. This type of memory is very strong in the young child, who cannot pull up memories at will until the age of six. For example, if you ask preschoolers, "What did you do at school today?" they will typically say, "Nothing." But if they receive other cues—if you start to sing one of the songs they learned at school or they see or smell something similar to something they experienced there—you can get an amazingly detailed rendition of the morning's activities.

The second type of memory that developed historically can be called rhythmical memory, in which history was carried in verse by poets or bards who would recite epic tales to remind people of their heritage. The rhythmical element makes memorization much easier, as when a young child sings his ABC's or recites "One, two, buckle my shoe." With such songs the child can go through the entire sequence, but he is unable to start in the middle or remember individual elements without reciting the whole verse from the beginning.

The third type of memory, picture memory, begins to develop in the third year and involves the child being able to use images and ideas. Lois Cusick, in the *Waldorf Parenting Handbook*, diagrams this progression in the following illustration, which also relates the three types of memory to the three major systems described by Steiner in human development: the limbs-metabolic system, which helps us move from place to place and is associated with localized memory; the heart-lung rhythmic system, which helps the young child easily learn songs and nursery rhymes "by heart"; and the head-nerve system, which is the last to unfold when the child is able to make images and later to remember more abstract ideas.[21]

HEAD-NERVE SYSTEM

THIRD YEAR		Picture memory (images, ideas)
SECOND YEAR	**HEART-LUNG RHYTHMIC SYSTEM**	Rhythmic memory (time)
FIRST YEAR		Localized memory (place, space)

LIMBS-METABOLIC SYSTEM

THE YOUNG CHILD'S SENSES

Considering the tremendous physical and psychological changes that take place in the first three years, it is especially important to protect the child's senses to promote healthy development. Because young children are not yet able to separate themselves from their impressions through thinking and reflection, it is as if they are all sense organ. Scientific studies have shown that the fetus and newborn are tremendously more sensitive than doctors believed even a few decades ago. According to Steiner, this sensitivity modulates but remains throughout early childhood:

> In the first part of his life . . . the child is, so to say, altogether a sense organ. This we have to take very literally. What is the characteristic function of a sense organ? It is receptive to impressions from the environment. If something striking occurs near him—for example, a burst of anger—then the reflection thereof goes right through the child. It will affect even his blood circulation and digestive system.[22]

Rainer Patzlaff goes on to explain, "Impressions are taken deeply into the unconscious physical processes and imprinted into the structure and function of the organs, into growth and form. This means that, in the education of very young children, the material as well as the social and human environment is of paramount importance."[23]

Paying special attention to the environment of the young child both at home and in child care or preschool is thus especially important. Almost all parents have experienced that their child can easily become overwhelmed when overstimulated by all the sights, sounds, and tastes at a children's party or at the movies. The opposite—the health-giving effects of a simplified environment and a rhythmical schedule for children of all ages—is less well known because the hectic pace of our lives doesn't support parents in having this experience. However, this relationship has been validated by Kim John Payne throughout his twenty years of counseling families. His suggestions in *Simplicity Parenting* form a practical and achievable way to enrich family life, from early childhood through adolescence.[24]

THE EMERGING SENSE OF SELF

Your toddler is very different from a baby, not only in her ability to walk and talk but also in her sense of self. By the time your child is eighteen months old, you will have no doubt that you are dealing with another human being of power.

A baby has what can be called participatory consciousness. There is no separation between self and other. Certainly the individuality is present and can be sensed in an infant, but it seems to surround the baby as the process of incarnation gradually occurs. The young baby participates in all the sense impressions of life without any distance, only gradually distinguishing various sensations, various adults, and all the things in the created world.

We have talked about the common occurrence of fear or shyness with strangers that most babies go through around nine months of age, and during the second year you will see other signs of the emerging sense of "I" and "not-I." During the second year, toddlers begin to feel themselves as separate beings, using their own name, starting to be possessive about toys, and starting to resist simple instructions from their parents. What psychologists call negativism is a normal sign in the second half of the second year of life. As the concept "no" begins to have meaning for them, children will pit their will against that of their parents.

In *The First Three Years of Life,* White writes, "Why a child has to become ornery and stay that way for a minimum of six or seven months is one of the mysteries that makes the study of early human development so rich and fascinating. . . . The next comparable step seems to occur at puberty and takes the form of adolescent rebellion. We leave it to other researchers to delve further into this fascinating problem."[25]

Steiner's explanation of such behavior is that the child's *I* is being experienced more strongly, making him more awake and more centered in the power of his individuality. These times occur at ages two to three, around age nine, and again around age thirteen. Finally, at age twenty-one the individuality is fully incarnated into earthly life.

The toddler's emerging sense of self is strengthened by the development of memory, which results in the first conscious use of the word *I*. Indeed, there can be no awareness of oneself without memory. Memory comes from an accumulation of experiences with the "not-I." Things that are painful—a knife that cuts, hard cement steps that cause a bump—interrupt the young child's participatory consciousness and separate the world from the self. Memory arises from these and other encounters, increasing the sense of the observer or the experience and the thing experienced. This sense of distance or separation is in contrast to the infant's unfocused consciousness, which doesn't distinguish between self and other, which participates completely in whatever sensation is at hand.

The emergence of memory, thinking, and the self go hand in hand, and sometime between two and three you will notice your child first saying "I" instead of calling herself by her name. Prior to this time she will say "Susy do it" or "Susy book," imitating what she has heard herself called. Saying "I" can only be done by the person herself, and the earlier ways of talking will disappear.

The age between two and three is an exciting time, one in which your child wholeheartedly says to the world, "Here am I!" This wonderful step in development can be accompanied by "self-will" as the child asserts her newfound power of individuality. Having an understanding of the changing consciousness of the child can help us gain perspective on the forces behind a child's actions and can help us offer guidance and correction (insisting on "right action") without our own emotional reactions muddying the waters. Examples of creative ways of coping with negative behavior will be given in chapter 7, "Discipline and Other Parenting Issues."

Having insights into your child's physical development and the changes in consciousness from birth through age three can help you understand and respond creatively to your child. In the next two chapters we will consider ways in which you can help your child's natural development during these crucial first three years.

RECOMMENDED RESOURCES

The Child from Birth to Three in Waldorf Education and Child Care, by Rainer Patzlaff et al. (Waldorf Early Childhood Association of North America). The first half provides a very cogent description of child development from birth to three.

Heaven on Earth: A Handbook for Parents of Young Children, by Sharifa Oppenheimer (SteinerBooks). Discusses how children learn and ways to create a nurturing environment for them.

The Incarnating Child, by Joan Salter (Hawthorn Press). Steiner-oriented work that addresses a child's devlopment through the second birthday. Highly recommended!

Simplicity Parenting, by Kim John Payne (Ballantine Books). Ways to protect the healthy development of children of all ages.

Waldorf Parenting Handbook, by Lois Cusick (Rudolf Steiner College Press). Valuable section on early childhood, as well as a description of the Waldorf (Steiner School) curriculum through adolescence.

CHAPTER 4

Helping Your Baby's Development

Before we consider ways in which you can encourage your baby's natural development in the first year, it is important to remember that your child is his or her own person, and more than the genetic blend of two individuals. Each person comes into life not only with unique characteristics that will unfold over the course of a lifetime but also with a unique individuality and destiny. This is reflected in the wisdom of many cultures and religions, and is also expressed by the Cherokee blessing, "May you live long enough to know why you were born."[1]

During pregnancy the mother has known this baby intimately, "from the inside out," for nine months. And yet when you look into your newborn's eyes, you realize that she is her own person, and you may have the sense of a very ancient and knowing being who is both familiar and a stranger to you. Who is this child? What will his or her life be like? What an adventure, finding out!

The experience of a unique spiritual being coming to you is sometimes felt by parents before the birth, or even before conception, through a dream about someone that they later recognize as this child or a "knowing" about the name of this child. I have found that when I ask parents what, if anything, they knew about their unborn babies, there will always be one or two in any group who were either aware of the moment of conception or were aware of a "being" who wanted to come to them shortly before they became pregnant. König describes this unseen process, of which we might be dimly aware:

> First the being of the child approaches the mother, and through this she finds the child's father. Later, however, the child's angel has a direct meeting with the mother's higher being and entrusts the child to her. . . . For most mothers this spiritual meeting remains subconscious, but its significance is a lasting one because from this meeting springs the well of the mother's love. This very special love which a mother has for her child, and which transcends all biological powers, is imparted to every woman when she meets her child's angel.[2]

This perspective, that on some level your child has chosen you (with all your imperfections!) and this life with all its joys and difficulties, can be helpful when you find yourselves overwhelmed with the twenty-four-hour-a-dayness of taking care of an infant or the sleepless nights of parenting a teenager. Before we turn to the practicalities of caring for a newborn, take a few minutes to think back on anything you knew about your child before he or she was born. What dreams did you have? Was there something special about how your baby's name came to you? What did you sense from your baby's movements while inside your womb? It can be helpful to keep a journal of your observations and feelings during pregnancy and throughout your child's first years—it's a great adjunct to the typical baby book.

STIMULATING AND PROTECTING THE SENSITIVITY OF THE NEWBORN

Birth involves a huge change for the baby. Psychologists have long told us this, but it has yet to transform birthing practices in most hospitals. It wasn't until the 1970s that the sensitivity of the newborn at birth was dramatically brought to awareness by the work of the late French obstetrician Frederick Leboyer. Medical science had fallen into the belief that babies didn't see, feel, or experience very much in the womb, during birth, or as a newborn. Leboyer himself said he had experienced three thousand deliveries before he realized that the newborn's cries were really made in distress.[3] Today it is hard for any thinking and feeling person not to be aware of how vulnerable the senses of a newborn are to sight, sound, temperature, and all the other experiences of the world.

Much has been written about the importance of stimulating your baby's senses, starting with maternal deprivation studies conducted in the 1940s, which demonstrated that institutionalized children without adequate stimulation from a primary caregiver show developmental lags that cannot be made up later. Later studies in Romania confirmed with brain scans that the temporal lobes, which receive input from the senses and regulate emotions, were dramatically less active in institutionalized orphans who had experienced extreme deprivation in infancy compared to normal children.[4]

However, American popular pyschologists and business interests have interpreted an infant's need for stimulation as meaning that you need to be constantly stimulating your baby with bits of colored plastic and flash cards. Rather than these artificial means, however, a baby needs the holding, rocking, talking, concern, and love of its mother or another primary caregiver in order to develop normally. More sensible child-development experts remind parents that infant stimulation is not something you need to do separately from caregiving.[5]

You will be providing most of what your baby needs for healthy development if you do the following:

1. Touch or hold your baby often.

2. Talk to him or her.

3. Spend time face-to-face, making eye contact.

4. Generally respond quickly to fussiness or crying.

Stimulation of your baby's senses is important for his or her development, but overstimulation can be detrimental. A baby does not have the ability to filter out unwanted impressions as adults do when, for example, they read while the television is on. A baby is bombarded by everything in the environment, and his only escape is to go to sleep in order to digest the constant flow of sensations. Steiner states:

> The child needs so much sleep because it is entirely sense-organ. It could not otherwise endure the dazzle and noise of the outer world. Just as the eye must shut itself against the dazzling sunlight, so must this sense-organ, the child— for the child is entirely sense-organ—shut itself off against the world, so must it sleep a great deal. For whenever it is confronted with the world, it has to observe.[6]

By remembering the sensitivity and needs of the newborn, you will gain confidence that you are providing your baby with the best possible start in life.

The Sense of Touch

Your baby is perhaps most sensitive to touch, the skin being our largest sense organ. The entire birth process is like a massage for the baby, stimulating her skin senses and getting her ready to breathe. The cold air hitting her skin at birth gives the baby her first strong dose of body definition, of inner and outer. This is in contrast to life in the womb, which is like being immersed in a warm bath.

Your baby's sensitive skin, which previously has only known water, will now be exposed to all of the elements of ordinary life. No wonder babies are so prone to rashes—it's quite an adjustment. Touch remains vital throughout your baby's life, and it's a pity that so many of the givens of modern child rearing, such as baby seats and strollers, serve to distance parents and their children and insulate the child from life-giving touch. Although babies need to be safely belted into infant seats in the car, holding and carrying your baby in your arms at other times is better for both of you. But how will you ever get anything done? Here is where the various types of slings and soft front carriers come to the rescue by leaving your (or your partner's) hands free for other tasks. However, a word of caution is necessary. Using vertical carriers before a baby can hold his head erect can place undue strain on the central nervous system, while using a sling that keeps the baby curled up too tightly or blocks all fresh air can limit free breathing. One of the best resources on selecting and using a baby carrier safely is still available as a reprint from *Mothering* magazine at www.mothering.com.[7]

Returning to the sense of touch, it is helpful to think about what kinds of materials you want to have touching your baby's skin and to choose fabrics that are soft, warming, and pleasurable against the skin. Natural fibers are especially beneficial because they breathe. If some kinds of synthetics make your skin crawl or make you feel as if you're sealed in an airtight container, consider that the effect is magnified for your baby. Not only do cotton, silk, and wool allow air to flow through the fibers, but wool also wicks moisture away from the skin and keeps your baby drier than other fabrics. Hospitals have found that premature babies gain weight faster when they are placed on wool sheets, but no one knows why.[8] Steiner would say that natural fibers can actually contribute to the body's vital energy, whereas some synthetics rob the body of energy.

The Sense of Sight

Your baby's sense of sight expands from the newborn's short focus from breast to mother's eyes to gradually take in more with each passing month. Your baby's security increases when the space he is in is small, like his depth of vision. This is one reason why your baby may sleep better in a small bassinet than in a large crib and why many cultures all over the world have a version of a cradle or Moses basket so the baby can sleep safely by the mother's side as she works.

Mothers all over the world tuck their babies into bed with them at night when they are small, and certainly while they are nursing. The American Academy of Pediatrics recently came out against "co-sleeping" because a small number of babies died in a given year, but they didn't report whether either partner had consumed alcohol or taken sleeping medications or any other drugs that increase drowsiness. Waterbeds obviously are not safe for co-sleeping. The benefits of sleeping with your baby include increased attachment and nighttime security for the baby. And it is certainly easier to nurse a baby in bed than to get up, go to another room and get the baby, and then sit up in a rocking chair before getting up yet again to return the baby to his or her bed. Some researchers feel that sleeping in close proximity with your baby helps regulate her breathing and decreases the risk of sudden infant death sydrome

(SIDS or crib death), which is also decreased if you put your baby to sleep on her back instead of her tummy. It's something you need to decide, and www.mothering.com is, once again, a valuable source of information.

One of the advantages of having a bassinet or hooded basket for your newborn is that it provides a small, enclosed space for naps during the day—and it gives you room to stretch out or be with your partner without waking the little one. An innovative compromise that offers the best of both worlds is the Arm's Reach Co-Sleeper, a three-sided bassinet that attaches to the side of your bed. Your baby is safely tucked in next to you, where she can still hear your breathing and feel your presence. The lack of a wall between your mattress and the baby's mattress makes it easy to reach your baby for reassuring or for nursing.

In the early weeks, bassinets may be draped with colored silk to fil-ter the light reaching the baby. A combination of blue and pink or rose silk provides an especially soft light, and such pieces are available from several online sources. Having a special blanket made of natural cotton or silk can help build up associations with sleep over the months and then can help your older baby settle into sleep when she is tired at night or at nap time. The sleepwear and the bed, together with the baby's skin, can be thought of as three "sheaths" that protect the baby in his or her contact with the outside world.

Is it necessary to take such care with a newborn? Certainly not in the sense of survival. Babies are hardy creatures and can even survive the fluo-rescent lights and Muzak in the preemie nursery. But it is helpful for us to be aware of how completely open to outside influences a baby is. Burton White, in *The First Years of Life*, states that the baby in the first six weeks

> is generally unusually sensitive. . . . It is perfectly normal for
> an infant to startle and cry at any abrupt change in stimula-
> tion during her first weeks of life. Such common reactions
> include a response to sharp nearby noises, or to jolts to the
> crib or bassinet, or to any rather sudden change in posi-
> tion, particularly when the baby has been inactive. A sec-
> ond, less dramatic indication of sensitivity at this age is the
> infant's avoidance of bright lights. A Phase I infant [birth
> to six weeks] will keep his eyes tightly shut in a brightly lit
> room or when outside in the sun. In fact, he is much more

likely to open his eyes and keep them open in a dimly lit room than in one at an ordinary level of illumination.[9]

The Sense of Hearing

Just as bright lights cause a baby to close down, loud noises will cause your baby to throw her arms and legs up in the startle reflex and begin to cry. Although you'll want to avoid slamming the door or dropping things near your baby, this doesn't mean that you need to tiptoe around the house all the time. Your baby should become used to the natural sounds of your household and will learn to sleep through most of them.

It is good to focus on the quality of the sounds that reach your baby's ears. One measure of quality is loudness; another is harmony and rhythm. One of the most pleasing sounds to your baby is your voice. Not only does she start to recognize your voice and your partner's, but if you hum or sing, she will be especially soothed. Many parents like to make up a little song for their baby that they start singing when pregnant; they have reported that the baby pays attention and is soothed by the song and seems to recognize it, even right after birth. You don't need to be a talented musician to sing to your children—even someone tone deaf can hum! Getting into the habit of singing will help your child's language development and sense for music and rhythm, and it's a delightful way to share together.

The quality of aliveness that comes through the human voice when you sing to your baby is very different from a recording of soothing music for babies, or even one of your own singing. There is a nurturing quality in things that come from living sources that disappears when they are transferred to a recording. Children, especially, have come into this life to be alive and to grow. That which comes directly from a living source connects them with life on earth and the forces of growth, while that which is mechanical is further removed from them. Devices now on the market that simulate the noise of a car going fifty-five miles per hour may drive your baby to sleep, but what an affront to a newborn's senses! Similarly, wh ite noise machines or creating a hum with a fan at nap time doesn't do your baby any favors.

It's obvious that your baby's experience is totally different when you or your partner sing to her (however ineptly) from when a CD player is the source of the sounds. Not only is the experience of a real person's presence missing with recorded music, radio, and television, but the quality of the sound is also different, regardless of the quality of the sound system. Steiner said that the quality of the sound from mechanical sources had a detrimental effect on the young child, both on the developing sensitivity of the ear and on the entire organism, because everything from each sense affects the entire body.[10] This is not so much the case with a child over the age of seven. Paying attention to the quality of the sounds your baby hears can only be beneficial.

The Sense of Warmth

A sense of warmth is especially important for your baby because her ability to regulate her body temperature is not yet fully mature. Also, an infant's head is so large in proportion to the rest of her body that the potential for heat loss is tremendous. Any outdoor person will tell you, "If your feet are cold, put on a hat," because so much of the body's heat is lost through the head. Many hospitals are beginning to put stockinette caps on babies in the nurseries, and it is a good idea to keep your baby's head covered throughout the first year. The baby's brain grows as much in the first year as it does throughout the rest of life, and for this process it is good to keep the head warm and protected.

A baby hat not only prevents heat loss but also keeps the fontanels covered. The fontanels are the "soft spots" in the baby's skull. The one toward the back of the head is harder to feel, but the one toward the front can take up to eighteen months to close. During this time the brain and central nervous system are just beneath the scalp instead of being under the bony layer of the skull. The fontanels should neither be bulging nor sunken when your baby is at rest (although they will bulge when she cries). Many parents have found that putting a hat on their baby has a calming effect when they are out in the world, for it seems to keep the baby more insulated from outside influences. I recommend fitted hats over the stretchy stockinette variety, because stockinette caps fit poorly and always tend to ride up and need pulling down. This can be irritating to the newborn—perhaps too much like the birth process she has just come through!

The sense of warmth is very important throughout early childhood, and it is important to keep babies and toddlers warm and protected from drafts so their energy can go into development instead of into maintaining their body temperature. You can't judge whether a child is warm enough by how you are feeling, or by what a verbal child will tell you. A better guide is whether or not the child's hands and feet are warm.

Don't let your baby get overheated, but it is important to keep all the organs warm, especially the organs of digestion. This is why formula has to be warmed to body temperature and why traditional remedies for colic often involve warm wraps on the stomach. It is also why babies should always wear an undershirt or onesie (usually in addition to other clothing). Traditional mothers in warm climates always keep their babies covered, to protect them from the heat of the sun and to protect them from drafts. In our culture we need to be especially careful when taking the baby into air-conditioned rooms to provide a blanket or clothing to cover the baby's skin and prevent her body warmth from dissipating.

The Importance of the Environment

During the first six weeks, your baby needs to adjust to earthly life gradually and to get her digestive system functioning smoothly. Because she sleeps so much and her perceptual abilities are so limited, any kind of "enriched environment" will be wasted on the infant. Be skeptical of commercial and media hype regarding the needs of the newborn.

If an "enriched environment" is wasted on your baby, an aesthetic one is not. Creating a feeling of calm in the room (and in the mother) communicates to the baby and helps with sleep, digestion, and peacefulness. Most of the commercial items for babies are expensive and unnecessary. If you do have the luxury of decorating the nursery, avoid garish wallpaper and cartoon characters. Greens, browns, and grays are also much more "earthy" than the infant or young child, who is still closely connected to heaven and doesn't yet walk firmly on the ground. The rose-pink-blue environment created by putting silks over the cradle or crib is especially soothing for young babies, and a color Steiner called "peach blossom" is especially suited to young children. Looking at the space in which your baby sleeps with attention and reverence adds those qualities to the environment. Adding a little table with fresh flowers, some photos or art reproduction, and some objects from nature like a pretty rock or shell can remind you of your own still center in the midst of all the demands of caring for a new baby.

Steiner suggested that many paintings by Raphael express higher truths, and he especially recommended that pregnant women contemplate Raphael's *Sistine Madonna*, which is also wonderful to have in a young child's room (note the faces of the unborn children in the clouds surrounding Mary). Meditating on this picture can reveal many things to the mother about both the nature of the eternal feminine and the incarnation process. About this particular painting Steiner said, "The painting of the Madonna with the child is the symbol of the eternal spirituality in people which comes certainly to the earth from beyond. Yet, this painting, through parted clouds, has everything that can only arise or proceed from the earthly."[11]

WHAT IS IT LIKE BEING WITH A NEWBORN?

Being with a newborn is sublime on the one hand and often shocking on the other—at least the first time around. On the sublime side, I have frequently walked into a room where a newborn is sleeping and marveled that anyone so small could fill the entire room. The poet William Wordsworth described a similar phenomenon:

> Our birth is but a sleep and a forgetting;
> The Soul that rises with us, our life's Star,
> Hath had elsewhere its setting.
> And cometh from afar:
> Not in entire forgetfulness,
> But trailing clouds of Glory do we come
> From God, who is our home:
> Heaven lies about us in our infancy!

On the other hand, I can still remember how difficult the first week was when I was a first-time mother. Having just given birth, you are wide open emotionally and physically. Hormones, starting to breastfeed, interrupted sleep, and roller-coaster emotions put a woman much more in touch with the beauty, vulnerability, and overwhelming aspects of life. Being a new mother or a new father involves a change in being, a stretching of who we are to take on the responsibility and the twenty-four-hour-a-day care of another human being, who (for a while at least) is completely dependent on us.

Most parents agree that the first six weeks are the hardest. Even after you recover from the birth itself, you will probably find the complete lack of rhythm doesn't give you any support. Life gets easier after these first six weeks, so if you can stay in communication with your partner during this transition time and have the sense that you are holding hands as you go under together, you will come back up together as well. It is easier with subsequent children because everything is more familiar. However, a second or third baby can be surprising in the amount of work he or she adds to a system where parents may already feel pressed for time. The key is getting adequate help so you can relax into what is happening and give up on things that aren't as essential, like cleaning the house yourself. Single parents, especially, need to arrange adequate support in advance.

Being with a baby involves doing a lot of repetitive things (diapering, nursing, washing clothes) that can look like nothing because they seem to involve maintenance rather than creative development. So when your partner comes home from work and asks, "What did you do today, dear?" you may think about it and burst into tears. I found I could accomplish one thing (one task in the world outside the baby) each day, if I was lucky, during the first two months. For someone who was used to being active and effective, that was a real shock.

How can this period of transition after the birth be made easier for parents? The most important thing is to get adequate help. This may mean having a relative come stay with you, hiring someone to come in and straighten up the house (postpartum doula support services are becoming more common, thank goodness), or going online to organize a care circle of friends to drop off a casserole or do a half hour of whatever is needed every afternoon during the first week or so.

To the extent you feel that you can relax and just be with your baby, you'll be more at peace. This may involve making sure that all other responsibilities are handled and that all deadlines fall well before your due date, or it may mean giving up on cleaning the house for a while.

When we finally surfaced about five days after the birth of our first child, every plant in the house was withered, and we were sad!

The first six weeks are a very special time to be together as a family, to just be present with your new baby, adjust to the changes in your life, and regain your strength and bearings. If you can honor the magnitude of the event, arrange for some help, and schedule few or no other activities, you may find your adjustment much less rocky. Allow yourself to be nourished by the wonderful energy that surrounds a newborn.

The energy of creation that is present at a birth is very powerful and holy. This is true at every birth, but it is more accessible if this energy is acknowledged and protected. Because babies are so close to the spiritual world, they call forth love and giving from all sorts of people—some of whom you won't have heard from in years. Learn to receive, to let people do things for you, to say thank you. Use the time to practice doing nothing, to just be centered in the heart or in your breath. If you have other children, you will be especially busy after the birth. See if you can find brief moments to just sit and watch the baby sleeping. Such moments nourish you for the constant demands of mothering. Try to take advantage of the connection to the spirit that your baby has and to which you are still open in the postpartum period. Life will return to a new "normal" soon enough.

WHAT IS IT LIKE FROM MONTHS TWO TO TWELVE?

Once you've emerged from the fog of the postpartum period and just when you think you've figured it out, your baby will have moved on to something new! Babies change so rapidly in the first year that you may always feel as if you're scrambling to keep up. This can make what might seem mundane—tending to your baby's physical needs for food, cleanliness, sleep, and touch—more challenging than you ever imagined. But don't undervalue the care you as parents provide, for the infant is being shaped by her relationship with both you and the environment. Parents' feelings and interactions have an impact different from that received in even quality child care. With more and more parents putting the baby in full-time child care at six weeks to return to their careers, we appeal to mothers and fathers to be with their child as much as possible in at least the first year of life! With the possible exception of your baby's grandmother, in your own home, no one can provide the calm environment and loving attention that the mother or father provides. The idea of "quality time" does not apply to an infant. She needs the constant proximity, the breastfeeding, the carrying, the being in a carrier or on the floor next to you while you do something.

No other mammal is born as helpless as the human being, and no other has such potential for development. In many ways a baby is not "ready" to be born when compared with other mammals, and yet it must be born after nine months' gestation or the head will become too large and calcified to fit through the mother's pelvis. But the baby's needs for being close to the mother's body do not stop at birth; they continue throughout the first year and longer. Most nonindustrialized societies practice some form of "marsupial mothering," with mothers carrying the baby in constant contact with the body up to the age of nine months—almost like a second gestational period. At that time there is a noticeable change as the baby becomes much more interested in the surrounding world, reaches for table foods, and is able to crawl and then walk on her own.

A different approach from the "in arms" mothering described above was articulated by Dr. Emmi Pikler, one of the leading European doctors who studied and worked with infants. She worked in a children's home in Hungary (where there weren't any mothers), and her work was developed in North America by Magda Gerber under the name Resources for Infant Educarers, or RIE. Helle Heckmann, who runs a Waldorf-inspired child care center in Denmark, says of Pikler,

> Through her observation of children, she was able to show the importance of confidence and self-reliance as well as the belief in "being able to," as fundamental to the child's development into a confident adult. By reinforcing the child's confidence in her physical capabilities, and by respecting each child's individual developmental path, we as caregivers and educators can meet the needs of the young child. Emmi Pikler has given me the courage to work with children in a respectful way.[12]

Heckmann translates that into her approach with infants and describes it as follows:

> There is no doubt that the infant thrives in love. Countless studies of the development of infants have shown that love and care are vital. But caring should not be mistaken for reaction and constant supervision. Show care and affection in situations when it is natural, such as eating and nursing, when it is natural to create a you-and-I situation, when it is natural to nurse, sing, chat, and get to know each other. The rest of the time it is important to leave the infant in peace and quiet to sleep or, when awake, to get to know herself without constant intervention from her surroundings. Often it is very difficult to show the infant this respect and leave her alone. Constantly satisfying our own need for reassurance and your need to look at your beautiful baby will often influence the infant's ability to be content with herself. Too many disturbances quickly lead to dependence on constant attention from the surroundings, and a vicious cycle of bad habits is created. By giving the infant peace and quiet for the first months of her life, she will get used to her physical life.[13]

Proponents of both attachment parenting and Pikler's more hands-off approach each have numerous arguments on their side. Parents and caregivers in both groups are caring, concerned, and consistent, and—when they are in touch with the being and the real needs of the child—both get good results, or what White would call "great kids." But when they fall off the tightrope, the former tend to err on the side of "smother love" or letting the child totally run the circus, while the latter tend to err on the side of rigidity or distance.

Steiner always encouraged people not to accept things by rote or on faith, but to test ideas for themselves. The key, as I see it, is not to follow any "system" or "expert" to the detriment of your child. Try to inform yourself, and ask, "What does the child need in this situation for his or her best development?" Use your head, listen to your heart, and make your best decisions based on what you perceive your child's needs to be and what you are able to provide in each situation. And then, if possible, evaluate what happened and grow from what you learned.

Although we have spent a great deal of time discussing different approaches to mothering, let's not forget fathers! The father's ever-expanding relationship with the baby also contributes greatly to the child's growth and development. This relationship can begin during pregnancy, as the father takes time to be in touch with the developing body and being of his child. In experiencing the birth with his wife, he finds his love and connection with this child strengthening dramatically. By sharing the care of the baby and seeing her grow, the father's relationship deepens, so that he finds other times and ways to be with the baby, especially if she is being breastfed. As the baby develops and is increasingly able to respond with smiles and play, the relationship of father and child deepens. In addition to the special love and protection a father can provide for his baby and his wife, there are many ways in which he can interact with his baby during the first year. Fathering is of benefit not only to the baby but also to the man, who allows the nurturing aspect of his personality to develop. Mothers enjoy seeing their husbands interact with the baby; in fact, studies have shown that marital satisfaction for women with children is connected with seeing their husbands active as a father.[14]

Here we will present no recipes for producing a "super baby." In fact, what most new parents need is confidence that they themselves are important and can provide the best possible care for their babies. However, based on an increasing knowledge of child development and the gradual nature of the incarnation process, certain principles and activities can be especially helpful for you and your baby.

PHYSICAL DEVELOPMENT

As we have seen, all babies go through a normal sequence of development that involves assuming control of the body. The differences in the developmental rates of individual babies have more to do with timing than with the order in which skills develop. Freedom to move the arms and legs ensures that muscles will strengthen and that processes such as language and cognitive development, which are related to physical movement, will unfold appropriately. If you are having serious questions about your baby's development, check with your family doctor or a specialist to reassure yourself that your baby is developing normally. This is especially true if you suspect a hearing problem or if your baby has frequent ear infections. So much of learning depends on good hearing!

Your baby does not need baby exercise courses or other fancy stimulation to develop well. Expensive infant stimulation and home exercise kits are a waste of money and make the false assumption that we know better than the baby which muscles she should move. You can have all the benefits of positive interaction with your baby without spending the money simply by enjoying being with your child and rolling around on the floor together. If you are doing something because it feels good in the moment (massaging your baby or watching him grab at something), then you are interacting positively. But if you are doing it for results (so he'll be serene when he grows up or will walk sooner), then you are out of the present moment and have fallen prey to the media hype that tells us we should help our children progress faster. The most important thing you can do in the first year is to provide a calm and loving environment for your baby so that she can grow and develop according to her own inner unfolding.

Your baby needs very little to play with in the first few months because her main task is to become accustomed to her body and develop her muscles (and hence her brain) through natural movements. Although your baby is still primarily a horizontal being, you can delight her with a mobile in which the objects are horizontal and thus visible to the baby (remember that what is visible to you is seen as a narrow edge by the baby in the crib).

Crib toys should not produce loud noises or flashing lights. It is important for safety to remove hanging crib toys when your baby seems nearly able to pull herself up to a sitting position.

Before a baby can sit up, it is good to have her near you on a blanket on the floor. Babies don't object to being on their backs or on their stomachs instead of sitting. Our culture is visually oriented, and we think that babies always need to be sitting up in molded infant seats when they are awake. Some researchers on developmental learning disabilities feel that babies should not be propped up into a sitting position by infant seats but should be given the opportunity to achieve the sitting position entirely unaided.[15] It is a question of not jumping ahead of the normal progression of development.

Once your baby can sit up, you'll find she loves to play with small objects, which are important in the development of physical coordination and intelligence. Especially valuable are toys and small objects that can be banged, thrown, or dropped. Think of things you already have that she will find fascinating. (Remember that everything ends up in the mouth, and small pieces that can break off are dangerous. Anything smaller than $1^1/_2$ inches in any dimension could get stuck in a baby's throat.) A wooden spoon, a beautiful shell, a cloth ball, and a small dried gourd can be favorites. Your kitchen is full of wonderful "toys"—measuring spoons, pots and lids, nesting bowls. The wooden rattle, of which the infant was unaware and which the three-month-old would hold or drop indiscriminately, gradually becomes interesting for its texture and sounds. Several sources of natural toys are listed at the end of this chapter. Although there is nothing wrong with chrome and plastic, it seems appropriate to honor the natural connection that young children have with the living world.

The playpen, which has fallen out of use, is another invention that doesn't take into account the real developmental needs of the child. Until the baby crawls, a blanket on the floor serves just as well, and a basket for toys can be handy for picking things up when the baby takes a nap. Once the baby starts to crawl, playpens are a real barrier to development.

When Your Baby Starts to Crawl

From a parent's point of view, development seems to go in phases. First everything is all right, then it's fairly difficult, then all is well again, and so on. Joseph Chilton Pearce, in *Magical Child,* speaks about each developmental step being preceded by a return to the matrix (structure, safety, mother) and then followed by a voyage out into the world to find new experiences and exercise new abilities.[16] The expansion and contraction is like breathing, and it is important for development that times of regression (inwardness or clinging behavior) be understood not as backsliding but as preparation for the next surge forward toward independence.

One such "regression" often happens just before a baby starts to crawl. You might find yourself carrying around this heavy child much of the time and wondering, "When will it ever change?" Then suddenly it does, and your baby is off, having mastered the first means of getting around on his own. Parenting changes with this event, because your baby is suddenly into everything. Planning ahead can save you a lot of grief and make this an exciting time in your lives.

Sometime before your baby starts to crawl, you will need to baby-proof your home, making it safe for and from the baby. Starting with the kitchen, where your baby will probably spend the most time, make sure that all poisonous and dangerous items are out of reach and put simple toddler locks on cupboards that you don't want the baby to get into. You should also check for unstable objects, such as a small table or a potted plant. Stairs pose a special risk of falling, but babies love stairs. An invaluable suggestion from White is to place the child guard gate about three steps up instead of at the bottom of your staircase. This gives your baby a place to practice climbing without the risk of getting hurt.

Making your home a safe place for the baby is one of the best things you can do to aid your child's development. The objects in your home provide wonderful stimulation for her, and you won't have to say "no" all the time. It is much better to let your baby roam than to keep her in a playpen, because babies need to crawl, need changing stimulation, and need to be around you. In his observations of families where children developed beautifully, White found that parents had made their homes safe and open to children rather than keeping them caged in playpens, where they rapidly became bored. He states, "It is my view that to bore a child on a daily basis by the regular use of a playpen for extended periods is a very poor childrearing practice. The same principle applies to the use of cribs, jump seats, high chairs and other restrictive devices" when they are used to limit a child's movement for long periods every day.[17]

THE DEVELOPMENT OF INTELLIGENCE

During the first year of life, the weight of your baby's brain can actually double. Brain cells, which become stimulated by picking up and relaying messages, develop new dendrite spines, and these neural pathways become myelinated, or insulated to make the pathway that has been created operate more accurately and faster. Your baby is learning constantly through her physical activities. As movements become more coordinated and are repeated hundreds of times each day, your baby learns eye-hand coordination and how to grasp something she sees. According to both Piaget and Steiner, these things that seem like the foundation of physical development are also the foundation for later intellectual development.

Between the ages of six and eight months a baby's interests usually change from her own motor skills to the world around her, and memory starts to develop. Interest in dropping, banging, and throwing small objects starts to teach the baby about cause and effect and temporal sequence, important foundations for later thinking. For example, the seven-month-old will repeatedly drop a spoon or toy from a high chair and watch where it goes. Toys that involve performing one action that causes another part to move are also favorites for a child of this age.

Understanding the gradual development of memory is also important when considering the growth of intelligence. Jane Healy concludes from her research in developmental neuropsychology:

> A child's first months lay the groundwork for paying attention, taking in bits of information to each of the senses, and practicing with body movements. During this "sensorimotor" period, the brain is not ready to deal with much beyond immediate physical experience. Around eight or nine months of age, the prefrontal cortex begins its long march toward maturity, and the child starts to use memory to link past and present experience: "Oops! Here comes the sitter—time to cry!"[18]

As the prefrontal cortex starts to develop, short-term memory and "object permanence" start to develop in the baby. A baby sitting in her high chair and dropping her spoon for the tenth time is not doing it to annoy you. Rather, she is observing the wonderful phenomenon we call gravity and playing with the idea of appearance and disappearance (which makes peek-a-boo a favorite game). In this play we can see a metaphor for the coming in and out of existence or manifestation that the baby is exploring by its very being. There is as yet no memory to give an object permanence; mother disappears and reappears as suddenly as the baby itself appeared in the physical world.

Babies around six to eight months of age also love to bang things and explore sounds. Having a cupboard in the kitchen that is the baby's (and putting child locks on the others) can be a real blessing. While you're busy, your baby can be occupied swinging the door, banging the pot with the wooden spoon, stacking the unbreakable bowls, or rattling the taped container with rice inside.

It is pointless to address a baby's learning ability in an abstract fashion from birth until eight months of age, because all babies go through the normal pattern of development unless they are abused or disabled. Jane Healy concluded from her study of developmental neuropsychology, "Your overall goal should be not to 'teach' your baby but to help her discover how to organize experience for herself. . . . Babies come equipped with the 'need to know'; our job is to give them love, acceptance, and the raw material of appropriate stimulation at each level of development. Your own common sense, augmented by current knowledge, is the best guide."[19]

However, the current pressure for early academic achievement and the American maxim that "faster is better" have clouded common sense when it comes to activities like teaching babies to read. Healy points out that even though babies can be taught to read words with enough condition-response training, they are not reading for meaning and are using a lower part of their brain, simply because the parts of the brain that should be used in reading are not yet developed. Such activities risk your baby developing habits that are hard to undo later (see chapter 11 for more reasons not to push academics onto younger and younger children). Let your baby be a baby. Play with her through language and movement and enjoy one another!

At this stage it is impossible to separate physical development and the development of intelligence, but one is not predictive of the other. In other words, a child who crawls at six months and walks at eight is not more intelligent or highly developed than a child who crawls at ten months and walks at fourteen. What is important for the development of intelligence is that the motions are gone through in each stage; the timetable is usually just a question of individual differences within the wide range of normal.

Researchers have been unable to find dramatic evidence of poor development in the first year in children who do poorly later, probably because they have not yet developed the deficit.[20] In other words, most parents manage to provide all that is needed for their baby's development in the first year. So relax, enjoy, and put your attention on the spheres that are more open to parental input during the first eight months.

EMOTIONAL DEVELOPMENT

A baby's sense of well-being depends on having her needs for love, warmth, touch, and food met. Emotional development is based on the love, trust, and touch experienced in the baby's first relationships within the family.

When you respond promptly to your baby's cries, she learns that the world is a friendly place and that your love and protection surround her. Parents who follow their instincts know this, and it's nice to find psychologists now stating that you can't spoil a young baby. Unfortunately, however, mothers are still likely to hear grandparents or perhaps even their husbands comment that they are spoiling the baby, or even that it's good for babies to cry. Surrounding your baby with love, warmth, and touch provides a secure foundation for later life that is almost impossible to make up for if it has been lacking.

Researchers have observed that babies usually cry only in response to discomfort until around four or five months of age. At that age a new kind of intentional behavior can be seen for the first time: crying so that an adult will pick them up and cuddle them. In other words, the baby has learned, through successfully having her physical needs met, that she can also cry for attention. It is important that she have confidence that an adult will come when she calls and that a pleasant experience results. This contrasts with babies in institutions, who learn that their cries won't bring a response, and as a result don't exhibit this new intentional behavior of attracting the attention of adults. Most professionals would rather see a baby between three and six months cry too much for attention than cry too little and risk receiving inadequate attention during the first few months of life.[21] Beginning to distinguish between the two types of cries is a valuable skill to develop. Because babies have neither reason nor a sense of time, you can't tell the child to wait or to stop crying. Many mothers and fathers find this a difficult time in their parenting that would be easier if we had more adults around!

During the months before your baby learns to crawl (perhaps between six and eight months), your baby may become demanding. She can see everything and wants to experience it, but she can't get to it. This driving force to crawl and walk is appropriate, but it can result in a baby who requires frequent changes of scenery, adult input, or carrying to avoid complaining. White, in his quest to find out what creates a pleasant, unspoiled three-year-old, as well as a bright one, has traced the origins of "spoiling" back to those parents who fall into a pattern of constantly responding to their six- or seven-month-old's cry for attention. "If you find that you are picking up your child and playing with her seven or eight times an hour for six or seven hours a day, you are probably moving into a pattern that will cause you some grief fairly soon," White states.[22]

I found this statement interesting because White is a sensible observer, and he must have noticed some sort of correlation. I pondered this observation for many years, because I couldn't figure out how he could suggest that you should ignore your baby's call for attention. I realized that if there is a potential problem, it must lie in the fact that one's circumstances have created a whiny baby who wants to be picked up six or eight times an hour. One of the ways to avoid this pattern is to involve your baby in your life. For example, parents with one or two other young children don't have this problem as often—they haven't the time. Also, the siblings provide interaction for the baby, so attention needn't always come from the parents.

It seems that White was observing the problems created when the baby becomes the center of attention instead of an observer of and a participant in family life. Ignoring your baby and letting her cry it out is not what he is recommending! Rather, he is suggesting that you realize that your baby is born into your family and needs to find his or her place there. You must find the middle ground between letting the baby become the center of the universe, and thus jumping to fulfill her every whim, and ignoring her out of some mistaken belief that you will spoil her.

It seems to me that two problems arise. The one we have just discussed seems to be solved by asking the question, "How can I be in empathetic connection with my baby and perceive what she needs in this moment?" The other seems to involve the problem discussed in the previous chapter, that modern life does not support what young children need and hence leads to problems of babies not being able to observe their mothers doing "real work" around the house. With the industrial revolution and the move to the cities, labor-saving devices not only changed the nature of home life but also created families in which women were isolated from other members of their families—indeed, from other adults altogether. So another way to avoid the baby's learning to whine louder and louder to get mother's attention is to have other adults about. Our culture, with its lack of extended family, puts a real strain on the mother. Earlier I mentioned a friend of mine who realized this truth from her experiences in Mexico (page 29). How much you hold and carry your baby can have an effect on him, but it also needs to be balanced with your own needs and emotional well-being.

The larger question with regard to many of the difficulties parents encounter has to be, "How can we overcome our isolation and find or recreate community?" Raising young children in isolation can be crazy making—I'm convinced it was never meant to happen. Everyone nods with a certain recognition that "it takes a village to raise a child," so how did we end up where we are today?

Two historical forces have served to isolate women and their mothering. The first was the pioneering impulse to strike out for the frontier, and the second was the migration to the cities. Although it was tremendously difficult for pioneer women to be separated from their community of women, life was so hard that children had to be incorporated into the process of helping the family survive, and rural life was at least healthier than conditions in the overcrowded tenements or factories. But with the dominance of city life, the isolation of mothers has continued and intensified as we have become increasingly mobile and tend to live far from all our family members.

If you find yourself home alone with your baby and are not having the time of your life, you need to reach out and find a network of support. You owe it to your children, your mothering, and yourself. Some suggestions of groups you might join include La Leche League, mother-infant groups, playgroups, and religious groups. Put up signs in the natural foods co-op or start talking to other mothers in the park. They're probably either as isolated as you are or they've found something worth sharing.

LANGUAGE DEVELOPMENT

As was discussed in the previous chapter, the first year is a critical period during which babies learn the sounds of a language and develop an interest in communicating with others. The baby has been able to hear sounds from the fifth month inside the womb, but most of the sounds the baby heard came from within the mother's own body or from her internal vibrations as she spoke. Only near the end of pregnancy does the expanded uterus begin to conduct outside sounds with any clarity. Some "prenatal university" advocates are trying to sell parents recorded messages or music with special earphones that attach to the mother's stomach to increase auditory pathways for future language or mathematical development. Just as Steiner says that you wouldn't want to stimulate the developing eye of the baby when it was in the womb, Jane Healy advises that "until we learn more about this topic it seems sensible to give the fetus a calm, stable start without an atmosphere of overstimulation or pressure. By all means talk and sing to your unborn child as you relax and rock, but reflect carefully before you start 'pushing' any type of learning." If you're still tempted by the hype associated with these items, she continues:

> Overstimulating parents, however, should think twice about an experiment in which duck embryos were subjected to abnormally intense auditory stimulation (noise); after the ducks were born they failed to learn their mother's call and showed other signs of abnormal attention and development. When you are tempted to turn up the stereo, remind yourself that 'augmented sensory experience' is probably not good for human babies either.[23]

Infants show a preference for their mother's voice and start trying to understand and remember speech sounds soon after birth. Nothing can substitute for the love and attention you give your baby. When you talk to her while changing her diaper, for example, you are providing loving stimulation and a model for language development. At around four months your baby will turn and smile when you say her name. This is a stage called prelanguage comprehension, because any name will work equally well, but regardless it is an exciting time. By eight months she will probably be responding to a few specific words, which usually include some variation of "mommy," "daddy," "baby," and "bye-bye," if English is the primary language in your home.

Babies prefer sounds that are high-pitched and respond especially well to the voice when it is rhythmical and melodic—hence the use of lullabies with babies throughout all cultures. Any time you hum or sing to your baby, you are doing her a wonderful service. Some parents worry that they "aren't musical," but everyone can hum, and songs can be extremely simple, involving only a few words and one or two notes. A simple musical instrument called a children's harp is very soothing at nap or bedtime and can also help parents bring the musical element to their young children. The harp is tuned in a special way, according to a pentatonic scale, so that anything you play sounds angelic—there are no wrong notes. Sources for the children's harp are listed at the end of this chapter, and music is discussed more in chapter 10.

TOYS FOR THE FIRST YEAR

American companies spent $2 billion on advertising to children in 1998, twenty times more than they did in 1988, and the amount has only gone up since then! Despite what Madison Avenue would like you to believe, your baby will develop quite healthily without your buying any toys in the first year. Helle Heckmann, director of the Danish child care center, Nøkken, states, "The infant has himself, and it is by observing himself and his limbs that the infant develops. That is why the infant should not be offered any toys."[24] However, every baby in America is going to have toys, so what principles can guide our selections?

What your baby needs is a balance of playing with objects, moving to develop physical skills, and interacting with people. Interaction can come through the daily care you give your baby—through breastfeeding or giving him a bottle (and, later, spoon feedings), and through changing and bathing her. Just make sure that you are attentive and aware of your baby as a human being during these times rather than treating her as an object or a chore that has to be accomplished. Talking and singing to your baby can lead to playing games as she becomes a little older. Babies love to play peek-a-boo after they are about six months old, delighting in the appearance and disappearance of themselves and the world. Simple movement games like "pat-a-cake" or "so big" also delight a one-year-old.

The following are the toys and equipment that I would recommend for babies in the first year:

- A rocking chair
- A children's harp, also called a *kinderlyre*
- An infant car seat (birth to nine months) and a child car seat (nine months on)
- A cloth sling for carrying young babies; a sling or backpack for older babies; a baby buggy or pram, if you can find one, and later a stroller for outdoor walks
- A crib gym (from six weeks until the baby is sitting)
- A stair gate placed on the third stair to allow for safe climbing practice (or you can construct three steps and a platform)
- A baby food grinder to prepare foods from your table for the baby (there's no need to give solid food before six months—and the food you make is fresh and salt- and sugar-free, unlike most processed baby foods)
- A large box or basket to keep toys in
- Several balls of various sizes, including a cloth or felt ball for the younger child (avoid foam balls, which can easily be pulled apart and eaten)
- Pots and pans (six to twelve months)
- Containers with lids and hinged boxes (seven to fifteen months)
- A box or basket with about a dozen safe objects (several large shells, pieces of driftwood, a pretty rock)
- Books with stiff pages

- Low four-wheeled toys that can be straddled (once your baby is walking)
- Water toys

The following items, however, are of questionable value:

- Pacifiers. After nursing is established, some babies still need to suck more than they need to eat, and a pacifier can be soothing during the first year of life, but its danger is that it replaces human interaction. Toddlers and older children who have a pacifier pinned to their clothing often have it stuck in their mouths just to keep them quiet.
- Props for bottles. Propping a bottle means that your baby is losing the love and attention that accompanies breastfeeding or bottle-feeding. Letting a baby fall asleep with a bottle in his mouth can result in serious tooth decay, because the juice or milk sits in the mouth and the sugars can encourage bacterial growth and "bottle mouth syndrome."
- Baby bouncer. This gets the baby vertical before she can stand, and the force of jumping can have a negative impact on the leg bones.
- Baby walker. Although babies love the mobility a baby walker allows them, it makes them vertical before they can stand and takes time away from crawling. It is also implicated in many accidents in the home.
- Playpen. Fortunately, Pack 'N Play and similar items are pretty much only used for sleeping these days. Better to babyproof your home than to confine your child!
- Swimming classes. Although these were formerly in vogue, many parents report having negative experiences with these classes and no real gains.
- Baby gymnastics. Your baby knows best how to move to develop! Gymnastics can be okay as an excuse to meet other parents if the children are just allowed to play, but it tends to be too stimulating and can place your baby or toddler at risk.

And, to conclude, these are some enjoyable activities to do with your baby that can help her natural development:

- Put an emphasis on touching, carrying, and skin-to-skin contact.
- Talk to your baby; focus on her as a person when you're caring for her.
- Hum and sing to your baby.
- Place a high value on contact with nature. Your baby will love to see the interplay of light and shadow when under a tree, and toddlers love sand and water play, indoors or out. However, avoid overexposure to bright sun.
- Recite nursery rhymes and play movement games, including peek-a-boo, pat-a-cake, "This Big," "Hickory Dickory Dock," and "Where's Baby?"

RECOMMENDED RESOURCES

Various Approaches to Parenting

The Continuum Concept, by Jean Liedloff (Addison-Wesley). The classic discussion of attachment parenting. Or see www.askdrsears.com or www.attachmentparenting.org.

LifeWays North America. Offers support for parents and child care providers through their LifeWays Early Childhood and Human Development Certification, a combination of part-time classes and guided work between sessions. See www.lifewaysnorthamerica.org.

Mothering.com. Natural mothering and online community with reprints from twenty-five years of *Mothering* magazine.

Mothering and Fathering: The Gender Differences in Child Rearing, by Tine Thevenin (Avery). Discusses the gender differences in parenting, both in society and in the home. Out of print, but worth finding online.

Mothering with Soul, by Joan Salter (Hawthorn Press). A Waldorf approach to mothering as special work.

Nøkken: A Garden for Children, by Helle Heckmann (Waldorf Early Childhood Association). Learn more about Heckmann's insights and program in Denmark. Available from www.waldorfearlychildhood.org.

Resources for Infant Educarers (RIE). Books, videos, training opportunities, and other information on the approach of Dr. Emmi Pikler and Magda Gerber. See www.pikler.org and www.rie.org.

Sophia's Hearth Family Center. Offers workshops and courses in New Hampshire for parents and professionals that combine principles from Waldorf and Pikler/RIE. At www.sophiashearth.org.

Things to Do with Your Baby

SONGS, FINGERPLAYS, AND LULLABIES
Giving Love, Bringing Joy and other titles by Wilma Ellersiek (with accompanying CDs). Hand gesture games and lullabies in the mood of the fifth. Available from www.waldorfearlychildhood.org.

Sing a Song with Baby and *The Wonder of Lullabies*, by Mary Schunemann. Songs, fingerplays, games, and lullabies, with accompanying CDs to help you learn them. By a consummate Waldorf songstress. Available from www.naturallyyoucansing.com.

SOURCES FOR TOYS
There are many online sources for toys for babies made from wood, wool, cotton, and other natural materials, including:

A Toy Garden (www.atoygarden.com)

Bella Luna Toys (www.bellalunatoys.com)

Nova Natural (www.novanatural.com)

Palumba (www.palumba.com)

SOURCES FOR CHILDREN'S HARPS
Bella Luna Toys (www.bellalunatoys.com) offers several lines, including Song of the Sea and Choroi. Also look on their site for their video, "Introduction to the Pentatonic Lyre," for a demonstration of tuning and playing.

CHAPTER 5

Helping Your Toddler's Development

ENCOURAGING BALANCED DEVELOPMENT

Between the ages of one and two, your toddler is improving physical mastery of her body and also developing facility with language. With the development of language, you will start to see your child use ideas and images in her mind rather than use physical actions to solve problems. This growth of thinking and memory interact with her behavior, so that a two-year-old is a highly complex social being. This aspect of development is marked by the emergence of individuality and personal power, the growing sense of *I*.

The main task of parents as first teachers during the time from twelve to twenty-four months is to encourage a balanced development. Physical development involves the freedom to practice new motor skills; emotional development centers around her relationship with her mother, father, or other primary caregivers; intellectual development comes primarily through exploring the world around her.

Your toddler's natural inquisitiveness is best met by letting it unfold naturally in a baby-proofed home, free from restraints. Much of her time will be spent exploring objects and mastering skills, such as taking things apart, stacking them up, and knocking them down. Hinged doors, stairs, and climbing up on a chair to look out the window are favorite activities. The toilet bowl is a favorite source of play, so be sure to keep the bathroom inaccessible. Outdoor play is encouraged because there are so many things to explore. Children in this age range love to swing and to play in the sandbox.

Because everything she explores still goes into her mouth and will be swallowed if possible, make sure that toxic items are stored out of reach in locked cupboards (toddlers love to climb). We wonder how children can swallow gasoline or cleaning fluid, but their curiosity is stronger than bad tastes or smells, and these children may swallow just about anything. Take time to recheck your home for safety when your child is between one and two years of age!

In terms of social development, a child in the second year will be focused primarily on her parents, not going very long without checking back in with them for nurturing, advice, assistance, or just making sure they are there. By being available when your child wants you and letting her explore without you, you are teaching your child both independence and security. And your encouragement and interaction when she brings you something to look at fosters her natural curiosity, showing that you value both inquisitiveness and learning.

Positive social interaction among two-year-olds is not very common. Their unconscious need to imitate means that one toddler wants whatever interesting thing the other has, and they usually lack the social skills to play together. Play will be more side-by-side than interactive, and a child of this age will need to be closely supervised to learn to touch with gentle hands and to wait when another child has a toy. Sharing is not a concept that comes naturally, but learning to wait until another child is finished can be an appropriate first step. LifeWays and some other home-based programs address the special needs of toddlers by caring for children of mixed ages. In this situation, toddlers can learn both social skills and imaginative play by imitating the older children, and thus learn them sooner than if they were around only their peers!

In terms of motor skills, you will find that your baby from the age of fourteen months is able not only to walk but also to climb. Running will also start to develop. Your eighteen-month-old will probably like sturdy toys that she can straddle while she walks. The ability to operate a tricycle usually isn't present until after the age of two, and such toys are best delayed until the child is older.

The best way to keep a balance in these areas of exploration, movement, and social interaction is to provide an environment where the child can explore by herself (with adult awareness of safety but not always with adult interaction). This will usually be your home, made safe and equipped with a few simple toys in addition to common household items.

Aids to Learning

Because of the natural impulse to want to provide the best opportunities for their children, many parents are turning to classes to help their eighteen-month-old learn to swim, read, become a gymnast, or whatever. Programs to teach infants to swim were very popular several years ago and have since drawn a great deal of criticism. Most parents' experiences were that early gains were lost, and their children's experiences were often heartrending. Trust yourself and don't do anything you don't feel good about. Putting your child into a frightening situation is not worthwhile. No classes are necessary for optimal or even enhanced development. If you do participate in any kind of group, make sure that you stay with your child, that the activity is appropriate for her age, and that the environment is not overwhelming on a sensory level. As mentioned before, a baby gymnastics class can be fun as a social experience for parents with cabin fever, but such classes can push children beyond their developmental stage. The toddler knows best which muscles to exercise to develop optimally. An excellent summary of reasons parents want their children to be in classes and why it is better to avoid them is contained in *Miseducation: Preschoolers at Risk* by David Elkind.[1]

Even a playgroup is more helpful for stay-at-home parents than for a child of this age; an ideal format might be a parents' support group during which one or two parents take turns watching the children while the others meet to talk. (They can also meet at night while the other parent watches the children!) Many Waldorf schools and LifeWays providers offer parent-toddler groups, as do many churches and service organizations such as the "Y."

Similarly, any kind of emphasis on intellectual development that takes time away from physical movement can lead to imbalance. There's a saying, "Don't push the river." Your baby is developing according to his or her own inner clock. Tampering with the mechanism by trying to speed up one area can lead to problems in other areas.

Some parents wonder whether their child will be missing out if she doesn't watch *Sesame Street* or other programs designed to promote early language skills. However, children learn how to use "before" and "after" in their speech perfectly well from hearing you speak—they don't need Grover to give a lesson on it! One study, cited above, showed that only language from living sources, not television, boosted children's vocabulary and knowledge of syntax.[2] Burton White corroborates this, saying, "Rest assured that if he never sees a single television program he can still learn language through you in an absolutely magnificent manner."[3]

The medium of television is totally inappropriate for the infant or toddler, who needs to be moving and actively exploring. Up until now, young children have been unable to sit long enough to watch the screen; if they did so with older siblings, it was more in an imitative and social way than because they were paying attention to what was being presented. Unfortunately, television producers have now studied what attracts toddlers and are offering programming designed to capture their attention. Videos such as the "Little Einstein" series marketed by Disney have been discredited for claiming benefits for young children. Don't buy their consumer arguments! A more detailed discussion of how the two-dimensional, flickering sensory stimulation from television is not what a young child needs can be found in chapter 12. In the meantime, it would be best for your child if you moved your television into a room where adults and older children could watch it without the images and sounds cluttering the environment of your baby or toddler.

As your child's first teacher, you have primary responsibility for him or her in the first years of life. One of the most important things you can do is to pay attention to all that surrounds your child. This includes the food, clothing, images, toys, sunshine, sand, and water. It also includes the less tangible "nourishment" that comes from your warmth and love and the emotions that surround your child. To help your toddler develop, work on yourself, which means cultivating patience and firmness and getting rid of blame and guilt when you are not the ideal parent. No one is, but it is the striving and the effort to grow inwardly that speak most strongly to children, who are so involved with their own physical and emotional growth. Our children come to see our faults and forgive us; our orientation toward inner growth through parenting fosters change within ourselves and is a great gift to our children.

If you understand your child's development, you will be less likely to do things that impede it, such as boring him by restraining him in an infant seat or high chair for hours every day. You will also avoid unrealistic expectations of your child, such as expecting her to remember that certain things aren't allowed or trying to reason with her. Remember the principles of imitation and movement when you correct her actions! This will make you better able to provide the correction and guidance that are needed, and to avoid the annoyance that can lead to you telling your child she is "bad" for exploring things you want her to stay out of.

DEALING WITH NEGATIVE BEHAVIOR

One of the challenges of living with the child from eighteen to thirty-six months is dealing with the negativism that he or she manifests. If you can recognize your child's emerging sense of self and power as something positive, you won't fall into the trap of thinking that you have done something wrong ("If only we hadn't moved," or "He must be selfish because I have a short temper"). You can take the adult and parental perspective of enjoying your child's development while providing the guidance and boundaries she needs.

Most first children suffer from too much adult attention, whether it is the result of love, insecurity, or mistaken ideals. With a second or third child, there just isn't the time to indulge her every whim, and life has to become more rhythmical and orderly or the parent won't survive. With my first child, I fell into the philosophical pit of not wanting to be authoritarian, and chaos reigned until I realized that I could (and should) insist on right behavior. This needs to be done with calmness and joy rather than anger, but with absolute conviction that the child will eventually learn what is expected. It is appropriate that parents be guardians and guides (less charged words than "authorities") and help children in the process of becoming pleasant as well as bright three-year-olds! Your children unconsciously trust you to know more about becoming adults than they do. Because they are just learning impulse control and the social graces, you must provide appropriate boundaries for them.

In observing families where parents had already produced "outstanding children," White found that "the effective parents we have studied have always been loving but firm with their children from early infancy on. The principal problem that average families run into in this area is allowing the child to infringe on their own rights too much."[4] This means, for example, that you set up your house so that the child has maximum freedom and requires a minimum of "no's," but then you are firm about what is not allowed. It is wonderful for your child to be curious, but he doesn't have to play with your makeup, which can be met with a stern "no," removing the child from the scene, and then putting the makeup in a less accessible place. There is no need to punish the child, because a toddler is unable to understand what he has done or to remember the next time.

Preventing your child from running your home becomes more of an issue when he starts to assert himself by saying "no" to you. One very useful tip for getting around the almost reflexive negativism of a two-year-old is to stop asking questions while cultivating an appreciation for the power of moving. Young children tend to be very verbal, leading parents to fall into the trap of relating to them on a rational level. Asking your two-year-old, "Do you want to . . ." invites a negative answer from a child of this age. Instead, positive and neutral statements such as, "It's time to brush your teeth for bed" can be very effective when combined with the absolute certainty that there is no other choice. Adding a bit of fantasy, movement, or song while going upstairs can also engage a child and circumvent negativity.

Keeping things the same as much as possible can also avoid problems with toddlers. Many two-year-olds hate change and fall apart during transitions between activities. Everything has to be a certain way or pandemonium breaks loose. This doesn't mean that you need to give in each time or put up with whiny behavior, but understanding the two-year-old's attachment to order can help you avoid problems. It is a phase that will ease in intensity as your child matures. You'll most likely find he's not attached to order as an adolescent!

However, sometimes your child will just be negative, and he may astonish you with the force of his refusal. When this happens, it is good first to acknowledge what it is that your child wants: "I can see that you really want to keep playing in the park. You have tears and are saying, 'No, mommy! No go home!'" This in itself may get your child's attention, and everyone appreciates being understood. After this heartfelt acknowledgment, however, you follow up with a statement of what needs to happen: "But it's time to go so we can make dinner for daddy. You can help me with the carrots when we get home." Again, presenting something imaginative can often help ("Let's hop to the car like that little bunny we saw. I wonder who will get there the quickest, mamma bunny or baby bunny?"). You might also provide a choice, either of which still accomplishes your aim, to help avoid a showdown ("Do you want to fly to the bedroom or hop like a bunny?").

If your child resorts to full-blown whining or screaming after you have acknowledged his feelings, it's important not to indicate that he can sometimes get what he wants by throwing a fit. You might physically remove the child from his location, either sitting and holding him, if that seems appropriate, or standing there with him like a big, boring lump while reassuring him that as soon as he's ready, the activities of life will go on again. While taking a few deep breaths yourself, you could ask yourself whether there is anything going on. Is he overtired or possibly coming down with a cold? Or there may be no apparent explanation. Sometimes one or two minutes of your leaving the room will calm a child right down. What's the point in having a tantrum when no one is watching? At other times singing a song or starting a favorite fingerplay can put the child in a better mood. Regardless of what method you use, you then need to lovingly and firmly follow through by insisting on the action that caused the meltdown. What doesn't work is becoming angry, hitting or belittling the child, or giving in and reinforcing that this behavior often gets results. Remember that intermittent rewards have been shown to encourage learned behavior more effectively than a reward that is given every time, so it's important to be consistent.

Knowing that you can set boundaries and correct behavior helps you maintain your patience and keeps you from allowing a child to run the household and then resenting it. Correction always occurs in the present moment, where the child lives. You can't expect your two-year-old to remember not to do that again, which is why time-outs or other punishment will not work. If you have an especially willful child, you may need to set the limits again and again during this period, but persistence pays off. Setting firm and consistent limits throughout the second year will usually prevent temper tantrums after the child turns two. Temper tantrums and the "terrible twos" are common, but they are not inevitable. White encourages parents to teach the child that he is terribly important, that his needs and interests are special, but that he is no more important than any other person in the world, especially his parents.[5] If a child moves into the third year without it having been made clear that he doesn't run the home and that you really mean it when you forbid something, you are in for trouble. Discipline and the importance of rhythm in home life in preventing behavior problems will be discussed further in later chapters.

ENCOURAGING THE DEVELOPMENT OF LANGUAGE AND UNDERSTANDING

Because we cannot really be certain what a child experiences when she contemplates an object, it is best to leave the toddler in peace until there is a natural break in her activities or she comes to you with something. Because of our lack of awareness and our desire to take advantage of teaching situations, we are constantly interrupting children to tell them the names of things when they are happily engrossed in an object. Instead, we can observe them and let them explore the world. In *The Young Child*, Daniel Udo de Haes makes the valuable suggestion that you do your teaching when you give the child an object, not when he or she is playing with it.[6] For example, you might say, "Water . . . water," when you give your daughter a bowl full of water and some measuring cups to play with, perhaps even picking up some of the water in your hand while you say the words. Then let her play by herself. Similarly, if she has discovered something fascinating in the yard, don't rush over to teach her about it. Wait until she wants you and then be there to comment on what she has found ("Bug. What a big bug!").

If we are conscious of the "silent language" of objects, then we can let our human language interact with it harmoniously. For example, after the child hears the wind rustling in the trees we might say "rustling," letting the child hear in these sounds something of what the rustling tree has first spoken to him. In this way it is possible for the child to experience through our words an inner connection between the language of things and the human language.[7]

With the toddler it is best not to speak about things but to let the things speak for themselves whenever possible. In other words, there is nothing harmful, and even something beneficial, in letting the doll say, "Good morning!" to the child or in personifying or animating objects and letting them speak for themselves. For the young child, all the world is alive, and everything does speak; the ability to distinguish reality from imagination lies in the future and will come naturally. As adults we tend to offer far too many intellectual explanations to our young children, having forgotten how to experience the world in movement and in pictures. If the personification of objects is done in a natural and responsible manner, it can strengthen an inward listening in the child.[8]

Around the second half of the second year, your child will become more interested in the pictures in books than with turning the pages. There is a value in bringing before the child a picture of what she has experienced in nature. Just as an artist can help us see everything, so a picture book can help the child recognize that others share her visions and experiences. With this in mind, pictures of everyday objects, far from being trivial, have great value in bringing before the child the most fundamental aspects of life on earth, and have the recognition value of mirroring the child's own experience. In this sense, a picture of baby's cup might be more valuable than an elephant, which the child won't yet have experienced! Thus pictures of the simplest objects, with no story thread, are satisfying for the child before the age of three.

Because the child is trying to experience the world and gain a picture of life as it is, it is helpful to put before her appropriate and accurate pictures of life rather than caricatures of a rabbit wearing clothes or cartoon depictions of characters. The young child does not have the sophistication to laugh at cartoon renditions of absurd events, which imply that the observer, like the artist, is placing himself over and against it in judgment and laughter. A picture book has value for the toddler when he finds in it a portrayal, created by adults with dedication and respect, of everything that has resonated in his inner being.[9]

Very few good books for toddlers exist, but if we understand the value of sharing the same book over and over (even several times in the same day), then very few are needed! It is beneficial to read only one book at a sitting because each book has its own atmosphere, and mixing them can clutter the child's experience, especially at bedtime. Similarly, too many pictures give the child no time to digest them and destroy the quiet intimacy that belongs with each picture. Children may bring another book to you and want more, but being clear that one story is enough will not only help your child live fully with those images but will also help convey the value of the individual experience in contrast to always having more of something.

It is also very valuable for your child if you draw your own picture book for her, preferably with her watching. Most adults think they can't draw, usually as a result of their own experiences in childhood. But the child is not concerned with our artistic ability. Rather, the magical quality appears when our attempts, which she invests with her own imagination, call forth her own inner recognition of experiences. By so doing, we show the child that her quest for the earthly world is understood.[10]

Another activity for toddlers is showing her a storybook whose pictures meet the above criteria but without reading the story. Simply comment on the pictures using simple language, such as "There is Mother Hen with all of her chicks. Peep. Peep. Peep." Then when we turn the page (or the child does), we can let him look at the picture for a while before adding our simple words. At first the child may turn the pages at random. Later he will want you to read or tell the story with the same words each time and will be nourished by their familiarity. As the years go by, stories can gradually be made more complicated, or you can begin conversations about a story, so that a good picture book can last from toddlerhood through the preschool years.

THE BEGINNINGS OF IMAGINATIVE PLAY

A young child's earliest play involves movement for the pure joy of it. Running, jumping, whirling, and standing on tiptoe are enjoyable in themselves. The imaginative element will start to enter in when your son or daughter hops like a bunny or rides a stick horse. In the second year you may have glimpses of imaginative play as your child begins to pretend she is eating or drinking or talking on the phone. Through imagination, the child is able to unite herself with the world at the same time that memory and thinking are separating her from it. Fantasy and play are like complementary opposites to memory and thinking. The creative power of imaginative play continues to develop throughout early childhood, blossoming between ages three and six.

For the young toddler, pretending first begins as imitation and is carried out as actions rather than words, like pretending to drink something from a real or an imaginary cup. As children approach the age of two, their growing facility with language enables their pretending to be more conversational and interactive. Simple toys further your child's imagination. For example, having a toy plate leads to talking about what is on it. This soon develops into preparing food, which can easily be done as a chair is turned into a stove top with an oven underneath.

A block can be used as a toy telephone and lead to conversational play, but your hand can do just as well. Many times, messages delivered this way can make the next set of activities into a game.

Mother (with hand to ear): Ring. Ring. Heather, your phone is ringing.

Heather: Hello.

Mother: This is Mommy. I need to buy some eggs. Get your shoes on and you can come to the store with me.

Heather: Okay!

Mother: Bye.

A bit of fantasy goes a long way in circumventing your child's negativism. For example, if you hold a washcloth like a puppet who is talking, the child may soon be convinced to rub noses with this talking friend. Or suggesting that all the little mice pick up the crumbs (scraps of paper) will immediately result in a "little mouse" helping you clean up the mess.

PROVIDING A RICH ENVIRONMENT
FOR YOUR TODDLER

You don't have to spend a lot of money on fancy toys to provide a rich environment for your toddler. Making accessible the items in your home, plus a few free or inexpensive items, such as a ball and a cardboard box, will provide your child with hours of valuable exploration. Your toddler will want to touch and explore everything in your home, seeing what it feels like, whether she can carry, empty, or fill it, and whether it comes apart. The toddler age requires constant supervision, because your child can hurt herself or other things the minute you turn your back. It's a time when you'll need to start teaching discrimination: it's all right to play with her toy telephone, but not the real one; she can play with the large necklace in her drawer, but not go into your jewelry box. It's understandable that it takes time for toddlers to learn the difference!

One valuable thing you will be teaching your child during this time is how to touch and how to care for things. Because your child is such an imitator, always demonstrate the behavior you want and make positive statements such as, "Touch the puppy gently," rather than "Don't hurt the puppy." Or "Here, sniff the pretty flower," rather than "Don't crush the flower!" You will also need to start teaching the lessons of "Sharp!" and "Hot!" by modeling the behavior of taking your hand or your child's away from the object in question.

Toddlers are delightful if you can view their being into everything as their way of exploring the world, of experiencing new sights and touch, of emptying, filling, exploring gravity, using their muscles. They have no sense of adult order or goal-directed behavior. If you want Jason to clean up, start putting the toys in the basket with him. He's glad to help, but he's equally glad to dump them all out again if you walk away from him. When you find yourself being annoyed, take a minute to enter into a toddler's world and you will realize that he isn't doing it to annoy you. Quite the contrary, he's probably doing it out of pure "doingness" and is quite oblivious to you. You can (and must) correct and teach him what is and is not acceptable, but you needn't be annoyed when you do it. If you want to get your toddler to do a specific action, the key is to model the behavior you want, while he or she watches and/or does it with you (you'll still end up doing 90 percent of it yourself, but that's the way it is at this age).

Even though it is necessary to know where toddlers are at all times, it's good to provide them with time and space to explore the world while you appear not to be looking. This has been called "benign neglect" because you're aware of what's going on but are not involved in it. Having a craft project such as knitting or crochet is an ideal way to be "busy"; reading, however, does *not* work! Independence is fostered by not always interrupting your toddler but being accessible when he or she comes to you for assistance or to share a discovery.

In addition to loving to explore, your toddler loves simply to move for the joy of movement. She will delight in running, jumping, climbing, pushing, and carrying. All of these activities help in the development of the large muscles and express the young child's nature: to be in movement. Aside from deciding which furniture it's okay to climb on and jump off, you can provide your child with a low balance beam made from placing a wide board over a couple of low bricks or blocks. If the bridge you have made is too challenging for your one-year-old, place it next to a wall; raise it as she becomes more skillful.

Toys that help with the development of large muscles include the very popular indoor wooden slide and ladder with crawling space underneath. Four-wheeled straddle toys that are low to the ground are also favorites of toddlers. A wooden cart, child's shopping cart, or doll stroller is a good toy for pushing. Make sure it is sturdy enough to take the child's weight.

Toddlers love to be outside, and a sandbox (covered to keep cats away) and a water table can provide long periods of enjoyment. Again, make sure that you have inspected your yard and have a locked gate or other means to keep the child away from the street. Most children love to swing, so a sturdy swing is good from age one on. Toys for sand and water play inside are also valuable when the weather is bad.

Many of the toys listed in the preceding chapter will still interest a toddler. As a guide for buying toys, always take into consideration safety and durability. A toddler will still pull things apart and put them in her mouth. As she becomes more adroit at manipulating objects, stacking boxes or nesting dolls are very popular. Wooden toys with moving parts are especially recommended for young children by Rudolf Steiner, who stated, "What a healthy toy it is, for example, which represents, by moveable wooden figures, two smiths facing each other and hammering on an anvil. Such things can be bought in country districts. Excellent also are the picture books where the figures can be set in motion by pulling threads from below, so that the child himself can transform the dead picture into a representation of living action."[11] The ability to have an effect on something and to transform it through movement suits the young child's nature.

Your child loves to stack things, so we suggest making a set of blocks by cutting the trunk and large branches of a tree into blocks of various sizes and shapes. Unlike the geometrically perfect blocks you buy in stores, these irregularly shaped blocks will be used throughout the preschool years for much more than stacking. Their unfinished quality lets the child use his imagination with them. They can easily become people, cans of cat food, or baby bottles; flat pieces from a trunk can be used as plates or cakes. Your preschool child's imagination will be endless. But your toddler will be most interested in stacking them up and knocking them down.

When purchasing toys, consider not only their safety but also their aesthetic qualities. Are they beautiful? How do they feel? What kind of picture of the world do they put before the child? Darth Vader figures, Transformers, dinosaurs, and chartreuse ponies with platinum hair are caricatures of reality that simply are not beautiful nor accurate representations of the world. Everything the young child takes in from birth through age seven has an especially strong effect on him—more so than in later years. The effect of toys and the power of imitation were strikingly illustrated by a photo that appeared in *American Baby* a number of years back. This prize-winning photo showed a preverbal child next to a Cabbage Patch doll, with the child copying exactly the inane expression on the doll's face. Such imitation is completely unconscious and would have been missed if the photographer hadn't been there. Such a photo captures in black and white how deeply sense impressions penetrate the young child and are manifested through the physical organs.

In another remarkable case described by professor of child therapy Alfred Nitschke, a ten-month-old baby girl was admitted to the hospital with extreme lethargy. She was unable to sit up, being doubled over in a jack-knife position; she had a listless expression and a blank gaze. No one had been able to diagnose the problem. Finally one doctor was inspired to notice that the child looked exactly like her constant companion, a floppy stuffed rabbit that was long-limbed and droopy, with large, fixed eyes. The doctor brought a new toy that was friendly looking and had a well-defined shape. The child soon became attached to the new toy, and within a few days her posture, appetite, and mood had begun to improve without any other treatment.[12] In contemplating stuffed toys or dolls for your children, you might remember these examples.

Especially for the young child, the simpler and more archetypal a thing is, the more possibilities it holds for the child. Steiner states:

> As the muscles of the hand grow firm and strong in performing the work for which they are fitted, so the brain and other organs of the physical body of man are guided into the right lines of development if they receive the right impressions from their environment. An example will best illustrate this point.
>
> You can make a doll for a child by folding up an old napkin, making two corners into legs, the other two corners into arms, a knot for the head, and painting eyes, nose and mouth with blots of ink. Or else you can buy the child what they call a "pretty" doll, with real hair and painted cheeks. . . . If the child has before him the folded napkin, he has to fill in from his own imagination all that is needed to make it real and human. The brain unfolds as the muscles of the hand unfold, when they do the work for which they are fitted. Give the child the so-called pretty doll, and the brain has nothing to do.[13]

Because the young child is not fully conscious of his own body, what he is most aware of in himself and others is the head. Thus a knot doll with a large head is quite recognizable and satisfactory to the young child. For a very young child, you can change the basic doll into a "baby" by stuffing the bottom like a blanket or pillow instead of making a body and legs from the two bottom corners.[14]

TOYS AND EQUIPMENT

In addition to many of the toys listed at the end of the previous chapter, the following will be enjoyed by your toddler:

- Low three- or four-wheeled toy that can be straddled
- Push toy, push cart, or doll stroller that is sturdy enough to lean on
- Wooden slide and climbing toy
- Wooden blocks in various diameters cut from a tree
- Wading pool or other low container for water play outdoors, plus bath or other water toys
- Sandbox and sand toys
- Outdoor swing
- Simple first doll of natural materials
- Indoor and outdoor balls of various sizes
- Wooden toys that have moving parts (pecking chickens, two men with hammers)
- Wooden nesting dolls
- Simple picture books with stiff pages
- Books with parts that move
- Large empty cardboard boxes to play in
- Crayons (age two on), especially beeswax crayons, as described in chapter 9

   The following are activities that most toddlers will enjoy:

- Let your toddler start "helping" with things you do (such as loading the dishwasher, stirring the cake, putting things in the trash, sweeping, folding clothes, or watering the plants). The tasks will take you longer, but this is true quality time.
- Help your child experience nature through walks, visiting the park, or feeding the ducks.
- Set up a "nature table" (see page 126) with things that you find on your walks, such as a pretty shell or a leaf. Change the color of the cloth and the themes to reflect the seasons.
- Your toddler loves to be lifted up to the ceiling as if she were an airplane, resting on your extended legs while you lie on your back.

A friend once told me that she liked the ocean so much because it was the only thing big enough to toss her around the way her father did when she was little.

- Simple hiding games are fun. You and your child can take turns hiding under a blanket (our children always played "lump in the bed" while we were trying to make it). Hiding objects in your pocket is also fun for toddlers, who love to find them. Chase, catch, and hug is a favorite game, too.

- Use a song or a bit of fantasy to accompany daily activities like brushing teeth or getting dressed. I made up a little tune for when I wanted my daughter to lie down in the bathtub and get her hair wet: "Mermaid, mermaid, swimming in the water. Mermaid, mermaid, see my little mermaid."

- Continue singing to your child! Include action rhymes whenever you can.

RECOMMENDED RESOURCES

Toddler Play

Children at Play: Using Waldorf Principles to Foster Child Development, by Heidi Britz-Crecelius (Park Street Press). Will help you understand how the child experiences the world through play.

Creative Play for Your Baby: Steiner Waldorf Expertise and Toy Projects for 2 Months–2 Years and *Creative Play for Your Toddler* (2–4 years), both by Christopher Clouder and Janni Nicol. Overview of the development of play, plus many items to make, with clear directions and beautiful photos.

Giving Love, Bringing Joy and other titles by Wilma Ellersiek (with accompanying CDs). Hand gesture games and lullabies in the mood of the fifth. Available from www.waldorfearlychildhood.org.

"Joyful Days with Toddlers and Preschoolers." Blog, telecourses, and other resources from Faith Baldwin Collins, a masterful LifeWays teacher. See www.joyfultoddlers.com.

This Is the Way We Work-a-Day, by Mary Schunemann. Songs, finger-plays, and games for activities of daily life, with accompanying CD by a consummate Waldorf songstress. Available from www.naturallyyou cansing.com.

Toymaking with Children, by Freya Jaffke (Floris). Directions for making knot dolls and other toys for young children.

Sources for Creative, Natural Toys

There are so many companies on the Internet these days! Favorites include:

Bella Luna Toys (www.bellalunatoys.com)

Nova Natural (www.novanatural.com)

Palumba (www.palumba.com)

A Toy Garden (www.atoygarden.com)

DVDs and CDs on Sensory Integration and Child Development

The following CDs and DVDs are available from the online store at www.waldorfinthehome.org:

"Brain in Motion: How Movement Organizes and Improves Brain Function," by Tim Burns

"Developing Healthy Sensory Integration in Nature," by Nancy Blanning

"Helping Our Children Get into Their Bodies," by Nancy Blanning

"Supporting the Four 'Foundational Senses' in the First Seven Years," by Ingun Schneider

"The Twelve Senses," by Daena Ross

"Understanding the Twelve Senses as the Basis for Learning," by Ingun Schneider

CHAPTER 6

Rhythm in Home Life

Creating a rhythmical home life will nourish both you and your child. It will also eliminate 80 percent of your discipline problems—I can practically guarantee it! Because the young child is so centered in the body and in imitation, rhythm is one of the most important keys to discipline. It both guides the child's life by creating good habits and helps avoid arguments and problems. So much of discipline for young children involves self-discipline on the part of the adults: keeping regular rhythms in home life, working on your own patience and emotional responses, being there when your child needs interaction. As an example, playing with your child first can free up an entire twenty minutes to read the paper, whereas telling him you'll play in ten minutes can result in all kinds of emotional disasters. Elizabeth Grunelius states:

> Much of a child's happiness depends on our success in conducting the daily life with and around him with a minimum amount of friction. Every time we may feel like stepping in with advice or an order or a correction, we might well pause for a moment to do two things: firstly, to ask ourselves whether our interference at this particular instant is really necessary; and secondly, to find out what the child is actually trying to do.[1]

In this chapter, first we will consider why rhythm is so supportive to every member of the family, and then we will look at the activities of daily life and some practical suggestions you will be able to apply immediately. Finally, we'll consider the rhythm of the week and then the rhythm of the year as it connects us to both nature and spirit.

CREATING RHYTHM IN DAILY LIFE

We are surrounded by rhythm in nature: the alternation of day and night, the phases of the moon, the cycle of the seasons, the ebb and flow of the tides. Our bodies are permeated by rhythm, in the beating of our hearts, the breathing of our lungs, women's cycles of fertility, and the circadian rhythms of our metabolism. But as modern human beings we have also established a life that is removed from the rhythms of nature. Through electric lighting we can work well into the night; we can shop at twenty-four-hour supermarkets; we can fly strawberries to Minnesota in January. Through technology we can live outside most of the rhythms of nature. As a result, we have often become unaware of the messages and rhythms of our bodies and have forgotten the importance of rhythm in daily life. Steiner describes it as follows:

> Rhythm holds sway in the whole of nature, up to the level
> of man. Then, and only then is there a change. The rhythm
> which through the course of the year holds sway in the
> forces of growth, of propagation and so forth, ceases when
> we come to man. For man is to have his roots in freedom;
> and the more civilized he is, the more does this rhythm
> decline. As the light disappears at Christmas time, so has
> rhythm apparently departed from the life of man. Chaos
> prevails. But man must give birth again to rhythm out of
> his innermost being, his own initiative.[2]

A baby, who has been surrounded by the mother's heartbeat and rocked by her breathing in the womb, emerges into earthly life and must find new rhythms, gradually developing from the fast and irregular heartbeat and breathing of the newborn to the rhythm of one breath to each four heartbeats of the adult.

A regular lifestyle, like the pattern of life in the womb, offers a stable environment during the rapid growth and changes in rhythm of the body during childhood. Children provided with this regular life feel confident about their world and are not concerned by uncertainty about when the next thing will happen. Rhythm in home life can also help calm a nervous or difficult child by turning the child's life into a series of events in which he participates, and from which he gains a new sense of security and competency. Regular mealtimes and regular nap- and bedtimes start orienting the child to a natural feeling for the passing of time. They go a long way toward preventing discipline problems, because bedtimes become something that happen as regularly as the sky turning dark—there is no one to argue with or complain to each night.

Grunelius summarizes, "The rhythm then becomes a habit, is accepted as self-evident and will eliminate many difficulties, struggles and arguments about eating and going to bed. . . . Regularity should prevail in as many of the child's daily activities as possible. It is the key to establishing good habits for life."[3]

She gives an example of how supportive rhythm is for young children and how much they learn through it by telling about taking care of a two-year-old child whom she bathed each day in the same way—first soaping her hands, then her arms, then her neck, and so on. When she took care of the child again after several weeks, the child spontaneously asked, "May I wash myself?" and proceeded carefully and happily through the whole sequence exactly as it had been done so many times before. The child was extremely satisfied with herself![4] This example amazed me, because it never occurred to me to wash a child in a regular fashion, thus providing the child with something it would then be possible to learn.

Andrea Gambardella, a Waldorf teacher, explains, "With the young child and the elementary school student this requirement for an outer structure continues to be vital to growth and emotional well-being. Learning that there is a 'time for all things' is a life's lesson. Now is the time for you to play and do as you will, now for a meal, now for homework, now to prepare for bed."[5]

Rhythm is also a blessing for parents, because it enables the daily activity of life to flow more smoothly, requires less energy, and becomes a platform that supports the family, its activities, and interactions. Many parents don't discover the secrets of rhythm until they have two or more children and suddenly there isn't enough time not to be organized! Regular meals prevent constant feeding and cleaning up or overhungry and whiny children; regular bedtimes suddenly free the evening for adult conversation and life again as a couple. The benefits are many, and yet it is often difficult to create rhythm in family life. It requires an inner discipline of its own!

Creating rhythm in one's life doesn't mean being rigid and dogmatic. There is still plenty of room for special activities and surprises (and sometimes the piper to pay the next day when the child has missed a needed nap or had a late, exciting evening—but it's worth it!). But freedom is not without form, and one is truly free when not hampered by a disorganized life. The rhythmic structure imposed on a young child and permeated with the parents' love is a discipline in the most positive sense of the word. And as your children become older, they will transform this outer structure into an inner self-discipline that will be invaluable for homework and getting other jobs done. Putting attention into these areas can help the quality of life for both you and your children from the time they are toddlers until they leave home.

A Word of Caution

Before reading the following practical suggestions, remind yourself that I'm not suggesting you have to do all these things to be a good parent! Rather, by mentioning so many different ideas, I hope that you will be drawn to adding one rhythmical element to even one area of your child's life. Most people are too busy to have every part of the day be a wonderful time for their children. In my house, breakfasts were efficient, without frills; there was no way, during the school year, that I was going to put special place settings on the table! So I focused my attention on bedtimes. For someone else, however, early mornings might be a great time for the family to be together, especially if evenings are shortened by a parent working late.

There are many blogs and e-zines today portraying a picture-perfect "organic" home life that may make you feel like giving up before you get started. Real life, like the tides, ebbs and flows. There may be chaotic times when all you can focus on is the two most basic activities: eating and sleeping. Because they always occur, they are an excellent place to start and are more than enough during challenging times! There is no point to feeling guilty on top of feeling overwhelmed—life happens!

I suggest you start by focusing on the area of your life that is going the least smoothly. It might be nap time, or it might be dinner, or it might be getting the children out the door in the morning. Whatever the area, think about what happens now, and how you could make things go more smoothly by applying some of the suggestions given here or by inventing some of your own. Having a regular rhythm, adding a bit of ritual like a song or verse, and avoiding too many choices can transform a hectic part of family life into an activity or transition that flows smoothly. Discuss your ideas with your partner, if you have one, agree on a new series of actions for an activity, and then start doing them with the children. You'll be amazed and supported by the results!

Mealtimes

Eating together is a major part of family life and can be an important force in bringing people together. However, attention needs to be focused on mealtimes so they don't become tense or chaotic or simply disappear because everyone is eating on the run.

When do meals occur at your house? Who is present? There are no right or wrong answers when it comes to rhythms and family life. You need to consider the needs of your family members and decide what works for you. The important thing is to bring your consciousness to your situation and work toward what feels best. We know a family where the father and three-year-old would have breakfast together on weekdays before he went to work while the mother got some extra sleep. It was a special time for the two of them that they really cherished. Similarly, work schedules will probably determine what time dinner happens and whether your children will need to eat before you do. Whatever you work out for your family, having meals at a regular time (and regular snacks for the children as needed) can provide an important anchor for rhythm in family life.

Now look at the setting. Do you have a table around which the family can gather? Any little touches you add, like a candle or fresh flowers, can help make meals a special time for the family. I found that, in the summertime, if I set the breakfast table the night before, even I felt nourished and cared for by waking up to a table that was inviting. And all the members of my family, who tended to get up and eat at different times during the summer, felt "held" by the family, even though no one else might be at the table with them.

Next consider the atmosphere. Are mealtimes relaxed and conducive to digestion? Small children in particular need to eat in calm surroundings, without the television or radio on. (The six o'clock news is enough to give anyone indigestion with their graphic reports of murders and other atrocities.) Similarly, the adults should be careful not to be negative about people or to dwell on disappointments of the day. Children take everything in and are unable to disconnect emotions from the functioning of their bodies.

Conversation at meals changes with the arrival of children. It becomes impossible to conduct adult conversation in the same way, and children need to be accepted as conversationalists at the table. Mealtimes then become a time for listening, sharing, and balancing conversations so that each child can bring something of himself or herself to the family's time together. The essay "Family Meals" in *Lifeways* shares many ideas for harmonious meals with growing children,[6] as does Shea Darian's book *Seven Times the Sun*.[7]

Beginning the meal with a spoken or sung blessing encourages feelings of thankfulness and ensures that everyone starts the meal together. Young children are especially nourished by whatever ritual you develop around your family's mealtimes. But you need to bring feelings of gratitude, not empty words said in haste! If you don't have any graces from your religious background, here are two that express an awareness of the connectedness of life and gratitude for our sustenance.

Before the flour, the mill,
Before the mill, the grain,
Before the grain, the sun and rain,
The beauty of God's will.

—UNKNOWN

Earth, who gives to us this food,
Sun, who makes it ripe and good,
Dear Sun, dear Earth, by you we live,
Our loving thanks to you we give.

—CHRISTIAN MORGENSTERN

It is important for children to learn to be grateful for their food and for the efforts of the cook in preparing it. Such an attitude will be fostered by the care we take in preparing and serving the food. This is another area in which cultivating our own gratitude and appreciation for the gift of life will resonate with our children. Handling a child's dislike of certain foods requires some creative thinking. You will need to set your own rules about what can be said about food and what needs to be eaten before a child can leave the table or have dessert. At our house we had a rule that no one could say food was "icky" and that they had to try one (or maybe three) bites of something. What about picky eaters? If you don't offer extra snacks or alternative meals, children are pretty survival oriented. It's sometimes helpful to realize that your job is to put wholesome, nutritious food in front of your child; it is his or her job and responsibility to eat and grow—something that you can't force. Usually the less said, the better.

So that meals can become a calm and harmonious experience for everyone, certain behaviors must be maintained. Sitting in the chair unless one leaves the room can be a minimal expectation, followed by learning how to ask for things politely. If a young child who is whiny or who throws a fit is immediately taken out of the room by a serious adult until he's ready to return, he will probably change his behavior within three minutes. No one wants to be away from the action!

Do your dinners have a formal ending, just drift off, or degenerate rapidly? Having children ask to be excused at the end of a meal is not an old-fashioned formality but a useful way to keep track of who's finished and can help a child clearly distinguish whether he should be sitting at the table or off playing (no coming and going, crawling under the table, chasing the dog, and so forth!). Although some families prefer that everyone stay at the table until a song or short verse is said to end the meal, we preferred that our children ask to be excused when they were finished. This gave them a short time to run around (outside of the dining room) and provided us with a chance to sit back and talk as a couple for a few minutes before we called everyone back to do their jobs of clearing the table, loading the dishwasher, washing the pots and pans, and so forth.

Mealtimes provide one of the earliest opportunities for each child to participate in family chores. While each child can take his or her plate to the kitchen, jobs that benefit the whole family, such as setting the table, clearing the dishes, and wiping the counters, can be rotated among the children. Even the youngest child can have his or her special task in contributing to the family meal, such as putting the napkins at each place.

Mealtimes will change as your children grow older. Meals are different with toddlers, teenagers, or children spanning a range of ages, but gathering around the table to eat and participating in the family's evolving rituals can become an irreplaceable part of your family's life together.

Nutrition

Although it is important for parents to be aware of nutrition, it is just as well to leave young children unaware of the intricacies of daily nutritional requirements. When a child is truly allergic to a food such as milk or peanuts, he needs to be able to tell people so he won't inadvertently eat it. However, your analysis of ingredients or searching for refined sugars will make preschoolers pick apart everything on the table rather than feeling that what they are being served is good. Allergic becomes a synonym for "I don't like," and any kind of shared snack becomes impossible because Liam doesn't eat dairy and Jennifer doesn't eat wheat and Michael is allergic to peanuts and Addie can't have anything with sugar in it.

Your child's trust that what you have given him to eat is good for him is equally or more important than the item itself; if three- and four-year-olds are excessively conscious about nutrition, it will only be divisive. I once saw at the lunch table two kindergarten boys who noticed that one had a huge lunchbox with a big thermos of milk, two white-bread sandwiches, potato chips, and a fruit roll-up, while the other had carob soy milk, a whole-wheat sandwich with tofu and sprouts, a piece of fruit, and a granola bar. These children, who were starting to become self-aware and more aware of the world around them, noticed the discrepancy. One said to the teacher, "My mother says that milk is good for you and helps your bones and teeth."

The other said, "My mom says that milk gives you mucus!"

"Who's right?" they asked together.

My eyebrows went up as I waited to see what my assistant would answer, and I was delighted when she wisely replied, "Your mother is right," which satisfied both boys.

We found that the preschool-aged children in our program had become so picky about food that serving any kind of common snack was almost impossible. The social experience of eating together was difficult to achieve at best!

Children instinctively feel that the world is whole and good and that whatever their parents give them is good for them. It isn't necessary to tell your child more than is minimally necessary for their health or is required to make distinctions about matters like vegetarianism. What you do will be more important than long explanations. "Our family doesn't eat meat" is usually enough for a child to know, and your telling friends and teachers will help keep the child from having to make choices. With something like trying to avoid sugar, if you feed your child wisely at home and tell grandma that you wish she would put away the candy jar before visits, then you may decide that the little bit your child eats at a birthday party or a friend's house may not be worth all of the intellectual and emotional investment required to tell the child he can't have it. These are issues you will have to discuss with your partner and decisions you will have to make based on your medical and philosophical convictions. I can only tell you as a preschool teacher that the awareness and misinformation children have about nutrition these days reflects an increased consciousness of the metabolic sphere that wreaks havoc with the unitive worldview of the young child.

Nap or Quiet Times

Young children need restful or quiet times during the day in order to be restored for play. Like the rhythm of breathing, the child's activities alternate between active play, during which the entire body is in motion, and quiet times, where he might enjoy a snack or a story. When a child focuses his attention on something close at hand, such as when he is making something, coloring, or modeling with beeswax, the activity brings the child into himself and balances his active play.

Many children today sleep very little and seem ready to give up afternoon naps at an early age. However, the afternoon nap is of great benefit to help a child digest the impressions of the day, and it provides welcome downtime for parents as well. The time can be spent sleeping or it can just be a quiet time during which the child has to stay on his bed or in his room. If the rhythm of a daily rest is maintained, the child will learn that this is a time to be by himself and not to call on mother or father. In our LifeWays program, all the full-day children sleep, and when I taught kindergarten, many of the five-year-olds would in fact fall asleep, even though they wouldn't ordinarily nap at home. The others would rest while playing silently on their mat with a favorite doll. Again, the same song is used each time to start and end nap time—and the ending is especially welcome because "Red Bird" (a felt bird on a stick) comes and wakes the children or lets them get up to play.

Recognizing the value of a quiet time for preschool and kindergarten children is the first step in instituting one. An hour in the afternoon without the children can also be a valuable time for parents to center and refresh their energies by resting or doing something they want to do. If your child is not used to a quiet time and you want to institute one, think it through first. What time will work for you? What are the parameters of acceptable behavior? For example, does the child need to sleep or can he just stay quietly on his bed? What kind of doll or toy, if any, will you make accessible to him? Will the room be darkened? What needs to be done in preparation? Going to the bathroom, washing hands, or putting shoes neatly under the chair? Will you sing or tell a story? A kinderharp is wonderful for calming a child and helping him go off to sleep. If you want to sit with your child until he falls asleep, look and act very sleepy yourself—eyelids drooping, not talking or answering questions, yawning, and letting sleep ooze from your pores. Putting your hand on a child's head or back can also be very calming. If you don't have such a nap time, you will probably find that your child comes home from a morning program and just wants to sit or play alone for a while after lunch anyway. The children have been so active in a group during the morning that a more inward time provides needed balance.

Bedtime

What is bedtime like at your house? Does the evening have a rhythm to it, ending in going to bed at a regular time and accompanied by a regular set of activities? A regular bedtime preceded by a set ritual can help calm your child and prevent arguments. It can also help him learn to do more and more of the activities involved in getting ready for bed by himself as he becomes older. This will also help him feel more secure when you have a babysitter if the sitter is taught to do things in the same order.

How a child enters sleep is important for refreshing the spirit as well as the body. Falling asleep and waking are portals to the spiritual world, the world of dreams and inspirations. How we and our children enter sleep and wake up can affect the quality of both sleeping and waking life. With a young child, the entire time after dinner is often focused on leading toward bedtime. Quiet play can be followed by straightening up the room, then by a bath when needed or washing up, brushing teeth, and putting on pajamas. Talking slowly or singing softly can help set a quiet mood for bedtime. Lighting a candle in the room and then whispering can help create a mood of calmness and sharing. A song, a story, a verse, or a prayer that unites the child's soul with the divine can all help a child drift peacefully into sleep. You might play some music on the kinderharp if you have one. If you have used a candle, you'll want to blow it out before leaving the room, but its warm, soft light can be very calming during the song and story. If your child has difficulty going to sleep, many more suggestions can be found in the essay "Sleeping and Waking" in *Lifeways*[8] and in *Seven Times the Sun*.[9]

Children love consciousness and cling to it, and thus they will stay up to the point of becoming overtired. They really can't be depended on to go to bed when they need to! When I first enrolled in the teacher training program at the Waldorf Institute, my children were in kindergarten and second grade and were going to bed at 8:30. One of the instructors talked about sleep and suggested that my children could easily be going to bed at 7:30. I thought, "Not my kids! Eight-thirty is hard enough!" But I decided to try this suggestion to see if it would work. To my utter surprise, the children went to bed an hour earlier without a fuss and slept an hour longer at night, even though they hadn't seemed tired on the old schedule. I was dumbfounded! I have had similar experiences, suggesting that preschool parents start their child for bed at 7 p.m. instead of putting him to bed at 11 p.m. To their surprise, it took less than three days for the child to get into the new rhythm, so that one boy even told his babysitter that it was time for bed in the early evening.

If your child goes to bed early, will he wake up at the crack of dawn? You will have to try it and see. A preschool child who wakes up bright and smiling with the sun can't understand why adults want her to go back to sleep! But most children will not wake up so early, and they can be taught to put on a robe and slippers, if it is cold, and to play in their room (often with something that has been set out after they have gone to sleep) if you need to sleep a little longer.

Mornings

The transition out of sleep is also an important time, and focusing attention on this time of day can help both adults and children. How do you wake up? Many parents have found that getting up a half hour before the rest of the family gives them a quiet, centered time in the morning that affects their whole day. Or, if they don't get up early, they arrange as many things as possible the night before: what clothes each child will wear, jackets or snowsuits and mittens if needed, bags for school, lunches, the breakfast table, and whatever else is needed. The biggest problem with mornings is that they are often rushed, which makes children move even more slowly and puts everyone in a bad mood.

Assuming you wake your child, how do you do it? Margret Meyerkort reminds us:

> It is important for both children and adults that the experience of the night-consciousness be allowed to stay more or less actively for a while just below the level of the day-consciousness. For here rest the hints, understandings, reassurances and sense of the spiritual world. Therefore the alarm-clock needs to be kept well away from the young child, for it is such a cold, stern and literally shocking awakener. After such an awakening, the child could be disgruntled for hours afterwards. Instead the parent can hum a melody or sing a seasonal or morning song.[10]

Holding a young child up to the window to see the light of the new day is also a nice way to start the morning.

Because a child is still in a kind of night-consciousness after awakening, he often can't cope with any kind of questions for the first ten or fifteen minutes. He simply doesn't have the day-consciousness to come up with the answer, so try to avoid questions and choices. Make your choices together the night before, about what to wear and so forth, so that morning doesn't have to become a battleground of the wills.

Once your child is fully awake, do the events of getting ready for the day have a particular order? Remember that doing things in an orderly way gives a child something to learn and makes it much more likely that your child will remember to brush her teeth and hair when she is school-aged, or won't forget even though it is Saturday. Think about your mornings: getting dressed, eating breakfast, brushing teeth, brushing hair; what about making the bed (together at first)?

Greeting the day is something that children love to do with a verse or a song. If you don't know any, here are two suggestions:

> Morning has come.
> Night is away.
> Rise with the sun
> And welcome the day!
>
> —ELISABETH LEBRET

> Good morning, dear earth; Good morning, dear sun!
> Good morning dear stones and flowers every one!
> Good morning dear busy bees and birds in the trees!
> Good morning to you and good morning to me!
>
> —UNKNOWN

Here is a verse by Rudolf Steiner that can easily have hand gestures added as you point to your eyes, your heart, make a circle like the sun, and put your head on your hands in a resting gesture.

> With my own eyes
> I see the world,
> The lovely world of God.
> My heart must give thanks
> That I may live
> In this, God's world,

That I may wake
In the brightness of the day,
And may rest at night
In the blessing of God.[11]

THE RHYTHM OF THE WEEK

Helping your young child achieve a sense for the rhythm of the week is more easily accomplished if special activities regularly occur on a specific day. If you tend to go to the park once a week, going every Tuesday will give your child a sense of this activity as a punctuation mark for the week; it will also help you organize your other activities. If you often bake with your child, could you do it every Monday, adding another rhythmically recurring event to your child's life?

In former times work was done according to the days of the week as expressed in this traditional verse:

Wash on Monday
Iron on Tuesday
Mend on Wednesday
Churn on Thursday
Clean on Friday
Bake on Saturday
Rest on Sunday

This kind of rhythm is still observed in the Amish communities and, rather than being boring, it creates for them a pattern in the chaos of having so much to do in daily life. While most of us no longer live according to such rhythms of work, if we appreciate their value for the young child we can do certain activities on set days, or shop together on a certain day, so the child starts to feel at home in the week and its recurring rhythm.

Within the pattern of the week, something needs to be said about the Sabbath, which used to be a very special day in which no work or play occurred during the observance of religious practices. If your family doesn't go to church, temple, or mosque, this special day (Sunday, Saturday, or Friday) may have lost its sense of a day for inwardness, for communion with God, oneself, nature, or the family. Think about what your family does on this day. Whether or not you go to church, would it be nourishing to do something regularly, like having a special breakfast, getting out into nature, or having spiritual study for adults with Bible stories told to the children? What would be meaningful for your family?

The days of the week all have specific qualities, colors, grains, activities, and planets associated with them. For example, Tuesday is associated with Mars (which is reflected in the words *mardi* in French and *martes* in Spanish). Since Mars is the god of war in Roman mythology, the theme could be considered strength and energy, and activities could involve heavy chores, sports, and so forth. The Waldorf-inspired *Living Home Kindergarten* curriculum discusses the various qualities in greater detail for anyone who is interested in learning more (see the resources listed at the end of this chapter).

CELEBRATING FESTIVALS AND THE RHYTHM OF THE YEAR

The rhythm of the year is marked by the changing relationship of the earth to the sun, producing the seasonal changes we can often take for granted. Many of the major religions acknowledge and incorporate our experience of the year into the celebrations of their festivals, for example using festivals of light around the time of the winter solstice.

Many people today feel a renewed need for festivals and meaningful celebrations or rituals in their lives. Even if they have turned away from the religious upbringing of their childhood, they are still seeking new ways of creating community and celebrating meaningful events in their lives (such as marriages), or finding new ways to approach the meaning of Christmas despite the commercialism surrounding it today. The celebration of festivals is not only important in individuals' lives, but it is also important socially and for the possibility it provides to step out of "ordinary time" and be connected with something more abiding. Steiner felt that renewed awareness of the celebration of festivals could form a valuable link between the earthly and divine worlds.

I encourage you to explore the deeper meanings of the festivals of the year within your religion or heritage and find ways to celebrate them that are meaningful to you and that can nourish your children. Because I came from a Christian background, my greatest familiarity was with the Christian festivals, but I have also learned a great deal from the Jewish, Buddhist, and Moslem parents of my students, who celebrate their festivals with their children in a living way and shared their efforts with our classes. *Celebrating the Festivals with Children* and several other books listed at the end of this chapter can provide helpful backgrounds on the inner meaning of festivals and ways to celebrate them.[12]

Festivals, Family and Food relates numerous stories, recipes, and craft ideas for celebrating the major and lesser-known festivals of the Christian year with children.[13] Remember that, with young children, the preparation for the festival—the baking, making special presents, decorating, and singing special songs year after year—is as important as the celebration itself. Be sure to include your children in all of the preparation activities! In trying to convey the inner spiritual realities of a festival to a young child, remember that what you do speaks more loudly than what you say. The care you put into making a present teaches more about giving than a lecture on divine love. In bringing festivals to young children, tell the story in simple images they can follow. Then the story, like the one of King Haman and Mordecai accompanied by noisemakers and the Hamantaschen cookies, will be a wonderful celebration for the young child. An example related to Easter comes through a story from the Waldorf kindergartens in Britain about a caterpillar who wanted to be like a flower and worship the sun.[14] Mother Earth told him that there was a way of transformation, but it was almost like dying and being born again in a new form. The brave caterpillar becoming a flower that can fly is an image of the resurrection in which nature mirrors the Easter miracle as well as our own potential for inner transformation.

Christmas is a festival that young children relate to naturally because Jesus as a baby is very near to them. The celebration of Advent with children makes a time of inner preparation more visible both to them and to us. The Advent calendar, with its magic windows, and the Advent wreath that can be lighted each night as a story is told, can help keep the inner aspects of Christmas from getting lost in the flurry of activity.

In addition to whatever religious festivals you celebrate with your children, you can enrich your own and your children's lives by observing the passing of the seasons. Seasonal songs, foods prepared in special ways, and seasonal activities all help raise our awareness of the changes in nature that surround us. Both *Festivals, Family and Food* and *The Children's Year* suggest a wealth of things to do with your children, and *The Living Home Kindergarten* program comes in four volumes corresponding to the four seasons.

You can bring a bit of nature into your home through a seasonal table, a place where you can keep special things, like the shells collected at the beach during the summer or a special birthday card from grandma. The colors of the cloth on this little table can be changed with the seasons, just as the objects on it change to reflect the changes in nature.

CELEBRATING BIRTHDAYS

Children's birthdays are special festivals that parents can find either delightful or a real strain. In planning celebrations for children, remember, the simpler, the better. Try to avoid sensory overload. If you don't actively enjoy a place, chances are your child shouldn't be there either. It is unfortunate that so many parties for young children now occur in pizza or ice-cream parlors with blaring music, nauseating clowns, or "singing" mechanical characters and video games.

Many suggestions for delightful birthday celebrations at home can be found in *Festivals, Family and Food*. With a group of children you can do some movement games, or try decorating "treasure bags" and taking a walk in the woods, or making "fairy gardens" out of moss on a paper plate and decorated with acorns and a pretty stone that the children find.

A birthday celebration, even just within the family, is a way of saying, "We're glad you were born!" Ways of letting the child be special that day can include having a special drawing or crown at her place at breakfast, letting her choose what will be cooked for dinner, or whatever traditions you develop. Think of traditions you might want to start, such as making a card for your child each year that includes several photos of that year—riding a tricycle, getting a new kitty, going on a trip. Such cards can be saved and become things that will be treasured when the child is older.

For the young child, a birthday story about his or her coming down to earth over the "rainbow bridge" is often told in Waldorf early childhood programs and is beautifully recounted in the children's book *Little Angel's Journey*, listed at the end of this chapter. The story involves a little angel or "star child" who wants to come down to earth after having dreamed of or seen its parents on the earth. The big angel says it would be possible to become an earthly child by traveling over the rainbow bridge, which reaches from heaven down to earth. The little angel finally agrees to leave its wings behind when reassured that they will be safely kept until his or her return. Then the little angel crosses through the many colors of the rainbow, while on the earth the seasons change three times. Then it becomes very dark, almost like going to sleep, and when the little angel opens its eyes, there is the loving woman and the man with the kind heart who were in the dream. And the little angel knows it has found its earthly home as the parents welcome him or her and say, "And your name will be . . ." Such an image nourishes a young child by affirming that we know there is more to him or her than just the body.

Birthdays provide us with an opportunity to note the passage of time, which seems to go by so quickly when we see how our children grow and change in the course of a year. Birthdays, holidays, and the changing seasons all provide a familiarity and rhythm that can nourish us as well as our children. Through the turning of the days, weeks, and years, a rhythmical lifestyle is one of the greatest gifts we can provide the young child.

RECOMMENDED RESOURCES

Rhythm and Family Life

Beyond the Rainbow Bridge, by Barbara Patterson and Pamela Bradley (Michaelmas Press).

Gateways, Spindrift, and other books in the series by Margret Meyerkort (Wynstones Press). *Spring, Summer, Autumn,* and *Winter* contain a wide variety of poems, songs, and stories of the seasons and many contributions for festivals. *Spindrift* contains material from many different cultures for use throughout the year. *Gateways* contains sections on morning, evening, birthdays, and fairy tales.

Lifeways: Working with Family Questions, edited by Gudrun Davy and Bons Voors (Hawthorn Press).

Making a Family Home, by Shannon Honeybloom (SteinerBooks).

Prayers for Parents and Children, by Rudolf Steiner (SteinerBooks).

Rhythm of the Home. A quarterly e-zine with many contributors. At www.rhythmofthehome.com.

Sanctuaries of Childhood: Nurturing a Child's Spiritual Life, by Shea Darian (Gilead Press).

Seven Times the Sun: Guiding Your Child Through the Rhythms of the Day, by Shea Darian (Gilead Press).

Simplicity Parenting, by Kim John Payne (Ballantine Books).

The Spiritual Tasks of the Homemaker, by Manfred Schmidt-Brabant (Temple Lodge).

This Is the Way We Work-a-Day, by Mary Schunemann. Available from www.naturallyyoucansing.

Waldorf in the Home. The website www.waldorfinthehome.com provides articles and nearly two hundred DVDs and CDs of keynote presentations and workshops by leading Waldorf educators, including:

> "Family Matters: Homemaking 101 for Busy Parents," by Rahima Baldwin Dancy

> "Life as the Curriculum for Young Children," by Cynthia Aldinger

Work and Play in Early Childhood, by Freya Jaffke (Floris).

Festivals, Birthdays, and Seasons of the Year

Birthday, by Heather Jarman (Wynstone's Press).

The Birthday Book, by Ann Druitt et al. (Hawthorn Press).

"Create Your Own Family Celebrations." DVD by Esther Leisher from www.waldorfinthehome.org.

Festivals, Family and Food, by Diana Carey and Judy Large (Hawthorn Press).

Festivals Together: A Guide to Multicultural Celebration, by Sue Fitzjohn et al. (Hawthorn Press).

The First Jewish Catalog, by Richard Siegel et al. (Jewish Publication Society of America).

The Islamic Year: Surahs, Stories and Celebrations, by Noorah Al-Gailani and Chris Smith (Hawthorn Press).

Little Angel's Journey, by Dzvinka Hayda (Trillium Forest Press). Retells the Waldorf birthday story of the child coming to birth over the rainbow bridge.

The Nature Corner: Celebrating the Year's Cycle with a Seasonal Tableau, by M. V. Leeuwen and J. Moeskops (Floris).

Sing Through the Seasons, by the Society of Brothers (The Plough Publishing).

Homeschooling: Waldorf Preschool and Kindergarten

A Journey through Waldorf Homeschooling Kindergarten Curriculum, by Melisa Nielsen. Available at www.waldorfjourney.typepad.com.

Kindergarten at Home with Your Three- to Six-Year-Old, by Donna Simmons. Available at www.christopherushomeschool.com.

"Little Acorn Learning." Monthly Waldorf-oriented guides and e-books from Eileen Straiton, available at www.littleacornlearning.com.

The Living Home Kindergarten. Waldorf-inspired homeschooling program in four seasonal volumes, plus monthly consultation with a Waldorf teacher. Valuable throughout the early childhood years. Contact Live Education! at www.live-education.com.

Waldorf in the Home. The website www.waldorfinthehome.com provides articles and nearly two hundred DVDs and CDs of keynote presentations and workshops by leading Waldorf educators, including:

"Homeschooling: Which Style Is Right for You?" by Regina Mason

"Waldorf Preschool and Kindergarten: Preparation for Life," by Daena Ross

CHAPTER 7

Discipline and Other Parenting Issues

THE QUESTION OF DISCIPLINE

As mentioned at the start of the previous chapter, having a rhythmical home life will eliminate 80 percent of your discipline problems, so please don't read this chapter without first having read that one! And you may have gotten the idea by now that all discipline starts with self-discipline by the parent. We aren't using the word to mean "punishment." In fact, "discipline" comes from the same root as "disciple," so we're actually asking how can we raise our children to become devoted followers of their highest ideals, not how can we browbeat them into obeying us.

The very fact that discipline is an important issue for parents is symptomatic of our times. Many parents know more about what they *don't* want to do regarding the discipline of their children than what to do, or what the results of their approach will be. Because many parents today don't want to be authoritarian, they even question whether they should ever insist that their child do as they ask. Studies have shown that children do best when their parents are authoritative, charting a middle course between the extremes of being authoritarian or permissive. Authoritative parents effectively and consistently set limits for their children. Children naturally look to parents, as trusted adults, as knowing more about the world and how to behave in it than they do. Children are eager to become confident and competent and to make a contribution—to grow up. At the same time, they lack impulse control and have trouble deferring gratification, so it can be frustrating to them when they aren't able to do what they want or have everything they see.

Remembering Your Child's Basic Goodness

Fortunately, calling children "good" and "bad" when they do something we do or don't like has fallen out of favor, because feeling judged and labeled can have lifelong effects. I encourage you to go a step further and not even think of individual behaviors as "bad" and "good." Marshall Rosenberg, in developing an approach to living called Nonviolent Communication, or NVC, encourages us to see emotions and behaviors as arising when basic needs are either met or unmet.[1] As a simple example, when our need for harmony and cooperation is being met by seeing our boys playing together without fighting, we feel happiness and contentment. But, when their play devolves into hitting, feelings generated by our unmet needs for harmony and cooperation may make us less than effective at restoring domestic tranquility. Instead of being able to step in with a strategy that includes some imagination or a suggestion that will help one of them wait for the other to be done with a certain toy, we may act out of our annoyance, or we may even express annoyance that has been building up over several days. Then what we do (our unconscious "strategy") is most likely to result in a bigger scene. We've all been there when that happens.

Although the basic principles of NVC are fairly simple, actually getting in touch with your own and your children's needs is not something that comes naturally to most people, because we weren't raised that way. My first reaction to this approach was "I don't have any needs"—but I had plenty of anger, which I eventually came to understand was a result of denying my needs. So this approach is important for helping you acknowledge that *your* feelings and needs are part of the equation.

But what is going on with your children? Let's say your son, who is two, is resisting your efforts to put on his shoes and get out the door. Two fundamental principles of NVC can be very helpful here. One is to look for the unmet needs underlying the emotions, and the other is to have empathy for and acknowledge what the child is feeling. This doesn't have to be done on a verbal level, however, which would often lead to way too much talking about emotions with the young child. Similarly, trying to teach your young child to articulate his feelings and needs is way beyond his developmental level. However, cultivating empathy for a young child's perceptions and reactions is a valuable skill that we can learn as adults, though it can be challenging if adults didn't provide that for us when we were young.

First, acknowledgment: what can you say that lets your child know that you get it, that he's being understood? "You'd really like to do this yourself!" Or maybe it's not about self-sufficiency, but he's feeling rushed or wants to go barefoot. Make your best guess and watch his response. At the same time, you can take note of any physical needs he might be experiencing: Did he wake up several times during the night? Have things been rushed this morning? Is he cutting his two-year molars? Often your acknowledgment of his actions and wishes will be enough to defuse the situation.

Then follow up by repeating your request for "right action," which might sound something like this: "I understand that you don't like feeling rushed. Another day we'll have more time by getting up earlier. But this morning we need to see if your shoes make you able to run as quick as a bunny to the gate." It's important to follow up with your request, but a little imagination or distraction can go a long way. Sometimes it can help to a give a choice of two options that both still accomplish your aim: "Do you want to put on your shoes and hop to the car like a bunny, or put them on and fly like an eagle (in my arms)?" If you have a child who resists transitions, I suggest letting him know a few minutes in advance rather than setting up a pattern of negotiating after every request.

If you and your two-year-old have fallen into some undesirable habits with one another, some of the suggestions in Harvey Karp's book *The Happiest Toddler on the Block* can be helpful.[2] Although I take exception to a few of his techniques and find his description of toddlers as "little cavemen" a bit limiting, in general I found his approach practical and useful.

While it is appropriate to teach children where and how certain behaviors work—and where they don't—discipline means more than correcting undesirable behavior. It also means guiding the child to develop in a healthy way physically, emotionally, and mentally. We guide the baby largely by nurturing his physical body; we lead the toddler by ordering the rhythm of her day; and as the child becomes older, we take her by the hand and try to be an example ourselves. Once the child reaches school age, he is guided most by stories and the spoken word.[3] How to guide a child depends on his age, personality, and the nature of the parent-child relationship. Even within the same family, differences due to temperament and age mean that all children do not have to be treated in the same way—only fairly.

It is impossible to speak about disciplining a baby in the sense of correcting her or making her do something, because the baby's will is both very strong and not under her conscious control. A baby doesn't do things either because of us or to spite us, and she can't change her behavior because we want her to, even if we insist upon it. This can either strengthen our patience and develop our nurturing capacities as new parents, or it can result in extreme frustration. We read from time to time about tragic cases of injury or death from shaken baby syndrome, when parents are isolated and fail to get the help they need with their own anger or frustration. Taking care of an infant is not easy, and newborns cry an average of one to four hours a day. Anyone can experience transient anger toward a crying baby, but if the impulse to shake or hit is strong and recurrent, please find local help or start by calling an agency such as the National Child Abuse Hotline (800-422-4453).

Imitation and Example

Instead of getting angry or trying to reason with a young child, who doesn't have the memory or consciousness for reasoning, keep in mind the principles of example and imitation that are so effective with the child under the age of eight. If you want to teach a certain behavior to your child, one of the best ways is to actually perform that behavior in front of (or with) him. This demands that we get up and actually do something rather than giving the child orders or directions. For example, instead of saying, "Don't eat with your fingers," pick up your spoon and very purposefully go through the motions yourself while stating the positive, "We eat with our spoon." Or instead of saying, "Go clean up your toys," we need to go with the child and do it together, while saying, perhaps, "It's time to put your toys away."

Movement combined with the smallest amount of fantasy, song, or good humor can go a long way toward getting the child involved in an activity. For example, when you are cleaning up with your child, you can ask the truck driver to steer the truck to its garage or get the cowboy to ride the stick horse over to the stable. Another strategy is to join in the children's fantasy rather than interrupt it. So, if the children are involved in play, ask the train drivers to move the train out of the walkway while you start moving the chairs with them instead of interrupting their fantasy by telling them to move out of the way. What about things you've told your child a hundred times? For example, you've told your five-year-old "Don't slam the screen door!" at least that many times, but to no avail. Try gathering your intention, meeting him at the door, and saying with good will, "We close the door quietly," while you move his hand through the motion of gently closing the screen door. That will probably do it. If not, a second time is probably all that is necessary. Movement and stating what it is you want to have happen, rather than what you don't, communicate with children in a way they can understand.

Whenever possible, state the positive. Say, "Pet the kitty gently," while you demonstrate how to do it rather than shrieking, "Don't hurt the kitty!" Sentences with "don't" will communicate your displeasure, but the brain often doesn't process every word, so the message may in fact register as, ". . . hurt . . . kitty!" It's a lot more effective to say, " . . . gentle . . . kitty," instead.

This approach—always trying to say things positively—takes practice and awareness. But the power of "yes, and" is astonishing. For example, if your three-year-old wants to ride the bicycles to preschool and you need to take the car that day, you could say, "Yes, that would be fun! . . . And today I need to take the car to go shopping afterward. We'll ride the bicycles again another day." We think that "another day" wouldn't be satisfying to an older child or an adult, but it's magical how affirming young children find it.

Not Expecting Results

It isn't until elementary-school age that a child is ready to respond consistently to words that are not accompanied by your actions. With the preschool-age child, you need to correct and demonstrate the right behavior again and again, but you can't expect children to remember it. Their memories simply aren't that mature yet. There will be slow improvement over time, but the "learning" that does occur takes place through gradual maturation and through forming habit patterns. For example, early in the year at Rainbow Bridge, several children couldn't sit calmly during snack time. "We sit with our feet in front of us," we repeated again and again as we reseated the child or showed our own straight way of sitting. After several months the children were able to sit calmly during snack time, both because they were older and because the lesson had been repeated so many times that it had begun to penetrate the body. Gradually the child who couldn't stay in his chair could calmly eat and wait for "Red Bird" to come and choose who would blow out the candle, signifying it was time to go and play. But it took a month or two of constant repetition with a group of new children.

Only around the age of five does the child have enough memory and perspective on the world to *begin* to remember what he should and should not do. I saw this stage with a little boy in the preschool who was corrected nearly every day for rough behavior toward the other children. We tried everything! As he approached five he started to remember *after* he hit someone that he wasn't supposed to do that, and he began to feel regret for both the action and the situation that would follow. But it took even more maturity for him to be able to start remembering *before* he struck out; because of his fiery temperament, it was more difficult for him to get control of his emotions than for many children. It was a real effort and a test of patience to work with him and to constantly insist on the right behavior, which he was eventually able to master.

Steiner describes this change in a child around age five:

> Previously, unable to understand what it ought or ought not
> to do, it could only imitate, but now, little by little, it begins to
> listen to and to believe in what its elders say. Only towards
> the fifth year is it possible to awaken in a child the sense of
> what is right or wrong. We will educate the child rightly
> only if we realize that during the first seven-year period—
> that is up to the change of teeth—the child lives by imitation,
> and that only gradually will it develop imagination and
> memory as well as a first belief in what grown-ups say.[4]

Steiner gives another example of a young couple who were distraught because their young child was "stealing" money from a jar in the cupboard. Steiner explained that the child was only imitating having seen the mother take money from the jar. He explained that only after the age of five can the child *begin* to have concepts of right and wrong sufficient to support or avoid the idea of stealing. Prior to that time the child is acting out of imitation.[5]

When You Say "No!"

Despite moving with your child and stating things positively, there will be times when you need to say "no" and your child needs to know that you mean it. Elizabeth Grunelius, the first Waldorf kindergarten teacher, said that she found only three reasons for having to say no to a child:

1. When what he wishes to do would be harmful to himself, such as going out on a cold day without a coat

2. When what he wishes to do would be harmful to others, such as making noise when the baby is sleeping

3. When what he wishes to do would result in real damage, such as using his crayons on the wall.[6]

In my experience, even in these instances it isn't necessary to start out with a head-on confrontation and battle of the wills. In the first case, you simply help the child put his coat on; in the second, you could suggest what he *can* do (either play quietly inside or go outside and play); and in the third case you give him a piece of paper and try to guide his activity into more appropriate channels. Where I would use a sharp "no!" is if the child were about to run out in the street or were about to bite another child. In these cases I might even clap my hands or I would jump up to intervene. If you seldom use "no," then it can be used rarely to startle and get a child's attention so she realizes that behavior is not to be repeated.

Short of that, deciding when something will be harmful to a child requires judgment, and the more you can fine-tune your judgment, the better for your child. If we can support our children in having their own experiences without excessively saying "no" and without interrupting them, they will learn a great deal about the world and about their own abilities. Climbing trees is an example. Yes, there is a certain amount of danger, but if I hadn't let my youngest daughter climb trees I never would have known that she really should have been born into a circus family that performs high-wire acts. As a child, she would climb up twenty feet and sit and play her wooden recorder, and now she is studying aerial dance! Once when she was four she got stuck up in a tree while my husband was away, so I had to get a neighbor to climb up our forty-foot ladder to help her (not for me, thanks!). The neighbors were hysterical and kept calling up to her, "Don't be afraid!" I had to explain that she wasn't afraid, just stuck!

It is important that before you say "no" to a child that you are sure what the child intends and certain of your response to that action. Sometimes it is good to pause for a moment and decide what to do first, because if you frequently change your mind, you can confuse him and encourage a habit of pleading until you give in. Being simple and consistent is important so that your child knows that you mean what you say, and that your word is followed immediately by action.

Negative Behavior

Many parents ignore their child's negative behavior until they either give in or lose their temper. We probably all know that pressure cooker feeling, when the steam is building up—unexpressed and sometimes unacknowledged—until we react out of all proportion to the irritation at hand. Other parents always keep their cool, but the child never feels acknowledged. For example, a woman with a baby and a two-year-old in one shopping cart and groceries in the other was ignoring the crazy behavior of her two-year-old, who became more and more annoying as he tried to get a reaction. By the time we were both at the checkout stand, he was having a full-blown fit. Although she was still able to ignore it calmly, we need to recognize that it is frustrating to children to be allowed to get crazier and crazier as they keep trying to get a response. There are a lot of calm but effective things she could have done along the way, like stopping the cart and saying it doesn't move unless he's sitting down; singing to him; engaging him by saying she'd let him get the pineapple juice, putting five things in the cart on the way to the pineapple juice, then letting him stand up and pick it off the shelf; or asking him to watch in the produce section and tell her when he saw the carrots.

Children don't have to be crazy or drive us crazy, but they do require—and deserve—creative interaction.

Young children can often be helped by modeling what it is they could say ("Let's ask him if you can have the truck when he's finished"), acknowledging that it's hard to wait, and then looking for something else to do in the meantime. Sometimes, however, a child who continues to raise a fuss needs to be removed from the action until he is ready to do what is needed (use gentle hands, wait for a toy, or whatever is at issue). Usually a couple of minutes is all it takes for a child to get himself back together and be ready to try again. This is not punishment or "time out to think about what you have done," but instant feedback that certain behavior is required in social situations. Remember that you need to move with the young child, not give orders. So out you go, away from the action, along with the young child and state that just as soon as he is ready to return, he can go back. Then you stand there absolutely stone-faced, so it's really boring to be in another room with such a parent while everyone else is having a good time. If this is not enough, offering a snuggle or getting him interested in something once you go back in can also help him reintegrate into social activity.

With negative behavior such as hitting, it is still best to emphasize the positive actions. "We need to be gentle with our friends." "We need to take turns." If possible, put your energy into the child who has been wronged rather than putting your attention on the offender. Obviously, spanking or hitting the child is providing a model of the thing you are trying to get him to stop doing. It sends a really mixed message, because our actions speak to a young child much more powerfully than our words.

Biting is one of the behaviors that deserves a sharp "no!" Just as the nursing mother needs to get the baby's attention and remove her from the breast when she bites, your displeasure is appropriate in response to this behavior with other children. Some children bite when they're struggling for a toy, while others will walk up and bite their parent or another child seemingly out of the blue. Others will bite whenever they get too close to another child (hence hugging other children is discouraged with these children!). Until this phase has passed, it is necessary to be extremely vigilant with a child who bites, and it can be reason enough to stop preschool for a few weeks to see whether the behavior improves with a break.

Our Own Emotions

Because children are so imitative, we need to monitor our own emotions and actions when interacting with them, for our actions and emotions speak louder than our words. How can we keep our own tempers at those times when we feel like throttling our children or yelling uncontrollably? One of the keys to discipline involves bringing one's own consciousness and objectivity to the incident—talking in a quiet voice, sticking by what you say, repeating it if necessary, and, whenever possible, actually moving with the young child.

Developing some success with this approach can help defuse your own frustration and make it easier to come up with "adult" and creative approaches to your child's annoying behaviors. But no one can do this all the time. When you are in a situation that has gone south, give yourself time to get into a better place and then reflect on what happened. What was going on for you? What were your triggers? What do you tell yourself that justifies your blow-up? (You might think, "He should be able to . . . ," "If I don't correct him now. . . ," or "No one respects what I say.") Try to imagine other responses and determine what you would need to do earlier to be able to use them.

Children don't do things just to annoy you. They're exploring the world and trying to figure out what works and how to get their needs met. Unpleasant situations with your child occur only in areas in which you have unconscious or ambivalent feelings. Otherwise, you'd be able to respond to the child in a way that wouldn't contribute to a downward spiral. This is one of the reasons why children behave so differently with their parents than with their preschool teacher or someone else who is clear about what works and what doesn't.

It can be useful to consider what your child might be gaining in a situation in which it looks like both of you are losing. For example, if your child is whining, she must be getting what she wants from it some of the time, even if it's just more interaction with you or a negotiated settlement. Remembering that loving your child is more important than "straightening him out" may help you call a halt when your child's behavior and your own are both spiraling out of control. Too many parents remain silent until they overreact from a string of annoyances that have been smoldering. As a result, the child often feels underacknowledged and thus makes life miserable to get attention, while the parent is feeling overwhelmed much of the time. If this is happening to you, it's probably because you are denying your own needs and could use some help setting effective boundaries sooner. In this case, find a friend you can talk to, talk to a family counselor who can provide a more objective perspective, or attend parenting classes. Even an online class with individualized counseling can help (I recommend Joyful Days with Toddlers and Preschoolers with Faith Collins, listed at the end of this chapter). Somehow you need to acquire new knowledge and new perspectives, as well as ways of defusing your own emotions. This is especially true if you were abused emotionally or physically as a child, but it can be true for anyone. Your child is providing you with the opportunity to fix what is broken—before it becomes broken in him or her as well.

Living with young children is both demanding and rewarding. It requires attention to create a harmonious life, and there is often very little time for other activities (this is where extended family or support systems are a must). Children are young only once. They will soon be away at school and there will be much more time for your own activities. Understanding the nature of the young child can help you raise a happy and well-behaved child, as well as a bright one, and can help you have fun and find satisfaction in the process while you continue in your own growth.

WHY DOES PARENTING TAKE SO MUCH ENERGY?

It takes a tremendous amount of energy to nurture a baby or young child. Even preschool and kindergarten teachers find that they must get enough sleep to replenish the kind of energy that young children seem to demand. Your best intentions will come to nothing when you are excessively tired or irritable. The first thing that is necessary for a happy and healthy baby or toddler is to have a happy and healthy mother. This means you must be sure you are eating well and taking vitamin supplements for at least as long as you are breastfeeding. Interrupted sleep, especially in the first few months after birth, can compound fatigue and complicate the adjustment to new parenting.

Babies are nourished by your love and care just as they are nourished by food. The reason that parenting young children takes so much energy is that the life forces of the mother and baby are interconnected throughout the first three years. Young children are surrounded by and consume what Steiner calls "etheric" or "life energy" (we might call it "vitality" or "life force") from their parents, caregivers, and teachers. Mothering is deceptive, because sometimes it seems as if you're accomplishing so little, so why should you be so tired? However, caring for young children draws on your vital energy, and you need to replenish your own vital forces in order to continue to feel good in your mothering.

Three things that can really help replenish this energy are sleep, artistic activity, and meditation. Try to make sure that you get enough sleep by scheduling a nap when your baby or toddler naps. Maintain a quiet time for your child every afternoon when he or she stops napping— as much for yourself as for the child. As a preschool teacher, I always found being in bed by ten an essential part of my preparation. Otherwise, I couldn't stand the noise and couldn't keep my emotions on an even keel.

Artistic activity involves the same vital or creative forces that your infant or toddler is using, but it replenishes rather than depletes them. Playing a musical instrument, drawing, sculpting, or painting can all help mothers have more energy. Writing down your thoughts, experiences, and insights can also be helpful. The regularity of doing something like taking a walk each day can likewise be of great help in keeping your balance and replenishing your energy. Contact with nature can help us feel refreshed as well.

Meditation can be as simple as setting aside five minutes before you go to bed to center yourself in your breathing or concentrate on a single thought. Returning to your own center through meditation or prayer not only helps replenish your energy but can also help you maintain equanimity in the midst of all the stresses of parenting. A number of years ago I discovered that I had been involved in the caring professions all my life without having much relationship to the feminine aspect of the divine. This led me to explore becoming grounded in my body and on the earth through dance and deep tissue work, and to investigate how I could feel supported and nourished by the feminine. The books listed at the end of chapter 1 were especially helpful to me on the journey. Out of working with *The Woman Awake: Feminine Wisdom for Spiritual Life*, by Regina Sara Ryan, for example, I developed a practice of starting the day at Rainbow Bridge by visualizing myself sitting on the lap of the Great Mother and dissolving backward into the heart of love.[7] Needless to say, it was and still is transforming, as is a mantra a friend suggested to me, "What shall I do with this opportunity for love?"

In addition to setting aside time for meditation, set aside time to spend alone. Even an hour or two spent out of the house can help you in your mothering. Most women in nuclear families live isolated from other adults, so try to develop the social network you need.

Some fathers are primary caregivers while the mother continues to work; in that case, the above advice applies to them as well. When the father is working outside the home full time while the mother is at home, he can still play a vital role in helping the mother maintain her vitality. With a child under the age of three, this involves actively supporting her mothering emotionally and financially so that she is encouraged and strengthened in being with the children. I hate to risk sounding traditional by speaking of men as "providers and protectors," but there is some validity to that image when both partners apply it with consciousness. However, this does not excuse men from the need to develop their own nurturing side so they can assume coresponsibility for the children rather than depending on the mother to rise to every parenting occasion. Single parenting, with or without a husband in the home, is not an easy task!

CAN YOU WORK TOWARD RHYTHM WITH AN INFANT?

Part of what makes the first six weeks of caring for a new baby so hard is that the baby seems to have no pattern to its eating and sleeping—at least nothing you can depend on. Rhythm gradually does emerge from chaos, and life becomes easier over time as rhythm becomes established and builds a framework that can support you in your other activities. This lack of framework can be very disorienting in the postpartum period, comparable to when a person retires or a career woman quits work when pregnant and finds she can barely get out of bed in the morning because life has become so unstructured.

"Experts" in the 1950s told mothers to give babies a bottle every four hours (and not a half hour sooner!) no matter how loudly the baby protested. In reaction to this sacrifice of the individual to the clock or the book, the pendulum swung the other way in the 1970s, with most breastfeeding mothers nursing their babies whenever they were hungry or fussy. Demand feeding takes as its model nontechnological cultures in which the baby is carried in a sling next to the mother's body and can nurse any time she wants, which usually involves nursing frequently for short periods. Many mothers who take their babies to bed with them find this same pattern of frequent nursing continuing throughout the night as well, throughout the first year or longer.

Most people today agree that a young baby's needs should be met as they arise, and mothers are more likely to trust their instinct to respond to their babies with love and the breast. But when does this change? At six weeks, six months, two years, or later?

I would like to propose an alternative to the polar opposites of feeding on demand versus feeding according to a schedule, and that is gradually working toward establishing rhythm, which will change as the baby grows. One of the tasks of the growing child and one of the functions of parenting is to bring the child into rhythm. Consider how arrhythmical a newborn's breathing is. Sometimes she takes short gasps, while at other times she holds her breath—it's quite startling if you really listen to your newborn breathe. Babies' heart rates are also much faster than adults'. As the child matures, the breathing and the heart rate gradually become coordinated, and then around age nine they assume the adult ratio of one breath for each four beats of the heart.

Working toward rhythm does not mean slavishly going by the clock or letting your baby "cry it out." It does mean being aware of rhythms as they emerge and change, honoring and encouraging them. Working toward rhythm is especially valuable in dealing with naps and sleep and avoiding sleep problems. At first your baby requires sustenance during the night; it's a physiological fact. But after the baby's stomach and digestive system can get enough nourishment to last for an extended period, waking and feeding are for other purposes: simply from habit, to be comforted by your presence, or to play.

If every night you were to get up, turn on the lights, feed your baby, and talk to him, he would probably start wanting to be awake and playing at that time every night. Some babies can get day and night reversed, sleeping most of the day and wanting to be active at night. Nursing mothers are usually able to avoid these pitfalls by somnolently tucking the baby into bed with them and barely waking up while nursing.[8]

You need to decide your style of mothering and what is right for you and your family. As long as you are happy nursing your baby at night, there is no need to change. But when you grow tired of being awakened at night—and your older baby could be sleeping longer—it is possible to change his habit pattern. First, you need to gather your intention to stop nursing the baby when he awakes at night. Then, when he cries, you can go in and say, "I love you, but this is time to sleep." You might hold and rock him, or just pat his back and then go out. It isn't easy to hear him cry, but stay connected and go back in after three minutes and pat him again, saying, "I'm sorry you're so upset, but it is time to sleep," keeping your voice and actions very drowsy. You then go out for a longer time and repeat as necessary. The child soon learns that food will not be forthcoming, but he also doesn't feel abandoned because of your love and concern. Without the possibility of food or play, he will soon start sleeping longer without waking up. My own experience is that it generally takes three days or nights to change a pattern, but it can also take a week or longer.

There are so many schools of thought on what babies need and how to parent. I encourage you to trust your own heart and to be as aware as possible of your baby's needs and of what you are really feeling. If you're content nursing your baby all night, then that is working for you. But if you feel as though you'd appreciate uninterrupted sleep at night and are starting to resent the cry in the night or the constant nuzzling against your body, you should realize that it's all right and easy to change your child's patterns if it's done with love and awareness. Bringing the child into rhythm when the time is right is part of life in all cultures. Only you can decide when that time is for your baby, for you, and for your family.

WHAT ABOUT WEANING?

Doctors and even formula companies now admit that breastfeeding is the best start you can possibly give your baby. It's something you should continue as long as it feels good to both mother and baby, but any amount of nursing is better than no nursing at all. If you are considering weaning in the first month, chances are that you are having difficulties; it should be pleasurable for both you and your baby. Working with a lactation consultant can give you the help you need. Often doctors give the wrong advice, which is less likely to happen with women who are knowledgeable and trained to help nursing mothers. If you encounter special situations, such as going back to work or illness, La Leche League or lactation consultants can also provide the support you need to successfully breastfeed in these circumstances.

As you have probably figured out, I am not into authorities telling women what to do with their bodies. When women listened to doctors, they didn't breastfeed at all, which was clearly bad advice. Then American doctors recommended breastfeeding for six months, and now the American Academy of Pediatrics has extended the time to twelve months. The information and impulses from our formula-pushing culture need to be balanced by the information on natural mothering and extended breastfeeding provided by organizations such as La Leche League. However, I feel their emphasis on "child-led weaning" needs to be balanced by information that it really needs to be "nursing-couple-led weaning"—both your needs and emotions and the baby's count. It really is all right to stop offering your baby or toddler the breast when it comes to that time. Weaning, like death, is part of the shadow side of life. It involves the ending of one phase and moving on to another. Try to become aware of your own needs, comforts, fears, and questions that might either lead to early weaning or work against weaning when your child is able to move on to a more independent phase. You may have feelings such as "Breastfeeding is so pleasurable, why would I ever want to stop?" or "It's so wonderful to be touched and needed like this—do I really want my child to become more independent?" or "How will I show my love for my toddler in the next phase?" Being aware of your own emotional undercurrents can help you be more aware of your baby's real needs and more alert to the subtle cues that he or she is giving you. You may even find that there are spiritual realities that make weaning at nine or twelve months a natural event.

For example, some people working from Steiner's indications have observed that when the child achieves uprightness and walks (between nine and twelve months), he is freeing himself and asserting his individuality; they have felt that achieving similar freedom in the area of nutrition is appropriate at this time as well. Certainly the baby is able to eat and even reach for table foods at this age. One of the tasks of the first seven years is for the child to assert his individuality by overcoming or remolding the forces of heredity; because these forces are particularly strong in breast milk, prolonged nursing of toddlers is viewed with alarm by many working out of Steiner's view of human development.[9] American readers may be surprised, amused, or annoyed by the rigidity of some of the books by medical doctors working out of Steiner's indications who prescribe weaning at the "traditional time of forty weeks" (nine months). Since mothers were advised to wean by six months in some of the older versions of these same books written by European pediatricians, one has to try to distinguish between cultural influences and spiritual "facts."

However, it can be valuable to ask ourselves whether there is an observable truth behind what anthroposophical (Steiner-based) writers are noticing about the toddler's changing consciousness and needs in today's world. In her book *Mothering with Soul*, Joan Salter described how many women connected with the Gabriel Baby Centre in Australia felt that weaning at nine months was too early, so they were starting to wean around nine months and finishing by twelve.[10] The fact that Salter felt it necessary to justify this by using esoteric numerology to show how the nine is transformed into the twelve left me somewhat bemused, however.

Once the baby is able to eat table foods (around nine months), the nature of breastfeeding changes to fulfilling a need that is more emotional than nutritive. La Leche League speaks of baby-led weaning, pointing out that some babies really do wean themselves and others don't, continuing nursing until they are three or four years old. The League and *The Continuum Concept* by Jean Liedloff point out how common it is in less technologically developed cultures for children to be nursed for two or three years or longer.

Do these cultures provide a model of "natural mothering" that is valuable for us to copy? The development of individual consciousness, which is so advanced in the West, presents a fundamental dilemma. On the one hand, our extreme individuality has caused alienation, anxiety, competition, and the denial of the spirit. On the other, we can't escape it just because we can read about other cultures, whose group consciousness may not necessarily be appropriate for us in the world in which we live. However, something new is clearly needed or we're going to destroy ourselves. Steiner's answer is that our individuality is appropriate, but we must now go on to the next stage and find a reintegration of spirit and matter from our modern vantage point. To do this, we have to start where we are.

Although some mothers are content to take their cues from other cultures in nursing their toddler or even older child, I have encountered many mothers who are "suffering through" nursing an older child, anxiously waiting for their child to wean herself. I've even had mothers with nursing four-year-olds come to me for advice on weaning, terrified of the scenes and "trauma to the child" that they were sure weaning would produce. I worked with several mothers at the Birth Center who didn't want to stop nursing their toddler during pregnancy but found that once the new baby was born, they felt completely exhausted and overwhelmed. Yet still they didn't feel free to wean the older child. My feeling is that perhaps, in these cases, we should take our lesson from the cats, bears, and most other mammals who are more into self-preservation and preservation of the young than that. There is no way I can believe that an older child's sucking need is being well served by a resentful or exhausted mother. Babies and older siblings register and take in emotions just as deeply as actions. Breastfeeding is like making love—nothing is gained in suffering through it.

Regardless of how long you breastfeed (or bottle-feed) your baby, the question remains about when to start introducing solid foods. In our culture, pediatricians used to want mothers to introduce solid foods at three months (or earlier), either because a baby was not growing enough or (in my case) because he was too fat! The trend now is toward waiting until six months, but some pediatricians may suggest solids earlier. La Leche League has good advice about how and when to introduce foods, and if there is a history of allergy in your family, giving nothing but breast milk for the first year can help prevent sensitization to food and other allergies. There is no need to supplement iron for breastfed babies; they don't become anemic in the first year from a breast milk diet.

Steiner gave many indications about nutrition that vary quite a bit from information commonly available today. Interested readers can refer to *When a Child Is Born* by Wilhelm zur Linden[11] or *A Guide to Child Health* by Michaela Glöckler and Wolfgang Goebel.[12] One interesting thing I have gleaned is that what children eat before the age of three is what they acquire a taste for, and I have seen evidence of this many times. For example, we gave our youngest daughter almost no red meat before the age of three, following Steiner's indications that red meat is very dense and inappropriate for young children. Even though we aren't vegetarians, as a teenager she wouldn't eat most meat and preferred tofu. A friend brought up her child without any sugar or sweets before allowing occasional sweets when the child entered preschool. It was interesting to observe that the girl really had little taste for the cupcakes and other treats at birthday parties. This seemed to go beyond a desire to fulfill her mother's wish that she partake moderately of these foods.

CRYING BABIES

Since babies can't verbalize their feelings and needs, they cry for a wide variety of reasons. We are taught to see whether they are wet or hungry, but if they are not, we usually try to hush them up or ignore them. As we have seen, it is important to respond to a crying baby, not leave her to "cry it out."

The next time you hear a baby cry, notice what feelings and associations it brings up in you. Also take some time to think about how you respond to your baby's cues; are you more concerned with your own discomfort or the child's? Many valuable exercises to help parents understand their own feelings about crying, sleep, food, and so forth can be found in *Exercises in Self-Awareness for New Parents,* by Aletha Jauch Solter.[13] Her book *The Aware Baby* also offers much good advice about crying babies.[14]

Having a "colicky" or high-needs infant can be a real strain on parents. There are many techniques you can try—looking for food allergies, burping the baby frequently, putting warmth or pressure on the tummy, giving weak chamomile tea—but there doesn't seem to be any statistical correlation between causes and cures for colic. Limiting stimulation and trying to create a calm environment should certainly be the place to start. Above all, try to remain calm yourself, because it is impossible to calm a baby if you are tense and annoyed (remember how imitative they are on the physical level!). Also remember that you are not responsible for your child's personality or temperament. Sometimes the best you can do is just be there for the infant, lovingly holding her while she cries. Crying can be a great release if done in the arms of someone who loves you.

Vimala Schneider, author and founder of the International Association of Infant Massage Instructors, writes, "Forcing babies to 'cry it out,' hushing babies' cries by stopping up their mouths, and letting babies cry 'cathartically' can all be excuses for not taking the time to listen to what they have to say. There is no quick fix. A good parent—a good culture—must go through the sometimes difficult process of responding to babies' cues individually, with compassion and with common sense."[15]

One father describes his efforts to become more intuitively aware of what his daughter's cries mean:

> In the evening, after we put Tara to bed, she sometimes wakes up after about an hour or so. At this point, she starts to cry, and we do not respond immediately, because we want her to learn to go back to sleep. . . . The decision whether to get up or not is a function of the nature of the crying. There's a kind of crying that is whimpering, where it's clear she is still asleep, and a kind of cry that is screeching, and it's obvious she is awake and distressed. However, there are some in-between cries, where it's hard to tell how she's feeling.
>
> I found myself trying the following technique. Rather than listening with my ear or with my mind, I have started to try and listen first with my heart. I try and let the crying go to my heart and then, with my mind, examine how my heart is feeling and responding. Is she in distress? Does she need comforting? Or is she just complaining, feeling uncomfortable? The distinction is important, in that Wendy and I want her to feel completely trusting of our presence, but we also want her to experience, in small increments, taking

care of herself. I do not believe in having her cry herself to sleep, as some parents recommend at this point, where she really screams for long periods of time and exhausts herself. Rather, I suspect the process can be much more incremental and evolutionary, like the changing of the tides. Each night there are small changes that over time build up into a major shift. In my case, the learning for me here is in trying to respond first at an intuitive, feeling level and then consulting that feeling. This is a process I have been exploring for a while, but this feels like a new dimension of it.[16]

Some parents sleep with their baby in bed and respond to their baby's waking up by giving the breast while barely even waking up themselves. Others find that there comes a time when they want more space at night and then must get up to respond to their older baby or toddler. Once again, there are no simple formulas to determine the right or wrong way to parent your child. You need to feel your own way through the easy and difficult times.

WHAT ABOUT GOING BACK TO WORK?

With more than half of new mothers returning to the labor force within twelve months of giving birth, child care for children under three has become a reality of American life. Within the Waldorf movement there has been an increased emphasis on meeting the needs of the child from birth to three, and LifeWays grew out of this impulse, taking the home as the model for young children, even in child care centers. Nøkken, a Waldorf-based program for children in Copenhagen, Denmark, has around twenty-five children from age one (or when they can walk) until they are ready for first grade at age seven. All ages are together as a large, healthy family except when the younger children have a snack and nap. Joan Almon, past president of the Waldorf Early Childhood Association of North America, commented after visiting Nøkken:

> Prior, to my visit, I had been very concerned that those raised in child care centers would have a hard time nurturing their own children when they grew up. Within

most child care centers, children are stratified by age, so a three-year-old does not see an infant being cared for. There is little opportunity to learn about such things through imitation. That Nøkken was able to overcome this problem made a deep impression on me. . . .

As I watched the children at Nøkken play being mothers, I was struck by the thought that where it was once a village that raised a child, more and more there now need to be such life-filled centers to provide the nurture children need. . . .

A number of Waldorf early-childhood teachers in the United States and elsewhere are exploring ways to meet these needs of children. An imaginative picture is developing of a multi-age center that includes mixed age groups from infancy to age six, as well as children up to age twelve who come for care before and after school. It's possible also to develop activities for adolescents, to include the elderly as foster grandparents, or to offer courses for the elderly, for pregnant parents, and more. In such life centers, young children can feel embedded as they once did in their own homes that were part of an extended family or village. It is hoped that within a few years, a number of such centers will exist. There is a growing commitment for such work within the Waldorf early-childhood movement, which now numbers over 1200 programs in fifty countries.[17]

The Milwaukee LifeWays Center is an example of these principles being applied in an American context, and Rainbow Bridge LifeWays Program, which my daughter, Faith Baldwin Collins, and I established in Boulder is an example of such an in-home program. Photo essays on both can be found at www.lifewaysnorthamerica.org. The ideal would be to have such mixed-age, relationship-based programs available in every community, but the reality is that most nonmaternal care for infants is substandard.[18] Although it is clearly out of step with the times to say the following (like asking for books on birth in the feminist bookstore in the early 1970s), I nevertheless have to take the risk and suggest that if you can possibly stay home with your baby for the first year, you should do so. However, having spent four years doing mixed-age child care with one- to five-year-olds using the LifeWays approach, I have to say that I have found that children today seem to be much more eager to be with their peers than children were twenty years ago—and vastly more than my generation was!

Among contemporary early childhood experts, only T. Berry Brazelton, called America's favorite pediatrician, has swallowed hard enough to write a book about putting your child in day care. In his popular book *Working and Caring*,[19] he discusses what mothers need to consider in looking for child care for a baby or a young child, the emotions involved in going back to work, the concern about the primary caregiver replacing you in the child's affections, the increased number of illnesses and need for antibiotics, and so forth.

The reason parental care is so important is that it establishes a secure parent-child relationship and creates a calm and rhythmical life for the infant. No caregiver can match the enthusiasm and excitement of parents over a baby's accomplishments such as sitting up and walking. Such reactions reinforce the parents' commitment and love and contribute to the child's developing sense of self-worth and security. In addition, the parents are best able to be there to satisfy a toddler's curiosity about all the things she discovers. Although studies have shown that ideal substitute care situations do no measurable harm to children, all situations are not ideal, and no studies show substitute care as being better than any but the most abusive family.

Steiner explains the uniqueness of the mother-child relationship, which contemporary educators have also documented in the first three years. Steiner observed that the etheric or vital energy of the baby is connected with and protected by the mother's vital energy, which surrounds it like a sheath, just as the baby's physical body was protected before birth by the physical body of the mother. Just as the child's physical body is freed at birth, so the child's etheric body is gradually "born" over the first seven years, with an important freeing from the mother occurring around the age of three. This change is quite dramatic if you are alert for it; suddenly your child is much more independent, much more able to be away from you comfortably, and more able to participate in group activities. This is why Waldorf preschool programs have traditionally preferred to accept children around age three and a half, after they have gone through this freeing from the mother.

According to Steiner, the baby in the first year is still totally connected to the mother's vital (etheric) energy and nurtured by it. This seems to explain the psychic connection or heightened awareness that exists between mothers and their babies. When I was a Waldorf preschool teacher in the 1980s in Ann Arbor, Michigan, most mothers stayed home with their children or only worked part time. I observed that the children who had been in child care since the age of six weeks stood out quite noticeably: they tended to be sick more often and more used to antibiotics because their parents couldn't stay home for recuperation time; and they seemed less childlike, having dealt with the stress of other adults and groups for many years. David Elkind, in his books *The Hurried Child* and *Miseducation*, speaks of the high level of anxiety with which our children live, and how we push them to grow up and cope with things that should be beyond their years.

If there is any way you can stay at home at least during the first year, it is of tremendous value to your baby and can be rewarding for you as well. Your baby only begins life once and will grow up so quickly! But there is not a lot of support for mothers who want to stay home. Maternity leaves are usually too short, careers don't wait for many women who decide to have children in their late thirties, and today's lifestyles often demand two incomes. But if it is your heart's desire, work something out and find the support you need. The Mothering online community (www.mothering.com) is a real support for women who value what they do with their children. Many websites for working mothers can also be very helpful. Or perhaps you can arrange to job share, work from home, or work part time?

If you decide to return to work before your child is a year old, what kind of child care is best? Through his work with young children, White found that the best type of substitute care is individual care in your own home; fortunately, the number of agencies handling nannies and au pair programs is increasing rapidly. Second best is individual care in another person's home. Next is family child care, followed by nonprofit center–based care. Last is profit-oriented center-based care, which is often done as a franchise and pays little over minimum wage.[20]

Obviously, finding quality child care is one of the major dilemmas facing parents today. If you need to find a home or a facility for your child, take the time to visit and thoroughly check out several of them. How your child is cared for all day does matter.

HOW LONG DO CHILDREN'S SENSES NEED PROTECTING?

As a first-time mother I had no notion about protecting my baby's senses and took him with me to Kmart at ten days of age. Although I knew how zingy the fluorescent lights of big-box stores make me, it didn't occur to me that my baby was even more sensitive to the environment. What I learned about child development through the work of Rudolf Steiner and others was that during the years from birth through age six, every aspect of the environment has a more profound effect on the growing child than it will when he is older.

Obviously you're not going to be taking the same care to put silks over the bed with a ten-month-old that you might with a one-week-old! The toddler is much more "here" and is quickly adapting to earthly life. Preschool- and kindergarten-aged children can become desensitized to their environment, but it is still beneficial to maintain an awareness of the quality of their sensory experiences. For example, taking a child under the age of seven to the movies or to "baby dance parties" or rock concerts provides more stimulation than a young child can process. Even in the home, the sensory experience provided by any kind of screen time (DVDs, television, computer games, or an iPad) has been shown by neuropsychologists and ophthalmologists not to be good for the developing eye and brain of the young child, regardless of the content (this is discussed in greater detail in chapter 12).

In contrast, the natural world provides so many health-giving elements for the developing child, from sensory stimulation to freedom of movement to opportunities for imaginative and cognitive development. You can bring the natural world to your child both by ensuring plenty of outside time and by providing clothing and toys from living sources. Synthetics, those wonderful creations of the human mind, can be introduced when the child is older. It is especially important to continue to keep your child warmly dressed (but not overheated!) throughout early childhood, protecting the vital organs in the trunk with an undershirt or T-shirt and keeping little girls' legs warm when they are wearing dresses. It is also beneficial for children from infancy to age seven and older to wear hats whenever they're out in the sun—a habit we'd do well to imitate!

TOILET TRAINING

There is clearly a maturational factor involved in teaching a child to use the toilet, so starting toilet training too young is fairly pointless. On the other hand, there is also often a window of interest and opportunity that, if missed, can lead to indifference or power struggles with an older child. As parents have become more and more relaxed about toilet training (and more reluctant to do anything), disposable diapers have become available in larger and larger sizes. In 1962 about 90 percent of children were out of diapers by age two and a half. A study published in 1998 in *Pediatrics* found only 22 percent are trained by that age, and almost half of boys weren't trained by age three.[21]

Experts cite a number of factors for the change to later toilet training and the surprising popularity of the size 6 Pampers and Huggies: the advent of comfy, leak-proof disposable diapers that give children no inclination to train; our hectic lives; the Brazelton-led impulse to listen to kids more rather than dictating their development; and the fact that so many toddlers are so big for their age.[22]

In response to the swing of the pendulum described above, a more recent movement toward "diaper-free toddlers" has arisen, partly in reaction to the cost and strain on landfills of disposable diapers. There is even a movement for diaper-free babies, called "elimination communication," based upon developing sensitivity to the baby by carrying him or her all the time, as in rural India, for example. Although in our culture it is difficult to be so tuned in to your infant that you can catch every impulse for eliminating before it happens, it isn't difficult to observe when a toddler is interested in and physiologically ready for the process.

The "diaper-free toddler" folks recommend dedicating a three-day period to toilet training that involves giving away all the diapers, letting the child go bare-bottomed or dressing him only in loose-fitting pants (with no underwear) that he can pull up and down himself, and reinforcing every success using little potties that are readily accessible. Dr. Sears has published a book on the three-day method, and over a thousand families in the San Francisco Bay Area have attended preschool teacher Julie Fellom's training called Diaper-Free Toddlers. Although some children make the transition more easily than others, it seems to work! You can learn more by searching online.

Second children usually toilet train themselves much more easily than first children because they have a sibling to imitate, and because parents are much more confident about it. Remembering how imitative children are, let toddlers see how it's done, and provide a little potty around the age of two. Many children feel insecure sitting on the big toilet, so a potty chair can be very helpful. Making it a special present and praising children each time they use it will reinforce their new behavior. After a three-day marathon, there will still be occasional accidents, but patience and a cheerful, "Too bad, maybe next time you can run faster," will soon lead to effective results.

SEPARATION ANXIETY AND "HELICOPTER PARENTING"

There has been a lot written in recent years on mother-child attachment, or bonding, and what can happen when this breaks down through prolonged separation, as in the case of premature or ill newborns. However, we also need to realize that under normal circumstances the mother and child are also going through a separation process. They start out as one, contained within one body, united both physically and psychically. Instead of trying to create a bond at birth, the question arises, "How can the separation of birth not be so painful or prolonged that the mother disconnects from the child?" The obvious answer is through humane birth practices that encourage the mother and child to remain together. Increased contact helps bridge the separation and establish a new relationship rather than leaving the mother feeling let down and isolated by the passing of the old one.

This separation process of mother and child goes on throughout life as the individuality of the child asserts itself more and more. The mother must constantly let go of her image of the child and their relationship as it has been so the child can more fully be himself and a new relationship can be born.

We have talked about the nine-month-old's common anxiety about people outside the family, and the child's pattern of going away from and coming back to the matrix or source of security. However, separation is also painful for the mother, as anyone who has left her baby for the first time knows. The full breasts, the psychic connection, the concern about how the baby is taking it, and the worry that no one can possibly care for this child as well as she does all pull at a mother's heart strings. The same is true the first time the child goes to school, has her first date, or drives the car alone.

We want to protect our children, but we need to realize that they are not extensions of ourselves. Your child is in fact a unique individual who has chosen you to be his or her parents. The individuation process needs to be allowed to occur in order for the child to grow up in a healthy way. In fact, a failure of individuation can cause as great a problem as neglect.

We need to recognize a child as a unique individual from the beginning and do everything we can to avoid hindering her in realizing her full potential and destiny in life. How does this translate into action? For one thing, it means being watchful but not overly protective. (What if the mother of Sir Edmund Hillary, who first successfully climbed Mount Everest, hadn't let him climb the stairs as a toddler?) Perhaps it means letting it be all right for your child to climb a tree or climb to the top of the swingset at the park. Chances are your child will do fine if she undertakes it at all; children are fairly self-regulating if you don't help them into places they can't get to on their own.

Another way of putting this is, "How can we be as relaxed about our first child as we would be about our fourth?" Naturally, we can't be, because everything is so new. But the "benign neglect" and the interaction with siblings that a younger child receives are beneficial compared to the hovering "helicopter parenting" and the constant push into adult activity that first and only children tend to receive. As parents, we need always to keep our toddlers in our psychic awareness, but we don't always need to be interacting with them. Raising a child who can play alone, who is self-motivating, and who does not always need adult input is a real blessing. We need to hold our children in our love and awareness, provide a rich and safe environment for them to explore by themselves, and be there when they come back to touch base. This may happen every few minutes at first, or every few hours as they become older—or just at family meals as teenagers.

CABIN FEVER

Raising a child is a full-time task. Someone has to be attending to your child all the time. You as parents have a unique relationship with this person and should value both the time and the effort necessary to take care of a toddler. But the same person doesn't have to do it all the time: you can trade off, engage grandma, have a babysitter, nanny, or mother's helper, or work out trades with a friend who also has a young child. The at-home parent should do whatever is needed to maintain his or her own composure and ability to mother or father this young child. At the same time, don't undervalue your parenting or accept the comfortable illusion that "quality time" makes up for the constant demands of the toddler to be in relationship with you as he or she goes out to explore the world. If you must return to work full time, try to choose an environment for your child that is as much like a home as possible.

Some women—even those who have dreamed of being able to stay home with their children—are blindsided by the lack of value placed on mothering and the isolation and frustration created by our lack of extended family and lack of neighborhoods. Fathers who stay at home with their infant or young child while their wife works outside the home face additional challenges, such as being the only father at a parent-child class or not knowing any other men who are in a similar role.

Regardless of your gender or the amount of time you spend at home, if you find yourself dying to get away from your children, try exploring some of the reasons and possible solutions. Here are some things to consider:

1. Is your child especially clingy?

Could you simplify and change the environment to make more interesting things accessible to your child, encouraging his exploration of the world? Can you change your expectations of your child, relaxing and recognizing that "this too shall pass"? Decide to spend three days devoted to nothing but "being there" for your child and observing, without resentment and without trying to get twenty-five other things done. Perhaps your child will start to branch out as he feels the solid base of your uninterrupted support. As your child approaches three, having more children around is often easier than having only one. Can you trade days of child care with a friend, thus making your time with the children more intentional and giving you time away?

2. Do you find yourself engaged in constant conflict with your child?

List the times of day and the activities that lead to conflict. What could you do to change each situation (lay out clothes the night before, get up fifteen minutes earlier, have more ritual and rhythm at bedtime, change your reactions)? What attitudes and expectations do you have? If you are a single parent, can you enlist someone else to observe the two of you and give you some much-needed perspective? If you have a partner, what does he perceive about what is going on? What does he feel about it? Is he supporting you and correcting the child or ignoring the situation? Do you get louder to try to get a reaction from him?

3. Do you miss intellectual stimulation or adult companionship?

Can you find a mother's support group or join a playgroup? Can you go to the park once a week with a friend who also has a toddler? Satisfied mothers of young children seem to be much more social than single women. They are often going to visit a friend with children or having them over. Sitting in the park or visiting are not luxuries we have at every stage of life. Can you come to appreciate these activities?

Do you have a good relationship with your husband? Do you have evenings free? If taking care of the children goes on until 11 p.m., see chapter 6, "Rhythm in Home Life." What is happening sexually between you? Can you set a time once a week to spend time together, just the two of you?

Would learning more about early childhood help make your task seem more worthwhile and help engage your mind? Would a new activity, such as getting out to an art class, satisfy your need? Taking some time away can often improve your state of mind and your mothering. A friend who was a mother of five young children and lived by the airport got her pilot's license after the birth of her sixth child because within five minutes she could be hundreds of feet above all the dirty diapers and toys on the floor. In a similar vein, I took a course to become a travel agent when my children were two and a half years and six months. I see it now as one of the main things that kept me sane during a very difficult time. It provided intellectual stimulation two afternoons a week and was pure fantasy fulfillment (I never became a travel agent).

4. Do you feel at a loss for things to do with your child?

One friend expressed her frustration by saying, "But I find doing puzzles so boring!" In general, we need to enjoy our children rather than be concerned about playing with them. By this I mean that we need to have a positive attitude and provide them with things to do, but we do not always need to do the same things they are doing. Think of ways to involve your toddler in the things you do rather than trying to get them done more quickly without her. Once your child is older than two and a half, invite other children over and let them play with one another. It requires supervision and judicious adult input, but it allows the child to be in his element rather than constantly requiring adult input to play.

If you are still feeling dissatisfied, see whether you can discern why and discuss it with your partner or a friend. You don't have to settle for "getting through it" rather than enjoying parenting and being with your children. New knowledge and perspective, establishing rhythm and discipline, and understanding how children learn and play can all help you enjoy the adventure of parenting young children. It isn't always easy, but it's always worthwhile and rewarding.

OTHER PARENTING ISSUES

If you still have issues that haven't been addressed, you can skip to chapter 12, in which we consider additional parenting issues, such as television and screen time, immunizations, balanced development, preparation for life, and much more. Or write to me at my blog, www.waldorf inthehome.org; I'd be glad to respond!

RECOMMENDED RESOURCES

Beyond the Rainbow Bridge, by Barbara J. Patterson and Pamela Bradley (Michaelmas Press). A Steiner-oriented guide to nurturing children from birth to age seven, with an excellent section on creating balance.

"The Four Temperaments," by Rudolf Steiner, published in the book *Rhythms of Learning* (SteinerBooks). An introduction to the study of temperaments, which is a great help in parenting.

The Incarnating Child, by Joan Salter (Hawthorn Press). Addresses parenting in the first two years from the standpoint of Steiner's indications and the author's wide experience at the Gabriel Baby Centre in Australia.

"Joyful Toddlers!" Blog and telecourses from Faith Baldwin Collins, from her work as cofounder of Rainbow Bridge LifeWays Program. See www.joyfultoddlers.com.

Lifeways: Working with Family Questions, edited by Gudrun Davy and Bons Voors (Hawthorn Press). Issues of family life growing out of discussions by a women's group working with Steiner's insights.

Mothering and Fathering, by Tine Thevenin (Avery). Explores the gender differences in parenting and the value of both. Provides valuable perspectives if you find yourself constantly at odds with your spouse or pediatrician on parenting issues. Out of print, but available through Amazon.

Nonviolent Communication, by Marshall Rosenberg, Ph.D. (Puddle Dancer Press). Also available are CDs and DVDs by John Cunningham on nonviolent communication and Waldorf, from www.waldorfinthe home.com.

Waldorf in the Home. The website www.waldorfinthehome.com provides articles and nearly two hundred DVDs and CDs of keynote presentations and workshops by leading Waldorf educators, including:

"The Artistry of Discipline," by Claudia McLaren Lainson

"The Changing Nature of Authority: NVC and Waldorf," by John Cunningham

"Getting Your Children to Do What You Want Them to Do without Talking Yourself to Death," by Nancy Blanning

"Introduction to NVC," by John Cunningham

"The L.O.V.E. Approach to Discipline," by Cynthia Aldinger

"Loving Authority: Building Up, Not Tearing Down," by Penni Sparks

"Mothering Our Lively Sons!" by Janet Allison

"Spiritual Parenting," by Joya Birns and Cindy Brooks. Book and three CDs on how discipline and communication change with children in the three seven-year cycles. Insightful and practical.

CHAPTER 8

Nourishing Your Child's Imagination and Creative Play

THREE STAGES OF PLAY

Play has been called "the work of early childhood" and is recognized as activity that is self-directed, coming from the child herself without any external purpose or motive. In early childhood creative play can be seen as unfolding in three stages: play arising from the body, play arising from imagination and imitation, and intentional pretending.

Play Arising from the Body

While your child is first mastering new body skills, most play consists of pure movement without the element of fantasy. A young child loves to run, jump, walk on tiptoe, climb, turn around, or roll on the ground. Like a lamb in springtime or a young colt, your child delights in movement for the sheer joy of it. And such movement is an important part of muscle growth and the acquiring of motor skills. If left unhindered, your child knows best what movements she needs to develop in a healthy way—there is no need for special baby gymnastics.

Anyone who has ever followed a toddler around knows that she is constantly in movement and expends a tremendous amount of energy! Where does this driving force for movement come from? The energy comes from the process of metabolism, manifested through the movement of the limbs. The metabolic/will/limb system is one of three major systems in Steiner's way of looking at the human being; the other two are the nerve/sense/head system and the heart/lung/middle rhythmic system. These three systems all interpenetrate, and all are active and growing throughout childhood. But Steiner recognized that at different ages one or another system may be dominant. Not only is one system growing most actively, but it also has a major influence on how the child experiences the world and on how she learns. The metabolic/will/limb system predominates in the child under the age of seven; the middle rhythmic system dominates during the elementary school years; and the nerve/sense/head system is predominant beginning in adolescence.

7-year cycle	Dominant System	How the Child Learns Best
0–7 years	Metabolic/will/limb	Willing/Movement/Imitation
7–14 years	Heart/lung/middle rhythmic	Feeling/Imagination
14–21 years	Nerve/sense/head	Thinking/Analysis

Thinking, feeling, and willing mature within each of the seven-year cycles, but understanding how the dominance changes from one to another as the child grows can help parents and educators meet the real needs of the developing child.

The metabolic/will/limb system can be called the vital pole because it is the center of vitality—the center for the anabolic processes of assimilating food and turning it into new physical substance. The growth processes are enormously powerful in a young child, whose life and growth forces are so strong that wounds heal almost immediately. Contrast this with elderly people, whose life forces are declining and whose wounds and broken bones mend only with great difficulty.

The movements of a baby and toddler can be seen as an expression of the movement of the energy that is active within the growth and inner processes of her body. The baby kicks her feet in the air and watches the movement; she moves her hands and follows the movement with her eyes. At first her movements lack intentionality and control. Then she loves to drop things and to fling everything out of her crib, taking joy in the development of her own power. For the infant, the mere moving of her limbs is play enough at first, and a manifestation of the happy unfolding of her powers.

In *Childhood: A Study of the Growing Soul,* Caroline von Heydebrand discusses how the first games of childhood are bound up with the body and have hidden interplay with organic activities, with the swing of the breath, the rhythmic flow of the circulating fluids, and the forming and excreting of substances. "The small child piles up his blocks so as to be able to tumble them down again. This is more important to him at first than to build a house or a tower. He feels the same satisfaction in construction and destruction when playing with blocks as he does in anabolic and catabolic processes of his organism when they are healthy."[1]

Similarly, when a two-year-old scribbles with a large crayon on a piece of paper, you will see spiral, circular movements punctuated by up-and-down movements. The child is expressing the dynamics of his inner being, not trying to make a representational drawing. This aspect of children's art will be discussed more in chapter 9.

Play Arising from Imagination and Imitation

The time when a little child first begins to feel her movements no longer as expressions of energy but as intentional activities within the sphere of her imaginative games varies with every child, but it usually first becomes apparent to the observer between the ages of two and three. The first kinds of play you are likely to see are your child's pretending to eat and drink or talk on the telephone. This type of pretend play comes through the imitation of things the child has done or seen the people around her do. Thus if your child sees you picking up potatoes or balls of yarns and putting them in a basket, she will be happy to copy you and put pinecones or spools in her own basket. Then she will dump them out again, for a child's play has no utilitarian purpose; there is nothing she is trying to accomplish. Your three-year-old may imitate your sweeping by using her own little broom, but she will be completely involved in the gestures of sweeping and unconcerned about picking up any dust.

Without discriminating, a young child takes in everything in her physical and emotional environment. These impressions, which are taken in by the child without filtering or screening, find their expression in play. A child will imitate not only the activity but also the "soul mood" or emotions present when an action was performed. Thus if your daughter observes a worker hammering a nail with great anger, she will copy the movement and the anger; or, if you straighten up the room with annoyance, you will see your annoyance mirrored in the way she handles her toys. We must pay attention both to the quality of our emotions when we are around young children and to the quality of our movements. Once I was throwing together a cake in a great hurry. I told my four-year-old she could help, but I was going so fast I wasn't paying much attention to her. Suddenly I noticed something was wrong. "What's the matter?" I asked. "You're stirring it too fast!" she said through her tears. And she was right—my movements were an affront to her. I apologized and slowed down!

The progression of play from movement to imaginative play can be seen in a young child's relationship to a rocking horse. At first there is no concept of horse, there is just the joy of rhythmical movement. The idea of being a fast rider and "going somewhere" might come next; later the horse will be incorporated into a five-year-old's elaborate scenarios of being a cowboy or taking care of horses or using one to get away from wolves that are chasing him.

The age between three and five years has been called the age of fantasy because all of the intensity that went into learning to stand, walk, speak, and begin to think now finds its expression in imaginative play, which becomes a story without end. Beginning with the sheer joy of movement, your daughter becomes a bunny hopping or a kitty wanting some milk as the imaginative element is added. Then she begins to transform objects from one thing to another in a stream-of-consciousness flow of associations suggested by the objects themselves and her interactions with them. For example, a cylindrical piece of wood may serve as a can of cat food, then it can become a rolling pin for making cookies. The rolling pin now changes into a carton of milk to go with the cookies and a tea party is under way. If you're lucky, you'll be invited.

This kind of play is similar to dreams in the way one object and situation can flow into another, but it represents a high-level use of the child's creative fantasy. Play is the work of the child from age three on, the way in which she unites herself with the world and tries on all of the activities and roles she sees.

Intentional Pretending

When your child is around four and a half or five you will see a new element begin to dominate her play. This new element is intentionality, and it manifests as "let's pretend." Play now tends to be much more socially oriented; it is a group phenomenon in which as much time can be spent in planning "you be the mother and I'll be the sister and you be the dog" as in playing out the actual scene. Now play begins to arise more from within the child herself, and she is beginning to make a picture or mental image of what she wants to do.

The child now not only manipulates objects and concepts by having one thing turn into another, but she also has the self-awareness to plan ahead in pretending to be someone else. By being the mother, the carpenter, or the baker, she is assimilating the world as she experiences it and "living into" the adult world. This is the age when children love bits of cloth and simple costumes to play various roles. Or they will use dolls and table puppets to put on plays that they make up. Their powers of fantasy and intentionality are also clearly revealed when they model with colored beeswax or clay, paint with watercolors, or color with crayons.

EXPERIENCING THE WORLD THROUGH PLAY

Creative play is the way in which children get to know the world, and it has been called the work of early childhood. "There is nothing that human beings do, know, think, hope and fear that has not been attempted, experienced, practiced or at least anticipated in children's play." This opening sentence from *Children at Play* by Heidi Britz-Crecelius is developed further as she explains the various "worlds" the child experiences through play.[2]

The World of Space, Time, and the Cosmos

The tiny baby plays unconsciously with his hands and feet. Von Heydebrand states, "He stretches out to the moon or to the sunlight dancing on the ceiling, not only because he cannot yet estimate distances but because in the dim dawning of consciousness he has a closer relation to distant spaces than the fully conscious, grown-up person."[3] But he soon learns that although the wooden ring can be caught hold of, the brightly shining moon cannot. His first attempts at grasping objects thus become an adventure in learning about near and far, attainable and unattainable.

The young child is still closely related to the cosmos and delights in play that involves the sun, moon, and stars and their rhythmical movements in the cosmos. Such play includes the image of the circle in all its forms favored by young children: balls, bubbles, balloons, circle games. The ball, a perfect sphere, is a likeness of the earth, the sun, and the "heavenly sphere" that seems to surround the earth. Soap bubbles are delicate balls that float away on the child's own breath. And watching a balloon floating up to heaven can fill a child with delight or great sadness, depending on his temperament.

The World of Nature

It is through play that children come to know the natural world of animals and plants and the timeless elements of earth, air, fire, and water. Getting out of the sandbox and actually digging in the earth puts a child immediately into contact with the soil and a myriad of life forms: many worms, centipedes, pill bugs, and tiny spiders can be discovered. Similarly, teeming life is discovered when the child turns over a stone by the river or sinks down into tall grass. In a country setting, intimate encounters between children and animals and plants occur without our help; in the cities we may have to arrange for such encounters so our children do not remain strangers to nature for the whole of their lives. Climbing trees, picking fruit and flowers, and sowing seeds and watching them sprout are all important experiences for a child.

Air can be played in using kites, flags, pinwheels, windmills, tissue-paper parachutes, and large leaves or any light thing tied to a string. Fire is more difficult for children to experience in our age of central heating and trash pickup, but the joys of a campfire are well known, and Britz-Crecelius states that when a fire is built often enough with adults, the prohibition against lighting fires without an adult will be easier to enforce.[4]

Nature is all around us, even in the city. Contact with nature is renewing for adults, but its importance for children should not be underestimated and has been highlighted by the phrases "nature-deficit disorder" and "no child left inside," popularized by Richard Louv's book *Last Child in the Woods*.[5] Children are especially nourished by contact with the world of living things because their own life forces are so strong. Child psychologist Bruno Bettelheim reminds us that "the child's thinking remains animistic until the age of puberty. His parents and teachers tell him that things cannot feel and act; and as much as he may pretend to believe this to please these adults, or not to be ridiculed, deep down the child knows better."[6]

The Human World

Through play the child interacts first with his parents and those in his immediate family. He can very soon start to help the adults in their work, washing the car or putting away the silverware. Because much of the interesting housework and handiwork that children used to grow into through play is now done by machines, it is all the more important to let children participate in what you are doing whenever possible, as discussed in earlier chapters.

The Special Role of Dolls

Through play the child familiarizes himself with the world and assimilates it, making it his own. His senses become sharpened and he is better able to control the instrument of his body and to relate to nature and his fellow human beings. Play with dolls is important as one of the ways the child can externalize his own inner being. "Through the doll the child finds its own self," Britz-Crecelius states, offering in *Children at Play* many examples of how involved children can become with a favorite doll, so that adults have to be very careful not to commit the faux pas of denying the reality of such a doll.[7] Parents must treat these attachments with respect and stay alert to which dolls are "living" for the child, for it can change with time and circumstances. The favorite doll can become like an alter ego for the child, invested with a bit of the child's own emerging sense of self.

Because a doll plays many varied and complex roles, according to the circumstances, it is easy to understand that the more indistinct and undefined a doll's expression, the less trouble it will cause the imagination of the child. If the doll has a fixed character, it will most often be assigned a specific role in play; it is less useful as a second *I* than a soft doll with eyes but no mouth, which can easily be happy, sad, or angry.

Constant invisible companions are used by children in much the same way, and Britz-Crecelius states, "The disappearance of an invisible companion, the discarding of a doll, are important steps on the path of the child to itself. If, however, one removes them forcibly and before the child is ready, then one makes it unsure of itself."[8]

Dolls also give children an opportunity to imitate and work out the ways in which parents treat them. For girls, play with dolls is mainly a mother-and-child game, while boys' play with dolls is rarely that. Boys are also less likely to dress and undress their dolls, so their dolls don't need removable clothes and wardrobes as girls' dolls do. However, boys between two and six have a need as great as a girl's need for a doll that can represent a second *I*, a being the child clasps in his arms when he is beyond himself in order to come to himself again. Many people in our culture are shy of giving dolls to boys or want to make sure they represent "macho" images such as He-Man or G.I. Joe. However, our sons need to be allowed both to be children and to exhibit nurturing behavior just as much as our daughters!

Most psychologists also support boys being encouraged to play with dolls. Bruno Bettelheim states, "If parents feel relaxed about their son's playing with dolls, they will provide him with valuable opportunities for enriching his play life. For them to do so, it is not sufficient that they simply refrain from disparaging such play. Because of the still prevalent attitude that doll play is only for girls, both parents need to have a positive feeling about a boy's doll play if he is to be able to take full advantage of it."[9]

We need to put our attention into the quality of the dolls our children have. Not only their expression but also the quality of the material is important. Is the doll cold and hard or soft and huggable? Is the hair platinum and grotesquely matted after a week's play? A soft cloth doll with yarn hair and a neutral expression provides the child with a companion who can change as he or she does. Britz-Crecelius reminds us, "Walk, talk, cry, laugh, eat, drink, wet itself, blush, get a temperature, get brown in the sun—any rag doll, any nice, simple doll can do that in the hands of a child. The mechanical creatures on the toy market can do it much less well, and provoke every older or younger brother into opening them up to have a look—and rightly so! Because these are not dolls, but machines, whose mechanics leave no room for the little bit of the child's soul that seeks to enclose itself there."[10] Even eyes that close are very mechanical, as evidenced by a little girl who said of her simple doll with its wooden head, "My Tommy doesn't always need to go to sleep straight away, he can also lie awake sometimes."[11]

The beautiful doll and the anatomically correct doll can be a hindrance to the inner development of the child. Not only do they leave nothing for the child's imagination to supply, but they also provide more than the young child can hold in awareness. Young children are mostly aware of the head, as evidenced by their drawings. (This will be discussed more in chapter 9.) Giving a child a doll with breasts is projecting her out of her childhood into the teenage world. Barbie dolls and those with "attitude" like Bratz dolls form a multimillion-dollar enterprise that shortchanges the world of the young child.

THE IMPORTANCE OF PLAY IN INTELLECTUAL DEVELOPMENT

Noted psychologist Bruno Bettelheim defines a young child's play as "activities characterized by freedom from all but personally imposed rules (which are changed at will), by free-wheeling fantasy involvement and by the absence of any goals outside of the activity itself."[12] Not only is self-directed play important for the healthy creative and emotional growth of a child, but it also forms the best foundation for later intellectual growth. Bettelheim continues:

> Play teaches the child, without his being aware of it, the habits most needed for intellectual growth, such as stick-to-itiveness, which is so important in all learning. Perseverance is easily acquired around enjoyable activities such

as chosen play. But if it has not become a habit through what is enjoyable, it is not likely to become one through an endeavor like schoolwork.[13]

Kindergarten, as first conceived by Friedrich Froebel in the nineteenth century, was a place where children would play, as if in a garden. However, the push to teach to the test has squeezed self-directed play out of kindergartens almost entirely, as described by the Alliance for Childhood in their report *Crisis in the Kindergarten*: *Why Children Need to Play in School*.[14] The imaginative play of the young child, in which objects transform from one thing into another, is an ideal foundation for the symbol manipulation involved in later reading. We shouldn't skip the stage of concrete, although fanciful, manipulation of objects in free play by going directly into reading, writing, and math. The years from three to six provide a lifelong foundation for creativity that should not be undervalued or foreshortened.

Just as it is important not to skip steps like crawling in physical development, it is important not to skip play, which allows for the development of a wide range of experiences, so that what is first grasped through action can later be learned anew through thought. Thus when the adolescent studies the laws of levers and mechanics in physics, he will have had the experience of shifting further forward or back on the seesaw, depending on the size of his friend; or the study of trajectories will have had its foundation in throwing balls or skipping stones.

WAYS TO ENCOURAGE YOUR CHILD'S CREATIVE PLAY

Creating an Inviting Environment

Most children today are like descendants of the old woman in the shoe and "have so many toys, they don't know what to do." The spoils of Christmases and birthdays past are most often stuffed onto shelves or thrown together in a toy box or basket, so it is frequently more fun to dump everything out rather than imaginatively play with particular toys.

Helle Heckmann, who runs a Waldorf-inspired child care center in Denmark, describes this cross-cultural phenomenon:

> The abundance of the children's room must be every
> parent's or child's worst nightmare. "I'm bored." "I've got
> nothing to play with"—even though the shelves are full
> to the brim. Dust-collectors, a useless mess. Where is the
> love for the teddy bear, the doll, the car? The present which
> was given in love and did not drown in abundance is hard
> to find. The child does not need the toys—the toy factories
> need the child.[15]

So I invite you to contemplate your child's bedroom or play room and see which items don't seem to contribute to imaginative play or are never used in play. The weeding out can be done openly or covertly. Some parents have enlisted enthusiasm for the project by saying to the child, "You have so many things. Let's sort through the ones you don't play with any more and give them to the Goodwill so other children whose parents don't have the money to buy toys for them will be able to have some of yours." Other items can simply disappear into a box for a few weeks, to be brought back if they are missed—or passed on if they are not. One mother told me she sets aside a box of extra toys as a "rainy day box," which she can go to at times when her child really seems ready for new input.

You might also consider your children's toys from an aesthetic point of view. More than seventy years ago Steiner railed against giving children "beautiful dolls" instead of simple ones. But what about all of the grotesque and bizarre toys that today's children play with, which intentionally try to embody "the dark forces"? Does beauty matter? Young children are looking to know the real world, and to maintain the inner conviction that it is good, true, and beautiful. This deep inner conviction needs to remain in their unconscious to be drawn upon as teenagers. Such wellsprings are necessary if teens are to have any kind of idealism and ability to seek solutions to the problems and evil in the world instead of succumbing to nihilism and despair. Dr. Gilbert Childs, a noted British educator, writes that it is as if we are actually surrounding our children with ugliness as a principle.[16] It's something to consider.

Once you've appraised your children's toys and you can begin to see the floor and the shelves, you'll be much more aware of the individual toys. Then you can think about how to arrange them, because the way in which you display a child's toys determines to a large extent whether or not your child will play with them. Remember that much of play is suggested by the objects themselves as they spark associations in the child's imagination. When toys are piled together in a toy box or basket, they aren't inviting to your child, and you'll never have the possibility of your child's playing quietly by himself after waking up, allowing you to get another twenty minutes of sleep.

There are other advantages to creating order in your child's play space by making sure that everything has a "home." Having a place for everything can provide the child with a feeling that there is order in the larger scheme of things. And it is through play that a child develops habits for work. Helping your child use things and put them away not only teaches good habits in the present but can also be of help in the later development of thought processes. Dr. Gilbert Childs writes, "Such tidiness in practical affairs will assist the order of thought processes, so laying the foundations for clear thinking in adult years. Children learn to 'think with their hands,' and doing repetitive activities that are allied to household and human tasks in life strengthens their will-power."[17] Although it may seem like extra work to clean up with your child at the end of each day, arranging toys invitingly on shelves or tables will encourage your child to be self-motivating in his play. Arranging little scenes on tables or shelves will invite the child to "live into" the scene and start to play with it the next day.

Another aid to your child's play is having activity areas, if your home or apartment is large enough. For example, a play kitchen area with a child-size table and chairs and some kind of toy stove and dishes will provide hours of imitative play. Most of the play dishes, pots, and pans sold in toy stores last a few weeks or months before they are broken or dented beyond recognition. Adult items—wooden bowls, small pots, silverware, saucers, and pitchers, for instance—are sturdier and can usually be picked up inexpensively at secondhand stores. Wooden fruit can be found at many import stores, and a jigsaw can be used to cut pieces of bread from a scrap of plywood.

When you set up activity areas, remember that your child will most often want to play fairly close to where you spend most of your time. A play area in a dining room or family room is often used more frequently than a bedroom that is upstairs and far away from the main activities of the family. One such area of great enjoyment is a workbench with a real vise, small hammer, saw, and nails. Children enjoy the activities of hammering and sawing, and they can also make toys such as boats or cars. An old tree stump that can be kept indoors for pounding nails is a great way to engage children's excess energy. A doll corner is a special place where the dolls can be put to bed each night and greeted in the morning. Cradles, baskets lined with cloth, a small high chair, and a drawer for dolls' clothes all add to the play in this area. The kitchen or dining room table can serve as an area for painting, coloring, and crafts; these activities will be discussed more in chapter 9.

A few simple capes, hats, and accessories for dress-up can greatly enhance your child's play. Children love to play dress-up for the sheer joy of putting on and taking off fancy clothes; they also love to transform themselves into characters who can then act out roles in imaginative play—especially if several siblings or friends play together.

Toys for Imaginative Play

The less formed and more archetypal a toy is, the more possibilities it leaves for the child's imagination. In *The Love of Seven Dolls* by Paul Gallico, a little girl takes leave of the seven dolls she loves so much. The doll "Monsieur Nicholas," who repairs and makes toys, gives her "an oddly turned piece of wood that had not one but many shapes. 'For your first-born,' he says. 'It is a toy I have made for him that is not any, yet is still all toys, for in his imagination, when he plays with it, it will be whatever he sees in it, or wishes it to be.'"[18]

Shapes and forms from nature—gnarled knots from trees, pieces of bark, small pieces of branches, or one-inch rounds from a tree trunk—have that same possibility. This is where a large box or basket filled with "blocks" made from a tree trunk and branches will be used for much more than stacking and knocking down.

"Waldorf-style" dolls and toys and natural craft materials are now readily available from online stores, some of which are listed at the end of this chapter. You can also collect natural objects that can be used in many ways by children. Rocks, shells, pinecones, chestnuts, or walnuts, if made available in small baskets or other containers, will appear as part of the scenery, pieces of food, small animals, or whatever else is needed in the moment's play.

Outdoor Play

In addition to a sandbox, swing, and slide, one of the best outdoor toys for three- and four-year-olds is a climbing dome, also called a jungle gym. Such a small dome is just the right height for these children and will be used for climbing, hanging, sitting on, and playing rocket ship.

Another well-used toy will be a balancing board, which is not yet as narrow as a balance beam. By attaching crosspieces to the underside of both ends, the board can be laid securely across concrete blocks, be secured across two chairs of equal height, or be used in many other ways.

If you can make a small hill in your yard, it will be a constant delight for a young child to climb, run down, march up, sit on, and sled down if you have snow. You can also make use of any natural landscape features you have to encourage the creation of little secret spots behind the hedge, construct simple tree houses together, and otherwise make your yard a magical space for small children.

Trips to the park will be enjoyable for the large climbing and playground equipment that is there, but also try to schedule walks with your child down country roads or through a wooded area. And be sure to walk at the child's pace, allowing ample time for exploration and discovery. I was always amazed at what an eye my daughter had for tiny little things: flowers, bugs, bits of colored paper.

Don't be afraid of the elements. Although most people with children buy appropriate clothing for outdoor play in the snow, few people let their children play in the rain. Waterproof rubber boots, toddler rain pants, and a good rain coat can give your child lots of pleasure stomping through the puddles or playing in the mud. Similarly, be sure to go out when it's windy, letting your child be blown by the wind and fly kites or a large maple leaf attached to a string.

The children in Nøkken, the Waldorf-based child care center in Denmark, are outside for several hours each day in all kinds of weather.

"There's no such thing as bad weather," director Helle Heckmann asserts, "only bad clothing." Each day she and her assistants walk with the twenty-four children to a nearby park. She describes how Karoline and Johanne, both one-year-olds, have started stroking a tree together and laughing, continuing undisturbed in this experience for about an hour. At the same time, two older children are making dinner with the mud. She writes:

> What makes it so important that Sarah and Magnus can sit in a puddle underneath a tree in which the wind is blowing, and in deep concentration cook dinner? What do they shape when they shape the mud-balls? To me, it is definitely themselves—their inner organs. Mud, soil, sand, and water do not have definite shapes; they have the ability to constantly change. This is exactly what the 3- to 4-year-olds need as an identification with the surrounding world. Getting dirty is a sign of health.
>
> The four elements, earth, water, air and fire, are the basic elements which children are nourished by and from which they grow. No shaped toys—be they wood or plastic—can compete with these materials. The seriousness with which the children play, the deep concentration speaks for itself, and shows how important this "playing" is. Nobody needs to fight about anything—there is plenty of mud for everybody.[19]

When I've done workshops on early childhood, I've sometimes asked participants to introduce themselves and then share an early childhood memory. The overwhelming majority of people remember something to do with nature. Often it's just lying in a field and watching the clouds. Try to let your child experience nature and the seasons of the year. You'll probably find it refreshing and energizing yourself!

Encouraging Play by Modeling Meaningful Activity

We have discussed the strong imitative powers of the young child and his need to reenact his experiences of the world around him through play. One of the reasons that children can't play is that they don't very often see the adults around them engaged in meaningful activity that can be transformed in their play. So put attention into the domestic arts and ways in which your child can copy activities such as sweeping, setting the table, sewing, or fixing toys. As discussed earlier, this is primarily because most of our "work" has become mechanized, so there is nothing to see, and because we mistakenly overvalue direct interaction over letting the child observe and share as we do things.

NOURISHING YOUR CHILD'S IMAGINATIVE PLAY THROUGH STORIES

Play enlivens fantasy, and fantasy kindles and diversifies play. As the child becomes older, this creative imagination develops into the formation of images. This same ability later transforms into creative thinking. Developmental psychologists have confirmed that "the development of imagery in the thinking processes of children is an important part of child development, related to play patterns, to creativity, and to adult achievements."[20]

The faculty of imagination develops simultaneously as memory develops. In the third year, the child begins to develop memory and ideas through the separation of himself from the world in consciousness. As the *I* comes to experience itself as separate from the world, there is someone present to remember things. At the same time, the child is able to unite his increasingly conscious self with the world through his will in play, and fantasy soon follows. The two simultaneous developmental processes can be diagrammed as follows:

knowledge   will
↓   ↓
separation of self and   union of self and
world in consciousness   world in play
↓   ↓
memory/ideas   play/fantasy

You can nourish the development of your child's imagination by providing nourishing images from stories the child hears and limiting images the child receives from television, computer games, videos, and movies.

The Difference between Auditory and Visual Images

Images a child hears actively engage his own imaginative or picture-making processes. A good storyteller knows that she is weaving a cloak of magic around the listeners as she describes the characters and the unfolding action. Once I overheard my eleven-year-old say to her friend, "I like to read books without pictures best, because then I can picture them any way I want to." Perhaps this is one of the reasons why movie renditions of books we have read are never quite as satisfying as the originals.

Images we make of things we have read or heard are easy to transform in our imaginations or daydreams because we have already given them life by creating them with our mind's eye. Images we see, however, have a tremendous sticking power and are very difficult to change because they come to us already completed. Who can think of the Seven Dwarves without seeing Happy, Sleepy, Doc, and the entire retinue as Disney portrayed them? I was surprised when my two older children talked to each other about cartoons they had seen five years earlier, before we had gotten rid of the television set. But then I realized that I could still call up images from television programs I had seen when *I* was a child.

Television and movies don't have as strong an effect on adults as they do on children. For me, seeing *E.T.* was sort of like eating cotton candy—it didn't make too deep an impression on me—so I was amazed when a year later my children still remembered Elliot's brother's name! Not only do images from television and the movies make a deep impression on the young child, who is all sense organ, but their power also means that these images will be repeated in play as the child tries to digest and assimilate what he has taken in. Even an older child (and many an adult!) will continually talk about a movie right after having seen it in an attempt to digest it.

Because the images from television and the movies are so powerful and change so quickly, children often do not understand the story line and are left imitating the rapid movements and the other elements that make the strongest impression: chasing, shooting, crashing, and so on.

Also, because children are kept passive while watching television, they have all the more need to race about when they are finished. Young children's natural state is movement.

Images from television always reminded me of those automatic reflex responses that bypass the brain, like pulling back your finger from a hot stove before realizing what has happened. In a similar way, images from television and the movies seem to bypass the child himself and come out in frenzied movement, without the child having transformed them into his own unfolding story. As a preschool and kindergarten teacher, I observed a dramatic difference in the quality of play of children who did not watch television. Their inside play was much more imaginative and more likely to have a story line than that of other children, who were more likely to run around and attempt to catch one another. When a child arrived at preschool wearing a Batman T-shirt, the play immediately turned into chasing one another. I then asked the parents not to send their children in clothing with insignias so that imaginative play could find a little space in which to grow and flower.

Some parents are afraid that if they don't let their children watch television they will be seen as social misfits. On the contrary, they are often welcomed. After my children had been involved with Waldorf education for a couple of years, a neighbor said to me, "We love to have Faith over. She's so creative." Needless to say, I was pleased.

Children who do not watch television will still play games with their friends involving TV or movie characters, whose nature they can easily pick up from the plastic figures. But when everyone was playing characters from *Star Wars*, for example, the internal process of play was very different in the child who had not seen the film. The imagination was more active and original in the child who was not relating to the fixed visual images from the screen.

The Importance of Oral Language and Storytelling

In his book *A Is for Ox*, Professor Barry Sanders develops the thesis that true literacy, and the ability to reflect upon one's self and one's actions, which it encourages, can only be based upon a firm foundation of oral language. His book provides a fascinating and cogent argument why, as he states, "The teaching of literacy has to be founded in a curriculum of song, dance, play, and joking, coupled with improvisation and recitation. Students need to hear stories, either made up by the teacher or read out loud. They need to make them up themselves or try to retell them in their own words. Teachers need to provide continual instruction in the oral arts—from primary school, through the upper grades, and on into college."[21] He also shows that this continuing emphasis on the spoken word in schools needs to be built upon the oral foundation provided by the parents in the home, through conversation, singing, nursery rhymes, and stories.

It is significant that Sanders mentions lullabies and nursery rhymes, which are valuable for the rhythmical qualities of language in which they bathe the child. Some are built on tongue twisters or riddles, delighting a child with their playful sounds and associations. Others introduce the child to the concepts, values, and traditions of our normal waking consciousness.

In addition to nursery rhymes, three-year-olds especially love stories that are built on repeating phrases, such as "This Is the House That Jack Built" or "Little Tuppens," which is a story about what the mother hen must ask of each animal so that the oak tree will give her an acorn cup for some water for little Tuppens, who is coughing. Other simple repetitious tales with which you are probably familiar include "The Three Billy Goats Gruff," "The Little Red Hen," and "The Little Gingerbread Boy."

To encourage the transition from nursery rhymes to stories, parents are always encouraged to read to their children, so the children will be exposed to books and to reading. Having parents who read and older siblings who have successfully learned to read increase a child's eagerness to do the same. However, there is also a great deal of value in telling stories to your children. Not only do the children gain listening skills, but they also appreciate the fact that you are doing something creative with them. When you tell a story, you weave a magic web in which the listeners become engrossed, and there is nothing between you and the children to distract your attention or theirs. By telling a story rather than reading it, you are also free to note the effect the story might be having on the child.

With two- and barely three-year-olds, your stories can be simple descriptions of the world that your child experiences. For example, if he likes to feed the ducks in the park, you might make up something like:

> Mrs. Duck called her five baby ducklings to follow her into the water. Across the river they swam, because they saw Jimmy and his mother had come with the bag of bread crumbs. Jimmy threw some of the bread into the water, and "splash" went all the ducks as they snapped up the bread. Jimmy laughed to see how hungry they were. When all the bread was gone, Mrs. Duck and her ducklings swam away and Jimmy and his mother went home for nap.

Everyday events are great adventures for a toddler, and he loves to live through them again and again in story. It is important to describe things in a natural way, letting your words bring to mind what the child has experienced. Introducing ideas from fairy tales, such as an "enchanted stream" or a "poison well," would only confuse a young child who is still taking in the direct experience of the water itself. Telling simple stories from everyday life in a slow, deliberate way with a musical tone of voice will delight a two-year-old. A lot of what your two-year-old appreciates is the special time with you and the soothing quality of your voice, which can bring up images or create a mood of security or fun with its rhythms and rhymes.

Children who are three years and older love to hear stories from your own childhood. "When I was a little girl my mother worked at an olive cannery where they had great big barrels where the olives floated in salty water to make them taste good to eat. And there among the barrels my mother found a little gray kitten. . . . Well, what do you think we named her?" These stories, which have their basis in your experiences, can also stimulate your imagination, so that you start telling a whole made-up series of stories about the adventures of the kitten named Olive. Imagination isn't just for kids!

In stories for young children, although the animals might be personified (like Mrs. Duck), it is best if they are still true to their natures and their lives in the natural world, which the child is coming to know and love. Cartoon characters represent an adult level of sophistication that goes beyond the world of early childhood.

Children also love to hear stories about themselves, especially about when they were babies (now that they are so grown up!). They like to hear about things they said and did, the time they went to grandma's house, and so on.

When is your child old enough for stories? Obviously it takes a certain maturity of language development for a child to listen to a story. Until that time children are still totally immersed in experiencing things themselves. Take your cues from your child and start with very short stories, as described above, gradually working up to longer ones with repetition, and then into simple fairy tales.

The Inner Meaning of Fairy Tales

When the child is about four years old, you will find he is fascinated by fairy tales that are told or read. A simple story like "Sweet Porridge," from the Brothers Grimm collection, will delight even a three-year-old. They enjoy hearing of the little pot, so full of abundance, which overflows until stopped by the right phrase. At this age the children themselves have a sense of life's eternal abundance, which one child expressed when her mother told her that she did not have enough time to take her out to play: "But Mother, I have lots of time. I'll give you some."[22] A simple story such as "The Star Child" can later be followed by longer ones such as "Goldilocks" and "The Three Little Pigs." Some fairy tales are so rich and complex that they can nourish children up to the age of eight or even nine.

Most parents today are unfamiliar with original fairy tales as literature, having grown up with only the cartoon or Disney versions or stories retold by someone who took great liberties with them. Such renditions are of questionable value, and I found that reading the Brothers Grimm or British fairy tales in their original, unedited versions was an entirely different experience. As I became open to their possible inner meanings and read them with new eyes, I found a great wealth in their images.

Fairy tales have gone in and out of fashion over the centuries. During the age of rationalism, they were dismissed as nonsense and were a dying oral tradition when Jakob and Wilhelm Grimm, among others, made their collections by visiting village storytellers in the late 1800s. The title of their well-known collection of stories in German is *Kinder- und Hausmärchen* (Children's and Household Tales), which indicates their original nature as tales or "little reports" that were commonly repeated in the home and told to children. The tales rarely had to do with fairies, and instead they seemed to talk about a world that was somehow strongly connected to our inner life, even if it was different from our everyday experience.

Today there is renewed interest in fairy tales through the work of psychologists such as Carl Jung and Bruno Bettelheim, and writers such as Rudolf Steiner. Jung speaks of fairy tales as projections of the collective unconscious in an attempt to explain their cross-cultural similarities. Rudolf Steiner states that fairy tales are like "readings" or reports from the childhood of humanity, a time when people participated in a dream-like, experiential consciousness that radiated feeling and was filled with images. This preceded the development of our scientifically critical, observant, awake consciousness that is filled with ideas.[23] Both Jung and Steiner agree that all of the characters in a fairy tale represent elements within each individual, aspects of our own selves and our destinies here on earth. Prince and princess, animus and anima, spirit and soul—all are metaphors for our own striving to achieve a sense of union of the parts of ourselves, represented by the marriage at the end of many tales.

Some object to fairy tales on the grounds that they are too Eurocentric, they lack appropriate female role models, or they are too violent. With a little extra effort, however, tales from other cultures and those with an active female lead can be found. Harder to find are those in which the *hera* (the feminine form of hero) is female and the journey is a woman's journey (no dragon killing here!). There is often violence in fairy tales, and certainly a Hollywood rendition of a story can scare a young child and give him nightmares. However, when fairy tales are told in a melodic voice, without emotional dramatization, the moral pattern of the fairy tale emerges. In the journal *Ethics in Education*, Diana Hughes states that fairy tales speak directly to the natural morality in the child and to his or her sense of moral order in the world. When the good wins and the evil is punished, a child is visibly satisfied.[24] Through the adventures and triumphs of the main character and showing that evil is always self-consuming, fairy tales are usually a source of reassurance and comfort to a child. A subtler theme in several stories is that when one recognizes the potential for evil, it loses its potency. For example, once Rumpelstiltskin and his equivalent, Tom-Tit-Tot, have been correctly named, they lose their power and their temper.[25]

Bettelheim states, "It is not the fact that virtue wins out at the end which promotes morality, but that the hero is most attractive to the child, who identifies with the hero in all struggles."[26] There is not a fairy tale known that doesn't end with resolution and the successful growth of the hero or heroine. Steiner pointed out that the world of the fairy tale and the world of the young child are essentially the same: both worlds share moral absolutes, mobility of imagination, and limitless possibilities for transformation.[27] Bettelheim states that fairy tales can often help children resolve fears and build feelings of competence.[28] Neil Postman, in *The Disappearance of Childhood*, praises Bettelheim's demonstration that the importance of fairy tales "lies in their capacity to reveal the existence of evil in a form that permits children to integrate it without trauma."[29]

If you have trouble with a fairy tale or its images, skip that one and choose another, but don't change parts of it as you go along. The "true" fairy tales are artistic wholes in which actions and descriptions are very precise. They should be told as accurately as possible, without emotional dramatization. The report of the witch locking up Hansel and later getting pushed into the oven by Gretel will not frighten a child if you are not in conflict about the story!

To the extent that we as adults can "live into" the inner richness of a fairy tale, we and our children will be the more nourished by it. As a result, it is best if you do not give explanations to a child or ask him, "Why did Goldilocks go into the house? How do you think she felt when she woke up and saw the three bears?" Fairy tales should not be reduced to the intellectual or emotional level. They do not need any explanation or rationalization to be appreciated by the child. Just as humanity has passed through various stages of consciousness, so children are passing through these same stages. For this reason, they live with the fairy tale images and are warmed and fulfilled by them again and again. When we tell a fairy tale with an inner understanding and appreciation of its deeper meaning, it is as if the young child feels, "Ah! You understand, too!"

Sharing Fairy Tales with Young Children

First, it is important that you be comfortable with a fairy tale and at least open to and appreciative of its deeper meaning. If a particular story pushes your buttons, don't share that one with your children. Rather, choose a fairy tale that speaks to you, one you can meditate on and try to penetrate to its mood and inner meanings. You can become familiar with various approaches to the interpretation of fairy tales by reading some of the books listed at the end of this chapter, but ultimately you will need to let the fairy tale speak to you directly. Try reading it to yourself every night before you go to bed. By taking it into your sleep, you will gradually gain insight into it.

One way to match fairy tales to the age of the child is to look at a story's degree of complexity. In almost every fairy tale there is either a problem that must be solved or a confrontation with evil. The milder the problem, the more appropriate the tale for younger children. Conversely, the greater the evil, the more appropriate the tale is for older children.[30]

Similarly, there are often several trials of varying complexity. In "The Three Little Pigs," the pigs are too smart for the wolf three times before they finally overcome him. The tasks the pigs face are really not very scary and are addressed with a fair amount of humor, making this tale well loved by most four-year-olds. In contrast, the sister in "The Seven Ravens" must journey to the sun, the moon, and the stars in order to free her brothers; this is a tale for five- and six-year-olds. Even more complex tales, such as "East of the Sun and West of the Moon," are appropriate for school-age children. If a fairy tale is widely known in society, children are often ready for it at an earlier age. Also, if a storyteller particularly loves a fairy tale, she can often tell it successfully to younger children. With children of mixed ages (such as three- to six-year-olds in a Waldorf mixed-age kindergarten or homeschooling situation), stories can be told successfully even if they are appropriate for only some of the children; the rest will listen as if carried along by the other children. Udo de Haes points out that you needn't worry about toddlers in a family hearing stories that are being read to an older brother or sister. In such cases the toddler will be most interested in sitting close to his parent and listening to the cadences of his or her voice and will not pay the same kind of attention to the tale as the child to whom the story is addressed.[31]

When stories and fairy tales are translated into cartoons or movies, they lose their evocative quality and are often too powerful or too inane for young children. However, when stories are presented to children using table puppets or silk marionettes, the experience can have a very calming and healing effect. Even more simply, telling a story in nature and illustrating it with a little puppet that comes out of your pocket or who is "found" behind a piece of bark can be totally delightful; Suzanne Down's newsletters and puppetry kits, listed below, can introduce you to this magical world of puppetry in early childhood.

RECOMMENDED RESOURCES

Story Anthologies to Get You Started

The Complete Grimm's Fairy Tales, by Jakob and Wilhelm Grimm and Margaret Hunt (The Pantheon Fairy Tale and Folklore Library).

Fearless Girls, Wise Women and Beloved Sisters: Heroines in Folktales from Around the World, edited by Kathleen Regan (W.W. Norton & Co.).

Great Children's Stories: The Classic Volland Edition, illustrated by Frederick Richardson (Rand McNally).

The Maid of the North: Feminist Folk Tales from Around the World, by Ethel Johnston Phelps (Holt, Rinehart & Co.).

Spindrift. Stories and songs gathered by British Waldorf kindergarten teachers. Available from www.steinercollege.edu.

About Nursery Rhymes and Fairy Tales

A Is for Ox: The Collapse of Literacy and the Rise of Violence in an Electronic Age, by Barry Sanders (Pantheon). A fascinating analysis of the importance of the oral tradition in developing a sense of self, and the crises facing youth and society today.

Lifeways: Working with Family Questions, edited by Gudrun Davy and Bons Voors (Hawthorn Press). Contains two chapters on the inner meaning of fairy tales.

The Tao and Mother Goose, by Robert Carter (Theosophical Publishing House).

The Uses of Enchantment: The Meaning and Importance of Fairy Tales, by Bruno Bettelheim (Knopf).

The Wisdom of Fairy Tales, by Rudolf Meyer (Floris Books). Interpretations working out of the indications of Rudolf Steiner.

Puppets and Puppet Plays

Juniper Tree Puppets. Shares the magical world of Suzanne Down through monthly story newsletters, books, puppet-making kits, workshops, and trainings. At www.junipertreepuppets.com.

A Lifetime of Joy, by Bronja Zahlingen. A treasury of verses, finger games, stories, and plays for puppets and marionettes. Available from www.waldorfearlychildhood.com.

Toymaking with Children, by Freya Jaffke (Floris). Instructions for making table puppets and many more soft and hard toys found in Waldorf kindergartens.

Curative Stories

Healing Stories for Challenging Behavior, by Susan Perrow (Hawthorn Press). More than fifty stories that address everything from bullying to jealousy of a new baby, plus a guide to making your own stories.

Why the Setting Sun Turns Red, by Eugene Schwartz (Association of Waldorf Schools of North America). Seven stories illustrating the imaginative and objective approach taken by a Waldorf teacher to questions of discipline with kindergarten through high school–aged children.

Books to Inspire Creative Play

Children at Play: Using Waldorf Principles to Foster Child Development, by Heidi Britz-Crecelius (Inner Traditions). Describes how the child comes to know the world through play. Highly recommended.

The Children's Year, by Stephanie Cooper et al. (Hawthorn Press). Directions for soft dolls, knitted animals, and many other toys to make with children.

Earth, Water, Fire, Air, by Walter Kraul (Floris). Play that encourages exploration of the four elements.

Earthways, by Carol Petrash (Gryphon House). Simple environmental activities for young children.

Making Dolls, by Sunnhild Reinckens (Floris). Richly illustrated instructions for making several types of soft Waldorf dolls.

The Power of Play, by David Elkind (DaCapo). More on the importance of play.

Toymaking with Children, by Freya Jaffke (Floris). Instructions for making dolls, knitted animals, wooden trestles, and many more soft and hard toys found in Waldorf kindergartens.

Work and Play in Early Childhood, by Freya Jaffke (Floris). Discusses the pillars of rhythm and repetition, example, and imitation. Beautiful pictures from Waldorf kindergartens.

Play, Storytelling, and Sharing Nature

Waldorf in the Home. The website www.waldorfinthehome.com provides articles and nearly two hundred DVDs and CDs of keynote presentations and workshops by leading Waldorf educators, including:

"Creating a KinderGarden for Young Children," by Betty Peck

"Creating Play Spaces for Young Children," by Simone Demarzi

"The Greening of Story," by Suzanne Down

"The Hidden Depth in Fairy Tales," by Thesa Kallinikos

"Letting Stories Teach," by Eugene Schwartz

"Nurturing Love and Reverence for Nature with Our Children," by Nancy Poer

"The Rebirth of Play," by Joan Almon

"Re-Creating Play," by Joan Almon

"Sharing Stories with Children," by Daena Ross

"Sharing the Joy of Nature and Flow Learning," by Joseph Cornell

Toys for Creative Play

So many wonderful sources are available online! Here are a few of our favorites:

Bella Luna Toys (www.bellalunatoys.com)

A Child's Dream Come True (www.achildsdream.com)

Community Playthings (www.communityplaythings.com)

Juniper Tree Puppets (www.junipertreepuppets.com)

Nova Natural (www.novanatural.com)

Palumba (www.palumba.com)

The Puppenstube (www.thepuppenstube.com)

A Toy Garden (www.atoygarden.com)

Weir Dolls and Crafts (www.weirdollsandcrafts.com)

CHAPTER 9

Developing Your Child's Artistic Ability

UNDERSTANDING CHILDREN'S DRAWINGS AND DEVELOPMENT

How and why do children's drawings change over time, and what clues can your child's drawings give you about his or her development? A child often starts drawing before the age of two, either enthusiastically or tentatively grasping the pencil or crayon for the first time. But once he joyously discovers the potential of drawing, he will be delighted to color frequently and on any surface that presents itself! It has been shown that at whatever age within the first seven years that the child starts drawing, he will begin at the two-year-old scribbling stage. If the child is already past that age, he will go through all the early stages in rapid succession and stop at the motif corresponding to his own development. What are the stages and motifs you can watch for in your child's drawings? It will strengthen your appreciation for the being of your child when you observe his development as reflected in his drawings.

The following information is taken from the excellent book *Understanding Children's Drawings*, by Michaela Strauss, which is based on a lifetime of observations by her father, Hans Strauss, who left behind a collection of more than six thousand young children's drawings that he had assembled and annotated.[1]

Children's drawings can be roughly divided into three stages that are similar to the stages represented in their play. In the first phase, before the age of three, the child creates purely out of the movement that carries him. The process of creation arises in a dreamy way, out of the rhythms and movements coming from within his own body, so if you ask a very young child about his drawing, he will usually be unable to explain the content to you. In the second phase, between ages three and five, the child allows the arising picture to take hold of his imagination. While he draws he will tell you about the picture as it unfolds in front of him. After the fifth year, the child often approaches drawing with a definite idea or picture in mind: "I am going to draw my dog, Mitzy, chasing a rabbit."

Within each phase, certain motifs predominate, and the new ones don't appear until the child has reached the next developmental stage. For example, two types of movement dominate the drawings of children under three. These are a spiral movement and a perpendicular or vertical movement. At first the movements are very large, even larger than the paper, which barely seems to contain them. Strauss observed that until the age of three, spirals are always drawn from the outside in, only gradually forming a center that reflects the child's growing realization of self between the ages of two and three. The flash of ego consciousness is documented by the ability to draw the form of the circle, which, even if the child says "I" earlier on, rarely appears in drawings before the third year. It is also interesting to note that monkeys are quite good at drawing like young children—certainly their jumping and swinging give them an inward propensity toward movement and they have the interest and dexterity to use a crayon or brush—but they are unable to make a connected circle out of the spiral movements that they have in common with the child under three.[2]

Strauss suggests that the spiral movements of scribbling are echoes of the movements of the cosmos and of the flowing rhythms of the fluids within the young child's own body. Similarly, she suggests that the vertical element that appears along with the spiral one is an expression of the child's own recent experience of standing upright.

At the same time a child is able to form a circle, he will probably make crossed horizontal and vertical lines for the first time. Soon the cross will be drawn inside the circle, and circles will also be drawn with a dot inside them. Both examples reflect the child's first experiences of inner and outer in his increasing consciousness during the third year.

After the third year, the circle and crossed lines are fused into a unity, and they continue to appear in more diverse variations until the fifth year and beyond. However, changes continue to occur during this time. The point and the cross, having crystallized as "I" symbols, begin to transform and to radiate from the center outward. At first the radiating lines will stop at the edge of the circle, and then they reach out like feelers beyond the edge of the circle.

As the child continues to develop, trees and people are frequently drawn. Strauss shows how the forms of a tree and a human being are the same for a young child and represent his own changing awareness of his body. First the focus is on the head, with a trunk extending down from it (a floating tree or "pillar person"). It is not until the child is older that the legs become divided and firmly planted on the ground. Around the age of four the child's focal point shifts from the head to the trunk, and a ladder pattern emerges in children's drawings, like the branches of a tree or the branching of the spinal column and the ribs. For the first time drawings now have left-right orientation around an axis of symmetry, like the body around the backbone.

Children at this age also draw people with arms coming off of the head or with huge fingers, reflecting their increasing connection with the world: now they are reaching out and getting into everything. The feet, which take the longest time to be developed in drawings, are thick and heavy, rooted to the ground. The child draws the human being not as we see it, but as he experiences his own self and body. The inner life processes, not the external form, are the determining factors.[3]

The house is another theme through which the child represents his changing relationship between self and world. Drawings of a very young child often show a circle or "head person" inside a larger circle, like the child in the cosmos or the baby in the womb. As the close unity between the self and the world gives way to separate individuality, the spherical "cosmic" house becomes more square in form and anchored near the bottom of the paper. In the third year, the form of the square or box appears for the first time surrounding the person. The narrowing of the perception of cosmic realms through the acquiring of selfhood—the process of becoming an "I"—resembles an encapsulating of the soul. A child may draw a person looking out of the house, and the connections between inner world and outer world can be seen in the doors, windows, and chimneys that now begin to appear.

Using color as a new means of expression is added to the drawing of lines in the middle phase, at ages three to five. Before the third year the child tends to use color mostly to emphasize the line, but toward the fourth year children will draw color for its own sake. Strauss writes, "Touched by the nature of colour, the soul of the child becomes creative. When the world of feeling comes into drawing, the world of colour comes into it too."[4] Before the child uses color for drawing objects, he uses it in drawings to cover a surface, exploring the qualities of colors by filling in areas in a dramatic and somewhat symmetrical "checkerboard" fashion. It is just at this age that block crayons (described in the following section) enable the child to cover large surfaces and increase his color experience.

Around the age of five children will start making illustrative drawings and want to represent objects and scenes from life or stories. These narrative-illustrative drawings will start to wrestle with the elements of space and changing perspective. The profile of the face and the triangle both appear for the first time, and the triangle can become the focus of multicolored geometrical designs that kindergarten children love to make.

When elementary-school-aged children draw a tree and house, the forms look more as we have come to expect them to look, but close observation of such drawings can also reveal interesting things about the inner life of the older child. One very dreamy boy I knew never drew his people touching the ground, even as late as the second grade. And a kindergarten boy in my class drew a sad figure between two houses. He said that one was a house and one was a fire station, but from conversations with his mother I knew that his parents were divorcing and he was spending time with both his mother and father—a sad little boy feeling himself on the road between two homes.

The relationship of children's art to their developing consciousness parallels the developing consciousness of humanity as expressed in primitive art and its evolution over the centuries. Just as the first babbling of a baby is unconnected with particular racial or national characteristics, this first picture writing is also universally human. In this early period of the first seven years the language of symbols is the same the world over. Both Strauss's book and *The Incarnating Child* provide many illustrations of children's drawings, which can become another pathway to increasing your understanding of the changing consciousness of the young child.

Coloring with Block Crayons

Using block rather than stick crayons enables your child to cover an entire page with color with very little effort. By using the flat edges rather than the corners of the block crayons, the child can create bands of color rather than outlines. Within these broad bands of color, forms grow naturally. The yellow streams down and outward; the red is concentrated and strong; the blue gently curves and surrounds. Into these gestures of color spring forms, without demanding precision and intricacy.

When you make a picture in front of a young child, every breath, every thought, every peaceful, careful stroke you make feeds and instructs the child. A picture you carefully and lovingly make for your child is a gift on many levels. It need not be great art! If at night you make a picture for your child from her own experience of the day's activities, with what wonder your child will wake up to this gift, just as the Rhyme Elves often left a little poem and drawing of important events for Sylvia in the *Seven-Year-Old Wonder-Book.*[5] Such pictures can be kept in a special collection, perhaps in a special box or drawer.

You'll find your own appreciation of color and artistic ability increasing as you color and paint with your child. All children have innate artistic ability. If they are given watercolors rather than marking pens, if they can color on blank sheets of paper instead of "keeping within the lines," then this ability is more likely to remain alive and accessible to them throughout their lives.

The block crayons used in Waldorf schools are made of sweet-smelling beeswax rather than paraffin and can be purchased through several online stores.

THE EXPERIENCE OF COLOR

Children have natural artistic ability that can easily go undeveloped or become stifled by inappropriate activities; this often results in frustration and beliefs such as "I can't draw." Helping your child's artistic ability unfold is a great gift you can give him. Though he will not necessarily grow up to be an artist, he will maintain a living relationship with color, will be able to appreciate the play of light and shadow with a sensitive eye, and will feel confident about expressing himself through some artistic medium and find enjoyment in the process.

The world of color is directly related to the way we feel. Colors affect our attitude to life and our moods, which are then expressed in colors. Even our speech reflects this relationship—"green with envy," "feeling blue," "livid with rage," "seeing red," "rose-colored glasses," "jaundiced view." You could say that the very substance of the world is color. Color is to the spiritual life what food, air, and water are to the physical life. As these nourish our bodies, so color nourishes the soul and spirit.

The world of nature is bathed in color. Color comes and goes seasonally, and indeed it does so each day with the coming and going of the light. Just as sunrise and sunset express their own moods through color, so the mood of spring, with its cold earth and moist air, is very different from the mood of fall, with its warm earth and cool, dry air.[6]

Children love colors and unite with the colors that flow toward them from their surroundings. Children's feelings are also strongly affected by colors, so that one color may produce a feeling of well-being while another calls up a feeling of discomfort. Because children are so much more receptive than adults, their experience of color is all the more intense.

In the first seven years the young child takes in everything with his total being; body, soul, and spirit are still united. The young child is completely open to experiences of color in the environment, and for this reason we need to create environments that reflect this sensitivity to good artistic qualities—colors, forms, wall decorations, sounds, and toys. This achieves a deeper effect than "art education" offered in a few spare hours.

The psychological effects of color on people are now being recognized and are beginning to be put into practice in places such as hospitals and mental institutions. When we consider the psychological effects of color on children, Steiner says that the complementary color must be taken into account up to the age of nine:

> A "nervous," that is to say excitable child, should be treated differently as regards the environment from one who is quiet and lethargic. Everything comes into consideration, from the color of the room and the various objects that are generally around the child, to the color of the clothes in which he is dressed. . . . An excitable child should be surrounded by and dressed in red and reddish-yellow colors, whereas for a lethargic child one should have recourse to the blue or bluish-green shades of color. For the important thing is the complementary color, which is created within the child. In the case of red it is green, and in the case of blue, orange-yellow.[7]

I saw this phenomenon in my kindergarten when each day the largest, rowdiest boy would immediately head for the costume rack and put on a huge red satin shirt. When he had it on, he was somehow more settled within himself. I was unaware of the idea that the complementary color works more directly on the young child until I read about it in Steiner's writings. As adults we experience the phenomenon briefly if we stare at a bright red circle and see a green circle when we look away. According to Steiner, the inner experience of the complementary color is stronger for the young child than the experience of the external color; only in the course of time do children experience colors as grown-ups do.

Ordinarily we think of colors as attributes of objects. But to the inward vision of the soul, the essential natures of colors can be revealed. Goethe's *Theory of Colours* forms a basis for much of Steiner's writing on color.[8] Steiner states:

> Goethe draws our attention to the feelings which the colors arouse in us. He points out the challenging nature of red, and his teaching is as much concerned with what the soul feels when it beholds red, as with what the eye sees. Likewise he mentions the stillness and contemplativeness

which the soul feels in the presence of blue. We can present the colors to children in such a way that they will spontaneously experience the shades of feelings engendered by the colors, and will naturally feel the colors' inner life.[9]

Parents and teachers are therefore advised to let children live and work in the world of color, to immerse themselves in the feelings color engenders, as early as possible. In *Painting with Children* Brunhild Müller states, "Not only do children perceive the color but at the same time they sense its quality, they feel in themselves its intrinsic nature, and they are conscious of the non-material essential being of such color. This consciousness is lost as the child grows older, and by the time children go to school, they experience colors as attributes of objects (the blue ball, the red roof and so on)."[10]

It is appropriate to expose the young child to activities such as painting and crayoning in a way that emphasizes the experience of color rather than approach these activities as "lessons" during which the child has to imitate the adult or achieve an end product or finished form. Such experiences of art are valuable for the young child as pure color experiences. Such experiences can also lead to abilities that can be transformed throughout the child's life.

WATERCOLOR PAINTING WITH YOUNG CHILDREN

One of the best experiences of color for the young child comes through painting with watercolors on wet paper. Colors are in their own true element in water. Their waving, shimmering, and streaming nature is manifest the moment they lose their heavy and earthy hardness. Rauld Russell, who wrote *How to Do Wet-on-Wet Watercolor Painting and Teach Your Children*, explains it thus:

> A wet paper surface lends flowing movement to color.
> Color in a thin sea of water can move, mingle, change,
> lighten and darken, just like feelings and emotions. To
> fix all the richness of inner life, all the potentiality, into a

rigid form with hard boundaries (as one would do in "dry" painting) can evoke "hardened" images of life. The application of wet-on-wet most truly corresponds to the soft, unfinished, still growing nature of the child.[11]

No one paints like kindergarten-aged children, because they are totally unself-conscious. If you are not familiar with children's paintings done in this wet-on-wet technique, two inexpensive books with color illustrations of such paintings are *Painting with Children* by Brunhild Müller and *Echoes of a Dream* by Susan Smith, both listed at the end of this chapter. You can easily do this kind of painting with your child, and the results are beautiful.

Supplies

The thought of stocking up at an art supply store may be intimidating to you, but you only need three tubes of color! In Waldorf early childhood programs we use only the primary colors red, yellow, and blue, which allow an infinite number of other colors to appear on the paper under the child's excited gaze. Russell reminds us that "because watercolor painting reaches into the deep psychobiological processes that affect a child's growth, for a very young child you will want to choose a bright medium lemon yellow, a cobalt or ultramarine blue, and a rose-crimson red. The purity of the color is essential." He recommends Stockmar, Grumbacher, Winsor Newton, or other artist-grade watercolors. Inexpensive acrylics will not work.[12]

It is also worthwhile to invest in some good-quality paper such as Grumbacher or Aquabee all-purpose paper or Strathmore 80- to 90-lb. painting paper. Less expensive paper will not bring out the luminous quality and intensity of the colors and will shred into paper-towel consistency before your child finishes a painting. Large sheets of paper are expensive but can be cut into four pieces, and you and your child only need to paint one picture each session. This kind of painting is special; it's not like covering as many sheets of copy paper as possible with paints from a box.

While you are at the store, buy yourself and your child a large flat brush (at least ³/₄ of an inch wide) rather than a pointed brush. The flat brushes enable a greater experience of color and discourage outlining.

Other items you will need include:

- A set of three baby-food-sized jars for each painter
- Pint-sized jars for premixing and storing each color (you may need to store them in the refrigerator to keep them from spoiling)
- Similar jars for rinsing brushes between colors (the advantage of jars over cans is that they don't rust, and the child can see the changing color of the water as he paints—fully as interesting as the painting itself)
- A wooden or Masonite board (16 x 20 x $1/4$ inches), handy both for painting and for keeping the paintings horizontal so they don't run while drying
- A clean sponge for wiping off the wet paper before starting
- A sponge or cloth for each painter to wipe her brush on
- Smocks or painting shirts

Preparation

Children love to help with the preparations for painting. Putting on your smock and getting out the materials will almost always produce a willing helper.

- Prepare the paper by cutting it to size (a two-year-old will need a smaller piece than a five-year-old). In the Waldorf early childhood programs we always round off the corners of the paper because the rounded form is more fluid and suitable for the young child than the square form. The rounded form also frees the children from painting around the outline of the paper, which many will do with a square sheet.
- Squeeze some color from the tube into your mixing jar and add water to dilute it to the consistency of a light syrup. You'll need more paint for yellow than you will for blue. Then put a small amount of this premixed color (a maximum of $1/2$ inch) in each painting jar so little will be wasted if it becomes muddied or spilled. You can store the extra and refill the small jars as needed.
- Put the individual sheets in water to soak. A sink will do; a plastic tray is helpful if you have many children painting.

- Let your child help put the painting boards down and fill the water jars. Arrange the three paint jars on each board and give a dampened sponge to each painter to wipe her brush on. Keeping the brushes until everything else is ready will prevent enthusiasm from carrying everyone away prematurely.
- Now put a sheet of paper on the board and wipe it off with the sponge that is reserved for this purpose. If the paper is too wet, the colors will float away and dry into puddles. But don't wipe it too dry, either!

Starting to Paint

The first time you use these techniques with a young child, you can mix up just one color. Then, over the first several sessions, the child will experience what yellow, blue, and red have to tell him when each is used all by itself.

You will want to demonstrate for your child how to wipe the brush dry on the edge of the water jar and then on the sponge before it is dipped into the color so that later on greater control can be achieved.

When you introduce two colors, demonstrate how the paintbrush needs to be rinsed before changing colors. I often said something like, "Peter Paintbrush needs to take a bath and wash his hair before he puts on his new clothes. And he needs to dry his hair on the sponge first to see if it is clean." We would look at the sponge to see if it was clean, and if so, Peter would go into the next color. Wiping the rinsed brush on the sponge both tests for cleanness and removes excess water. That simple technique is all you need to teach during painting—you don't need to provide lessons or themes—but keep a watchful eye, as young children don't always remember to rinse their brushes. Simply let the child experience the colors as they unfold in his painting. Because young children are so imitative, it is best for you to do a similar kind of color painting without trying to bring form or meaning to it. Let your child lead you rather than the other way around.

When you start working with two colors, your child will be delighted to discover what happens when yellow plays with blue, for example. The children's experiences with color are alive and active when they paint in this way, so they will have had a living experience rather than an intellectual idea that "yellow and blue make green." Not having had the experience of such things myself as a child, I can recall being ten years old and trying to remember whether yellow and blue made green or blue and green made yellow. Children who paint in this way never have that intellectual dilemma!

Over the weeks you can introduce yellow and blue, yellow and red, and red and blue before you put out all three colors at once. You won't need more than the three primary colors until your child is in grade school. For suggestions on how this approach to painting can evolve with older children, see the books and DVDs listed at the end of this chapter. From a foundation of having experienced the colors, older children are gradually able to bring forms out of the colors, rather than trying to paint forms based on outlines like a coloring book.

Children's Experience of Painting

Three-year-olds are often satisfied with a single color, and they are finished painting only when their color jar is empty. If a three-year-old is given two or three colors at the start, he will probably paint the colors on top of, rather than next to, one another, and a muddy surface will result. But if you begin with a single color and only gradually add the second and the third, your child will soon learn to paint by laying the colors next to one another.

Four- and five-year-old children paint with the colors next to one another on the paper, and they will happily share their discoveries of the new colors or the forms that have appeared on their paper. Five- and six-year-olds will approach painting with more of a plan, just as they now approach free play with an idea of what they want to do. Before they dip their brushes into the first color, they often have an image of the color they want to use or an object, such as a tree, rainbow, or heart, that they want to paint. The watercolors and damp paper make it difficult to paint solid outlines, which is good for the further development of the child's fantasy forces. Many times when the children add a new color to the already started form, they will have a new sense association that will interact with the fantasy. These older children will gladly tell you or another child something about their picture, such as which color they especially like or what content they discover in the painted picture.

Be receptive to any comments your child makes, but refrain from asking, "What is it?" or "What does it mean?" The child has had a color experience that may or may not result in any completed forms. Also, it is better to praise the beauty of the colors or the nature of their interaction rather than the artist. This postpones self-consciousness and the element of judgment.

A child who is precocious or "overly awake" can be helped by the fluid qualities of painting. According to von Heydebrand, "Color surfaces or waves of color flowing into each other, not strengthening or crystallizing into too hardened forms, bring the over-precocious child or too clever child back into the right condition of the more dreamy atmosphere of childhood."[13]

Once you have already put any favorite paintings on display on the refrigerator or walls, you will soon have a growing stack of colorful paintings that you can use for other purposes, such as birthday invitations, place cards, gift wrapping, crowns, book covers, or origami figures. Even those paintings that don't appear very interesting often have areas where the colors flow beautifully and that can be cut into wondrous things.

METAMORPHOSIS IN LATER STAGES OF LIFE

In addition to being a wonderful activity, there are other benefits of painting. When a child finds the colors used in this way as true to his own inner experience and being and then finds them again in nature, he will look at them with more sensitivity to the interplay of light and color. Even if it is not his destiny to become an artist, he will have a greater understanding and appreciation of the world, having been awakened to reverence.

There are other benefits less directly related to the artistic experience but still of great value in a person's life. These qualities in later life that were unconsciously influenced by the young child's experience of painting are discussed by Freya Jaffke in her article "About Painting and Human Development through Art."[14] For example, painting includes such processes as being careful, paying attention, waiting, following the course of the work, experiencing the laws of color mixing, and applying color in various strengths. Jaffke sees the following connections:

> All of these activities give ever-renewed stimulus to the gradually awakening soul of the child, helping him to grasp his physical body and make his sense organization and his limbs ever more responsive. One who at an early age has learned to pay attention to the strength or delicacy of color and to gradations in applying it will later find it easier to apply the same soul capacities in social situations, for example in self-assertion and in acquiescence or in the ability to hold conversations in which he brings forth his own arguments and is yet receptive to the responses of his partner. In a similar way, the adult process of logical thinking is helped by the inner order in the sequence of the steps of painting.[15]

As Jaffke points out, "sequencing" is best learned by the young child through doing, not by talking about what we did first, second, and last. She writes:

> Naturally, the child is not conscious of this. He does not reflect on what he is doing, but lives intensively in the activities. In this way he has experiences at deep levels which can wait there to be grasped by him consciously in later stages of life and to find expression in an ability to lead his own life. These effects reveal the true human justification for artistic endeavors in the preschool. Art is not an aesthetic add-on to "real life," but as an exercise of continual striving it can become the foundation of a truly human mastery of life.[16]

MODELING WITH BEESWAX

Another artistic activity your child will enjoy is modeling with colored beeswax. Beeswax has several advantages over clay. It smells nice, isn't messy, can be used over and over, and involves warmth, since the child must warm the beeswax with his hands before using it. Clay, on the other hand, is cold earth and tends to rob the body of warmth; for this reason, clay is often used with children over nine and beeswax with younger children. With a very young child or in cold weather, it may be too difficult for the child to soften the wax himself. In this case, it can be warmed a bit by your own efforts or by setting it next to a heater to give the child a head start.

The colored beeswax used in the Waldorf schools, which is available from Stockmar, makes a wonderful birthday present or holiday gift. To use it, warm a piece in your hands while your child does the same. This is a good time to tell a little story. Then start to make something. As with the other artistic activities, let your child make whatever comes to him without instruction. For preschool children, art is an expression of their inner experience, and it is inappropriate to try to make it conform to ideas imposed from the outside. Remembering the principle of imitation, do your beeswax modeling along with your child. I always found that by finishing last I was able to see the children's creations without them wanting to make what I had made, or wanting me to make the same thing for them! Very young children will simply enjoy the texture of beeswax, pinching and stretching it. As a fantasy element enters in, they will tell you what it is they have made (even though there may be no resemblance that you can discern). As they turn four and five they can become quite skilled and creative in what they make, and the figures can be placed on a little log in a special place to be played with or to wait until the next time they are warmed and transformed into something else.

MAKING THINGS WITH YOUR CHILDREN

Making things with your child or letting him imitate things he has seen you make are artistic activities that encourage creativity, dexterity, and aesthetic judgment. Because the preschool children often saw me sewing, they loved to work from their own sewing basket, and a couple of them made dolls that were much more creative than mine because they lacked a consciousness about how a doll "should" look. If you find yourself starting to make the dolls and toys suggested in this book, set up a sewing basket for your child. Imitating real work is one of a child's greatest delights.

Similarly, children love to embroider, at first using yarn with large plastic needles on burlap placed in embroidery hoops. In my program we were able to make designs on placemats, bookmarks, and "nature bags," which we used for gathering treasures on walks. The older children were able to use embroidery floss and sharp needles, and soon they learned how to safely handle the sharp scissors for making dolls.

You and your child can also make things out of bark, branches, and slices of logs, such as boats to sail, bird feeders, or doll furniture. The act of creation through the transformation of materials is one of the fundamentally human acts. Actually making something is so much more satisfying for children than cutting out shapes or fitting pegs into holes. Many wonderful ideas for craft projects can be found in the books listed at the end of this chapter.

FREEING YOUR OWN INNER ARTIST

One of the added benefits of doing these artistic activities with your children is that you can reclaim and nourish your own innate creative ability, which may have been squelched through lack of use or beliefs such as "I'm not good enough" or "I can't paint." One of the most exciting things about the LifeWays training and growing along with your child can be the rehabilitation of your own childhood and artistic ability.

Most of us, unless we had a Waldorf education, have probably managed to internalize the criticisms that our creative efforts received from those around us and have stopped having any kind of artistic or creative expression such as painting, writing, dancing, or singing. If you would prefer not to let your children have all the fun and want to unlock your own inner creativity, I highly recommend the approach outlined in *The Artist's Way: A Spiritual Path to Higher Creativity*, by Julia Cameron. She gives practical exercises and encouragement for attitude adjustments (which she calls "spiritual chiropractic") that can help harried parents and blocked artists alike reclaim their essential creativity.

Taking a little time for yourself not only can change your life, but it can also provide you with the creative and nurturing forces that you need for your parenting. According to Cameron, "A lot of times people think that art is decadent—they say, 'but what about all the starving people?' I say, if you are emotionally and creatively starved yourself, you don't have the sense of abundance necessary to be as helpful as you might be to others. If you are filling your own well, if you are caring for your own spirit, then you are able to effectively help others." The creative path goes well beyond creating art and into every moment of life itself.[17]

RECOMMENDED RESOURCES

Drawing and Painting

Analyzing Children's Art, by Rhoda Kellogg (Mayfield).

"Coloring with Block Crayons," by Sieglinde de Francesca. DVD available from www.waldorfinthehome.com.

Echoes of a Dream, by Susan Smith (Waldorf School Association of London). Available used from Amazon.

Painting in Waldorf Education, by Dick Bruin and Attie Lichthart. Available from www.awsna.org.

Painting with Children, by Brunhild Müller (Floris).

Understanding Children's Drawings, by Michaela Strauss (Rudolf Steiner Press).

"Watercolor Painting: Color Experience and Developing Form," by Kelly Morrow. DVD available from www.waldorfinthehome.com.

Craft Ideas to Do with Children

The Children's Year, by Stephanie Cooper et al. (Hawthorn).

The Christmas Craft Book, by Thomas Berger (Floris).

Earthways: Simple Environmental Activities for Young Children, by Carol Petrash (Gryphon House).

Echoes of a Dream, by Susan Smith (Waldorf School Association of London). Available used from Amazon.

Festivals, Family and Food, by Diana Carey and Judy Large (Hawthorn).

The Harvest Craft Book, by Thomas Berger (Floris).

Toymaking with Children, by Freya Jaffke (Floris).

Sources for Watercolors, Beeswax Crayons, and Beeswax for Modeling

Nova Natural (www.novanatural.com)

Palumba (www.palumba.com)

Paper, Scissors, Stone (www.waldorfsupplies.com)

A Toy Garden (www.atoygarden.com)

Weir Dolls and Crafts (www.weirdollsandcrafts.com)

Nourishing Your Own Creativity

The Artist's Way: A Spiritual Path to Higher Creativity, by Julia Cameron (Tarcher/Putnam). Plenty of practical exercises to explore your inner landscape and free your creativity in all fields.

The Vein of Gold, by Julia Cameron (Tarcher/Putnam). A journey to your creative heart.

CHAPTER 10

Encouraging Your Child's Musical Ability

MAKE A JOYFUL NOISE

Children love sounds. They love to make them—with their own voices, by banging a spoon on a cooking pot, by blowing into a wooden flute. And they love to hear sounds, because sounds give them exciting information about the inner structure of an object. They unconsciously absorb the sound that manifests the nature of the object when it is touched, knocked, or dropped. The baby with a rattle is expressing her nature to be in movement, but she is also listening to the sounds her movements produce that stop when she stops moving.

Movement is interwoven with sound for the young child. Neurologists have found that a child who is unable to make certain movements is unable to make certain sounds. The young child is naturally in movement. The child's movement often remains free-flowing prior to school age if she has not been repressed by the environment. The movement forms itself into long and short rhythms, but it doesn't manifest what we call a beat (a regular emphasis every so many counts) until the child turns nine. Around the age of nine the child enters a new relationship with the world and is able to feel and understand triads and scales.[1]

Speaking of the inner musical nature of the young child, Rudolf Steiner states, "We shall then notice that it is [the human being's] nature, up to a point, to be born a 'musician.' . . . It is a fact that the individual is born into the world with the desire to bring his own body into a musical rhythm, into a musical relationship with the world, and this inner musical capacity is most active in children in their third and fourth year."[2]

MUSIC AND COGNITIVE DEVELOPMENT

Seeing to your child's musical and movement activities in the preschool years might or might not make him a great musician later in life (that depends on musical talent and destiny), but it can lay the foundation for healthy development, which has ramifications in all spheres of life. Parents today are being bombarded with reports of the so-called "Mozart effect," a phenomenon that has gotten so out of hand that new parents are being sent home from many hospitals with a CD of classical music to play for their babies in order to make them smarter. All this is courtesy of the National Academy of Recording Arts and Science Foundation and the maker of Enfamil baby formula and is paid for by the state legislatures in Georgia and Tennessee. Florida even mandated that state-run day care facilities play such music every day. But what did the studies behind this trend really show?

The "Mozart effect" describes the results of a 1993 study in which college students who listened to ten minutes of Mozart's Sonata in D Major for Two Pianos scored eight or nine points higher on a spatial-temporal reasoning test than they did after experiencing ten minutes of silence or listening to relaxation tapes. Spatial-temporal reasoning is a key to the higher brain function required in mathematics, physics, and engineering. (It should be noted, however, that the increased ability was lost after one hour, and studies by other researchers have been unable to duplicate the results.)

The Mozart experiment actually began in 1990, when these same researchers discovered that the brain in a sense makes its own music. They made computer-generated models of neural firing patterns (electrical brain activity). When the research team fed these various brain patterns through a synthesizer, they heard recognizable but different styles of music. "Some sounded like Baroque music, some like Eastern music, others like folk music. In other words, the communicating neurons (nerve cells) 'play' music."[3]

This made the researchers question whether music itself might encourage those neurons to communicate, so they devised a study with preschoolers to see how musical training might affect their brain development. In their study, 111 three- and four-year-olds were randomly divided into four groups. One group received daily singing lessons and two 15-minute private piano lessons per week at school. A piano also was made available if the children wished to practice on their own. A second group received only the group singing lessons. Members of the third group received two 15-minute private computer lessons each week, while those in the fourth group received no lessons at all. At the beginning of the study, all of the students scored at the national norm on the tests. At the end of six months, however, those who received piano lessons scored an average of 34 percent higher on the tests of spatial-temporal ability, while those in the other three groups showed no improvement on any of the tests. The study was unable to follow the children to see whether the effect was lasting, but other studies with classically trained musicians have shown permanent physical changes in the brain compared to people who have not had extensive musical training.

Although this study showed that giving preschoolers piano lessons significantly increased their ability to perform the types of reasoning required for excellence in science and math, as a Waldorf educator, I would want to make sure that any music lessons are developmentally appropriate and presented in a way that use the appropriate part of the brain and not a lower part, as when babies are taught to "read" by memorizing flash cards. Given the dreamy state of consciousness of the young child, piano lessons would need to involve a lot of fun, not reading music or the pressure to perform. Still, this study might demonstrate to parents that if they're debating between investing in a computer (or sending an older child to computer camp) and buying an instrument and paying for music lessons, an active involvement with music could be more valuable in terms of brain development.

Musical development, mathematics, and spatial reasoning all result in similar brain activity. Both music and mathematics activate parts of the brain in or near the cortex, and there is a definitive relationship between mathematics and musical skills. The crucial window of development, as with language, is from birth to about the age of ten. So what should parents do to ensure optimal enjoyment of music as well as optimal brain development, in a way that is still developmentally appropriate for their child?

SINGING WITH YOUR CHILD

One of the simplest and best musical things you can do with your child is to sing. This can begin before birth and continue through lullabies and special songs that you make up for your baby. After you sing or say a nursery rhyme to your baby, listen and see whether she responds. Katherine Barr Norling, director of a parent-child resource center and school in Boston, writes, "I love singing, even to an 8-month-old, then stopping. Often, even such a young baby will respond by babbling back. One way to experience sound is to talk to your child. But don't stop there. Take that break and listen; allow him to answer in some way. There is so much children can learn even prior to speaking."[4]

Once your child becomes verbal, she will love to sing with you, the more so if you add gestures and movements to match the words. Singing involves the breath and the middle heart/lung sphere, whose development is emphasized between the ages of three and five. Its proper development forms the basis for later health and balanced overall development. Rudolf Steiner said, "You will be fostering all this if you give the child plenty of singing. You must have a feeling that the child is a musical instrument while he is singing. . . . Every child is a musical instrument and inwardly feels a kind of well-being in the sound."[5]

Julius Knierim, a music specialist working from the indications of Rudolf Steiner, observed that when they are by themselves, children younger than nine mostly sing at a much higher pitch than the music they have heard in their environment. They will also sing faster than an adult's rhythmic sense would dictate. Much of their singing is not yet rhythmically "correct" because their pulse-to-breathing ratio has not yet settled at the 4:1 ratio of adults and their voices are still light, nonresonant, hovering, and silvery. Children lack the complexity of adult experience and feel completely satisfied and fulfilled with simple melodies, whereas an adult would feel something was lacking and might long for more complicated harmonies and rhythms.[6]

It is difficult to simplify music enough for young children. Even a song with one note can be completely satisfying to them. Here is one song that I made up while looking out the window. It can be accompanied by hand movements that suggest the falling rain and by forming a circle with the arms to represent a puddle.

See the rain-drops fal-ling down! Mak-ing pud-dles on the ground.

When in doubt when choosing the pitch for your song, choose A above middle C. According to Steiner, the qualities of this note are associated with the sun and are especially suitable for early childhood. Here's a song that goes up and down from the A.

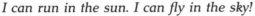

I can run in the sun. I can fly in the sky!

If you take off running and flying, your child will delightedly do it with you.

You can also make up songs to go with activities around the house, such as stirring or sewing. Songs can also ease transitions such as cleaning up the toys or going upstairs to nap. Waldorf teacher Mary Lynn Channer shares this transition song for nap time:

May I ride   piggy-back,   piggy-back,   piggy-back?

May I ride   piggy-back? And then I'll take my nap.

When you are telling fairy tales, remember how simply key phrases can become a song, like the following from the fairy tale "Snow White and the Seven Dwarfs."

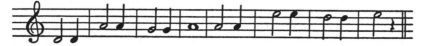

Mirror, mirror, on the wall: Who's the fairest of them all?

Many favorite folk songs and holiday songs that are part of our culture become old friends for your child when they come around each year with the cycle of the seasons. Some traditional songs contain the same kind of folk wisdom we find in nursery rhymes. For example, "Rock-a-bye Baby," according to Eileen Hutchins, "tells of the child cradled in the mother's womb and surrounded by the world of spirit (for spirit literally means breath or wind). But the time of birth draws near and child and cradle (or caul) are cast out into the world."[7]

Singing with your child is one of the joys of parenting. If you can't remember songs from your own childhood, several excellent anthologies (with CDs to help you learn, not to play for your child!) are listed at the end of this chapter.

MOVEMENT GAMES AND FINGERPLAYS

As an adult who hadn't moved much for a few decades, I found that putting movements to songs and verses wasn't my strong suit as a new teacher. I could remember "I'm a Little Teapot" from when I was three years old, but that was about all. But I decided to continue to ponder the movements that express the essential nature of various activities. Gradually the children taught me, and I began to understand more and more. Now I can do movements appropriate for preschoolers to any song or verse, but I certainly felt awkward and self-conscious when I started! Seeing how imitative young children are and how much it is part of their nature to move along with the words helped me rediscover this childlike part of myself.

Start with fingerplays and movement verses from your own childhood. Perhaps you remember "The Wheels on the Bus" or "Six Little

Ducks" or "Where Is Thumbkin?" The interaction with your child, her imitation of your movement, and the musical elements all unite in this kind of play that has delighted children for centuries and has great value for their development. Steiner points out how fingerplays and other tasks that develop dexterity in the fingers, such as knitting, help with brain development and later facility in clear thought.[8]

Circle games are also an ancient part of early childhood that delight young children. Modern ones like "Motorboat, motorboat, go so slow . . . Motorboat, motorboat, go so fast . . . Motorboat, motorboat, step on the gas!" are fun for their quality of changing speed and movement, but they lack the musical element. Older circle games such as "Ring Around the Roses" and "Sally Go 'Round the Sun" provide a picture in movement and song of the child's incarnating process. Jane Winslow Eliot, in her book on circle games, writes:

> Watch when a child falls on the ground. The shrieks are
> out of proportion to the damage done. It is because the
> little one has been shocked out of an enveloping cloud
> into a sudden realization of the solidity of earth. The soul
> resents this. When you ritualize this happening in the gar-
> ment of a game such as the lovely Ring Around the Roses,
> you lead the child lovingly, gently down to earth and she
> begins to enjoy the fun of it. Bit by bit the children don't
> mind staying.[9]

Ring games are joyful, sociable, and simple, yet they have all of the solemnity of a ritual in the way they are repeated over and over. Circle games contain rhythms that affect the beat of the children's pulses. They sometimes incorporate the ability to do tasks without self-consciousness, as in washing the clothes or brushing one's hair in "Here We Go 'Round the Mulberry Bush," while others deal with the interplay between the individual and the group, as in "The Farmer in the Dell" (a game that can be too intense for three-year-olds, who don't yet like being singled out and standing alone at the end). A child who does not want to be chosen should never be forced, for games that single out individual characters are too self-conscious for the very young child. The five-year-old, on the other hand, loves to be the farmer or the cheese and to be caught in the games "London Bridge" or "Oranges and Lemons." Younger children will enjoy these games if they can participate as part of the circle without being singled out before they are ready.

Steiner comments about the value of rhythmical games for young children:

> For early childhood it is important to realize the value of children's songs as a means of education. They must make a pretty and rhythmical impression on the senses; the beauty of sound is to be valued more than the meaning of words. The more vivid the impression made on the ear, the better. Dancing movements in musical rhythm have a powerful influence in building up the physical organs and this should likewise not be undervalued.[10]

PENTATONIC MUSIC AND THE "MOOD OF THE FIFTH"

The pentatonic scale has five notes in an octave instead of the seven we are used to in our normal diatonic scales. For example, a pentatonic scale built around A would have the notes D, E, G, A, and B, with no half steps (so the notes C and F are not included). If you look closely at children's songs and folk songs, you will see that many are written using this simpler scale.

Pentatonic music has the characteristic that it can go on and on without having an ending note that gives it a feeling of being finished (provided the song doesn't end on D, which changes the key from D pentatonic to G major). According to Steiner, these types of songs that are not grounded by a resolving note at the end are especially appropriate for the young child, who is not yet "firmly on the ground." Such music encourages the young child to stay in a dreamy state, so the greatest amount of energy is available for the healthy forming of the physical body. If this is done in early childhood, then the child's intellectual capacities will later wake up while he still maintains a strong contact with wonder, beauty, and creativity. In the Waldorf schools, pentatonic songs are used until the third grade, when the children have developed an inner emotional life that makes the major and minor scales more suitable for them.

The pentatonic scale was once used by most of humanity. The ancient Greeks used a pentatonic scale, and it was used in Europe until the Middle Ages. The Chinese scale is pentatonic, as was the ancient Egyptian. The quality of consciousness of ancient cultures was close to that of the young child—less earthbound, still on the threshold between two worlds. Pentatonic music and music in the "mood of the fifth" can have a healing influence on the young child by not rushing the child into fully incarnated earthbound consciousness and experience.[11]

A kinderharp (children's harp or lyre) is a small handheld harp that can be tuned to the pentatonic scale, which enables anyone to play beautiful music on it; all the notes sound harmonious together, and the quality of the sound is ideal for the young child. Such instruments, without sounding boxes, give a very pure experience of each note, without harmonic overtones. This simple, pure experience of the tones is ideal for young children and is recommended by Steiner over more complex instruments like the piano.

Kinderharps are lovely instruments for nap time and bedtime. Their music is very angelic and can really help calm a child and lull him or her to sleep. As children get older, they also like to pick out tunes on the kinderharp. Such instruments are used in Waldorf early childhood programs for the children to play (very carefully) and for the teacher to play at circle time, or at nap time in afternoon programs.

Kinderharps vary greatly in price and can be purchased from the companies listed at the end of this chapter. In addition, Choroi makes other pentatonic instruments such as a recorder (flute) made out of pear wood, and a klangspiel (xylophone or glockenspiel). Percussion instruments are not generally recommended for young children because a beat that is too strong can drive children too deeply into their physical bodies. This is in opposition to the fluid molding of their inner organs that occurs during the first seven years. Rock music has an especially strong beat and should be avoided for the young child.

I hope I've built a fairly convincing case for the benefits of simple, live music for the young child. We must remind ourselves again and again that the young child is all sense organ and monitor our children's environment for the quality of the sounds that surround and permeate them. In our culture not only do we also tend to be oblivious to the real nature of the young child, but unfortunately we also often substitute nonliving or mechanistic actions for living interactions. Thus instead of letting our babies sleep where they can sense our presence, we put on a recording of a heartbeat. Instead of holding and rocking them to sleep, we are told to turn on a machine that simulates a car going fifty-five miles per hour or to use the noise of a clothes dryer. Instead of reading to them and then letting them lie quietly until they fall asleep, we pop a CD of a professional reading a story into the CD player and beat a hasty retreat. Or instead of singing with our children and letting them help with what we are doing or play quietly near us while we work, we put on one of their DVDs to make them become passive and free us from them. Even though you may think that someone else singing children's songs is doing a much better job than you could possibly do and is providing a better experience, your child would not agree. Your child would always vote for you, because it is the "aliveness" that provides the real nourishment.

WHAT ABOUT MUSIC AND DANCE LESSONS?

Young children are naturally musical. Steiner describes it this way:

> The musical element which lives in the human being from
> birth onwards and which expresses itself particularly
> in the child's third and fourth years in a gift for dancing
> is essentially an element of will, potent with life. . . . If
> people had the right agility, they would dance with little
> children, they would somehow join in the movement of
> all children. It is a fact that the individual is born into the
> world with the desire to bring his own body into musi-
> cal rhythm, into musical relation with the world, and this
> inner musical capacity is most active in children in their
> third and fourth years.[12]

Is it, therefore, a good idea to start music and dance lessons at a young age? Unfortunately, most teachers of young children don't understand the principles of imitation and the importance of play and fantasy. They teach cognitively and put pressure on the child to learn a lesson or to do it right. Such a direct approach is far too self-conscious and can be stressful for the young child. While children need play that incorporates dance and music, most lessons are designed for older children, even though they may indicate that they are for four- or five-year-olds.

Elkind, in *Miseducation: Preschoolers at Risk*, develops a strong case that any type of lessons places preschoolers at risk with no real gain. Waldorf teachers would agree that most lessons are inappropriate for the young child. If you do consider any kind of lessons for your nursery or kindergarten-age child—swimming, gymnastics, modern dance, or sports, for example—be sure to observe the classes before you decide whether or not to enroll your child. Does the instructor teach through imitation? Are the things that are asked and done clothed in fantasy? Or is the instruction appropriate for a much older child? Does your child really feel comfortable being away from you? Would the classes be enjoyable or stressful for your child? Would classes be taking away time from play or just being at home (especially important for children who are already in preschool programs or child care)? Don't sacrifice the current stage of your child's development for some future achievement. If it isn't fun, it is better left undone at this age!

Steiner made two recommendations that aren't going to win him any points with parents today. He recommended that children avoid ballet and soccer. In ballet the fixed and artificial positions are foreign to the fluid and changing nature of the growing child. Ballet also affects the vital energy involved in growth and reproduction, as evidenced by the high rate of menstrual irregularities in professional ballerinas. The discipline and fixed positions of ballet are very different from the rhythmical movement that Steiner recommends when dancing with children.

In soccer the exclusive use of the feet and the head in hitting the ball puts undue emphasis on the extremities at a time when the grade-school child is centered in the middle sphere, the heart/lung area. Studies of the long-term effects of playing soccer following the work of neurologist Barry Jordan also found that Dutch professional soccer forwards and defensive players (those most likely to "head" the ball) were more likely to have subtle problems in everything from memory to visual perception than were midfielders and goalies. They had more concussions as well. Jordan also found that professional boxers who carried a specific gene linked to early onset Alzheimer's disease were more likely to suffer cognitive impairment than nonboxers, and he is also checking to see whether the same is true with soccer players.[13] Although your child won't experience the same kind of battering that professional soccer players endure, one can't totally discount Steiner's observation that such use of the head is not healthy for the growing child.

Returning from the soccer fields to the realm of music, unless your child is a musical genius who clearly needs a tutor at age three, there are many reasons to wait until elementary school before beginning music instruction. Unfortunately, most people who work with preschool children don't know how to teach from imitation and start by teaching how to read music. Even the idea of having to learn a lesson through imitation is too direct an approach for a young child. While the Suzuki method does work through the principle of imitation, the emphasis on recorded music is not consonant with the young child's need to hear live music and simple tunes. Performing at young ages, an integral part of Suzuki, introduces pressure and self-consciousness into the dreamlike world of early childhood. In the Waldorf schools children don't present anything before an audience until they are in the grades, when the classes share their poems, plays, songs, and recorder music as a class group with other students and with the parents at school assemblies.

Playing the wooden recorder is begun in the first grade in Waldorf schools, but the children learn strictly through imitating their teacher. Reading music isn't introduced until the third grade, when the child has reached a certain level of maturity and eye-hand coordination and is ready for the full range of musical experience, including the introduction of stringed instruments.

All parents want their children to develop according to their full potential, but an understanding of the inner development of the child leads to the realization that certain subjects and skills are best introduced at the age that corresponds to the child's inner ripeness for them. The desire to "do more sooner," which is a symptom of our spiritual materialism, can lead to skipping steps and hastening a child's development in one sphere without realizing the possible ramifications in another. These comments are not meant to provide a list of "Thou shalt not's," but rather are intended to encourage you to trust your own knowledge and your own heart to intuit what is best for your child. If parents do this, they won't subject their children to the "super baby syndrome" at the expense of the important years of early childhood.

RECOMMENDED RESOURCES

Fingerplays, Nursery Rhymes, and Circle Games

Dancing as We Sing, edited by Nancy Foster (Waldorf Early Childhood Association).

The Eentsy Weentsy Spider: Finger Plays and Action Rhymes, by Joanna Cole and Stephanie Calmenson (William Morrow and Co.).

Let Us Form a Ring, edited by Nancy Foster (Waldorf Early Childhood Association).

"Naturally You Can Sing." Various titles by Mary Schunemann, with accompanying CDs. Available from www.naturallyyoucansing.com.

The Original Mother Goose, by Blanche Fisher Wright (Running Press).

Singing Games for Families, Schools and Communities, by Anna Rainville (Rudolf Steiner College Press). Book with CD available from the Book Store at www.steinercollege.edu.

Waldorf-Inspired Song Books

Clump-a-Dump and Snickle-Snack, by Johanne Russ (Mercury Press). Pentatonic children's songs. Available from www.waldorfbooks.com.

Gateways and other volumes by Margret Meyerkort (Wynstones Press). Six booklets of songs and stories collected from the Waldorf kindergarten teachers in Great Britain.

Pentatonic Songs, by Elisabeth Lebret (Waldorf School Association of Toronto). Contains many songs for the seasons and holidays. Available from www.steinercollege.edu.

Quintenlieder: Music for Young Children in the Mood of the Fifth, by Julius Knierim (Rudolf Steiner College Press). Available from www.steinercollege.edu.

Seven Times the Sun: Guiding Your Child Through the Rhythms of the Day, by Shea Darian (Gilead Press). Book with many songs plus a CD. Available from www.gileadpress.com.

Other Selections

American Folksongs for Children, by Ruth Crawford Seeger (Doubleday).

The Lullaby Treasury: Cradle Songs from Around the World, by Mathilde Polee and Petra Rosenberg (Floris).

Pentatonic Instruments (Kinderharps and Recorders)

Bella Luna Toys. Offers the most complete selection, plus a DVD on how to tune your kinderharp. At www.bellalunatoys.com.

CHAPTER 11

Cognitive Development and Early Childhood Education

Parents naturally want to give their children the best start in life and do everything they can to ensure their intellectual development. In earlier chapters we indicated that the best thing you can do for your baby's cognitive development, once she starts to crawl, is to childproof your home and let her explore freely while she is near you. The baby needs to move and explore, and the objects in your home provide better stimulation than many expensive educational toys.

Once your child becomes verbal and begins to ask endless questions, there is a tendency to start providing rational and scientific answers. In *Miseducation*, Elkind points out that we must constantly remember that young children's verbal skills far outpace their conceptual knowledge. Because children's questions sound so mature and sophisticated, we are tempted to answer them at a level of abstraction far beyond their level of comprehension. As he points out, children are really asking about the purpose of things, not about how they work.[1] This gives us so much more room for creativity in answering their "Why?" questions. If we can't come up with a purpose-based answer, there is always the response,

"Why do you think?" Or, if you find yourself aboard a train of endless "Why's," there's always the startling closer, "Why, indeed?"

Elizabeth Grunelius, the first Waldorf kindergarten teacher, agrees that concepts are products of the mind at a more advanced age level, while images or additional observation will lead the child to arrive at his own answer. She gives the following example:

> Coming home from the beach, a six-year-old may ask, "Why are there waves in the ocean?" Instead of explaining, we may say, "Come, let me show you," fill the wash-basin with water and blow on it. The child will see the waves, repeat blowing on the water several times and get what is for him a more perfect answer than any explanation could furnish.
>
> Speaking about the child's reaction to the ocean, he will notice that the sea at times rises higher and at other times recedes, and ask about it. To answer him by telling him the influence of the moon is not to answer a child at all, who is not ripe to comprehend any more than the rhythmic sequence of the up-and-down movement of the water.
>
> We answer him with complete accuracy, however, if we let him hold his own hand over his breast so as to feel his in-breathing and out-breathing, and then tell him how the rise and fall of the sea resembles that breathing movement in his own body.[2]

ACADEMIC VS. PLAY-BASED LEARNING

There is tremendous pressure in our society to teach reading, writing, and math to children at an increasingly early age. The pressure on American education began in 1957 with the launching of Sputnik and has continued ever since. The result is that most public school kindergartens are now doing what was once a first-grade program, while nursery-age children have taken on tasks previously reserved for older children.

As publicly funded pre-K programs increase, the academic pressure on three- and four-year-olds increases as well. "Today we're asking kids to meet higher standards in K through 12," says American Federation of Teachers president Sandra Feldman in justification of this downward shift into the preschool. "But if we don't prepare them earlier, then they're not going to meet them."[3]

The fact that reading problems have increased and test scores have failed to improve using this approach has only produced greater pressure for kindergarten teachers to pound reading and math into young heads. Today even kindergarten teachers must use standardized curricula and make sure children can pass standardized tests that determine a school's standing and funding. Georgia's universal pre-kindergarten curriculum includes language, literacy, and math concepts. Although kindergarten teachers across the nation are increasingly unhappy, they feel powerless against the school boards and state legislators who keep mandating what they teach.

In the realm of private preschools and kindergartens there has also been tremendous pressure from parents to ensure that their children are successfully taught academic subjects early. This drive is motivated by the parents' desire to ensure their children's success in school and give them an edge on other children. In the 1980s parents who were professionals in their late thirties fueled this push toward early academics by utilizing baby flash cards, classes, and academically oriented preschools to help get their children into the "best" private elementary schools. However, the damaging effect of the "super baby syndrome" was pointed out by pediatricians and by authors such as David Elkind in his book *The Hurried Child.* In February 1987 *Newsweek* reported, "Now the pendulum may be swinging away from 'hothousing,' as the academic preschool phenomenon has come to be known. After years of internal debate, the early-childhood establishment has rallied against formal instruction of very young children on the grounds that it can lead to educational 'burnout' and a sense of failure."[4]

However, the rejection of early academics noted in 1987 never really took hold because of the digital revolution. Parents suddenly became worried that if their three-year-old wasn't computer literate, he or she would be locked out of success in the future. And some legislators felt that computer instruction was the tool that had been missing for teaching preschool children how to read and do math. Parents began buying software for their toddlers, and preschools were pressured to include computer instruction in their curriculum.

Questions about both the value and the misuse of computers in education have been explored in depth by developmental neuropsychologist Jane Healy in her book *Failure to Connect.* Through reviewing hundreds of studies, trying out hundreds of computer programs for children, and visiting hundreds of schools, Healy concluded that there is no advantage—and there may even be disadvantages—for children under the age of seven to use computers at all. For children in elementary school, she gives excellent guidelines for assessing and buying programs that really teach, and she also describes the importance of paying attention to factors such as how much screen time the child is putting in, the amount of glare he experiences, his posture, and so forth. Her book is a must-read for all parents and educators today.

WHY NOT INTRODUCE ACADEMICS EARLY?

Both Maria Montessori and Rudolf Steiner recognized that the young child should not be taught cognitive work directly. Montessori said that the child should be taught through the body, hence the wealth of special equipment (not called "toys") in a Montessori program for teaching such concepts as geometric shapes, weights, and so forth. Steiner went even further and said that concepts shouldn't be taught at all to children before the change of teeth. He placed the emphasis on creative play, imagination, imitation, movement games and fingerplays, crafts, and artistic activities until the physical body is more developed and the energy needed for its intense early growth is freed for forming mental pictures and memory work.

In noting the tremendous changes that occur naturally around the age of seven, Steiner gave indications of the problems that could arise by introducing early cognitive learning to children. Although it is possible to speed up development in certain areas with some children, tampering with nature's timetable can result in negative effects in other areas.

Whenever you call directly on the intellect and memory of the young child, you are using energy that is needed for physical development during the first seven years. The same forces that are active in the physical development of the young child are used later for intellectual activity. Attention to this factor in development during the early years can form the foundation for health and vitality throughout life. Obviously the child is learning a tremendous amount and developing cognitively during these years. Steiner simply means that parents should not address the intellect directly but instead encourage the child's learning through direct life experiences and imitative play. He explains:

> In the human embryo the eyes are protected and the external physical sunlight must not work upon their development. In the same sense external education must not endeavour to affect a training or influence the moulding of the memory, before the change of teeth. If we, however, simply give it nourishment and do not try as yet to develop it by external measure, we shall see how the memory unfolds in this period, freely and of its own accord.[5]

Some children can be taught to read prior to kindergarten, and even some babies can be conditioned to recognize flash cards. But based upon her research on brain development, Jane Healy reminds us that reading and writing are built on language ability—the power to listen carefully, understand what others are saying, and express ideas effectively. In *Your Child's Growing Mind*, she concludes:

> Even babies can be conditioned to associate two stimuli that are presented repeatedly, but this learning lacks real meaning for the child and may use inappropriate parts of the cortex instead of those best suited for the job. In fact, forced learning of any type may result in the use of lower systems since the higher ones which should do the work have not yet developed. The "habit" of using inferior brain areas for higher-level tasks (such as reading) and of receiving instruction rather than creating patterns of meaning causes big trouble later on.[6]

. . . Yes, even babies can be trained to recognize words. Babies, however, cannot read, tapping into a vast personal store house of language and knowledge that takes years to build. Most preschoolers, likewise, can be trained through a stimulus-response type of teaching. The human brain can be trained to do almost anything, if the task is simplified enough and one is willing to devote the necessary time and energy. Yet the brain power—and possibly the neural connections—are stolen from the foundation of real intelligence. Reading becomes a low-level skill, and there is a danger that it will remain at the level where it was learned and practiced.[7]

Healy points out that truly gifted early readers are insatiable in their desire to learn to read. They don't have to be taught, and they make instinctive connections with thought and language. These children usually learn without lessons from adults or older siblings. Other children, she says, can experience reading problems that are "created by forced early instruction. Many authorities believe that age seven is the right time to begin formally teaching reading. Studies in different countries have shown that when five- and seven-year-olds are taught by the same methods, the seven-year-olds learn far more quickly and happily than do the fives, who are more likely to develop reading difficulties."[8]

The common practice of having kindergarten and pre-K children fill out worksheets and copy lessons is also decried by most educators and developmental psychologists. According to Healy:

> Children under the age of six should not be expected to copy sentences. Meaningful copying requires brain maturation to integrate two or three modalities (looking, feeling, moving and sometimes even hearing a word). Little ones can copy at a rote level, but they're probably not using the circuits which will connect with meaning. Let it wait. Children of this age should not be sitting at desks doing academic tasks. Get their busy brains out doing and learning, not practicing low-level skills.[9]

Piaget, Steiner, and others have pointed out that children go through various stages in their development and thinking. The latest brain research has actually shown that the brain goes through a developmental and differentiating process. Healy, based upon her extensive research in brain development, has concluded that "the immature human brain neither needs nor profits from attempts to 'jumpstart' it. The fact that the phrase is being successfully used to sell technology [educational software] for toddlers illustrates our ignorance of early childhood development."[10]

In addition to causing children to skip developmental stages or utilize lower levels of the brain to accomplish learning tasks, early academics can take an emotional toll as well. According to Healy, "Studies show that four-, five-, and six-year-olds in heavily 'academic' classes tend to become less creative and more anxious—without gaining significant advantages over their peers. Youngsters in well-structured 'play'-oriented schools develop more positive attitudes toward learning along with better ultimate skill development."[11] Another study of young children looked at creativity along with academic gains. It showed significant reductions in creativity after even moderate use of a popular reading software system.[12]

THE VALUE OF PRESCHOOL

Today virtually all children attend kindergarten, and 63 percent of all parents say they plan to start sending their child to school by the age of four. This is more than four times the 1965 rate, and it will probably become greater as an increasing number of school systems and government-funded programs become available for younger and younger children. Well-off families can usually afford private preschools, and children from low-income households are eligible for Head Start—although there are not enough places available to meet the need. As an increasing number of states pay for at least one kind of pre-kindergarten program, the problem is that enrichment programs not only become the social norm but also soon become required by law. When Zell Miller, then governor of Georgia, first proposed the idea of publicly funding pre-K in 1992, his plan was denied as "state-sponsored babysitting." Georgia's universal pre-K program rapidly went on to serve more than 61,000 children, and Miller went on to advocate mandatory enrollment. When New York began funding pre-kindergarten programs, whose students had to be chosen mainly by lottery, it was with the goal of providing universal access. Unfortunately, no one is supporting—let alone funding—at-home mothering.

Nearly a quarter of families with children under three live in poverty. And the trend toward the early institutionalization of children is increasing as welfare reform values mothers joining the working poor over staying at home with their young children. With more than half of the mothers of children under four in the workforce at least part time, most children today have some kind of child care or preschool experience. Burton White suggests that the pressure to fund public preschool is actually the result of the lack of quality day care—public or private—because "there is no mandate in the law for child care and there is a mandate for education."[13]

Even mothers who don't need to work appreciate the social and learning experiences a part-time preschool program provides for their child, and the free mornings can give them needed time away from children or time alone with a new baby.

Long-range studies, like the one conducted by the High Scope Educational Research Foundation in Ypsilanti, Michigan, have shown that children from disadvantaged socioeconomic backgrounds gain an advantage from attending play-based preschool. Following 123 poor black youths with low IQs from the age of three or four up through age nineteen, this study compared the group who attended the preschool program at Perry Elementary School and had home visits from trained staff with a group who received no preschool education at all. Those who attended preschool went on to spend less time in special-education classes, had higher attendance rates, and graduated from high school in greater numbers. In addition, fewer received public assistance, were arrested, or became pregnant before age nineteen.[14] However, "for children from emotionally and financially stable homes, the advantages of preschool are less evident. While many experts believe that the early years are an enormously fertile time for teaching little children . . . some think that they learn best at their own pace at home. 'School for four-year-olds is indefensible on educational grounds,' says Burton White, author of *The First Three Years of Life.*"[15]

The experiences of life provided in a preschool or kindergarten can often be provided at home just as well as they can in a formal program. There is no need to seek out preschool if you and your child are doing well at home; there is also no need to avoid it or feel guilty if your child is eager to play with other children and welcomes the activities a play-based program can provide. LifeWays North America developed its "home-away-from-home" model to meet all of these needs without relegating children to an institutionalized model of care.

EVALUATING EARLY CHILDHOOD PROGRAMS

When you first begin to investigate early childhood programs, you will find they vary greatly in their philosophies and activities. In the 1980s, Waldorf early childhood programs were viewed as something of an anachronism, and as a result student teachers from universities would ask to visit to see what a "play-based program" looked like. Now that it has been shown that such programs are on the leading edge of brain development and are the best preparation for academic work later, one can hope that many more play-based programs will be started and they will be easier to find! That is certainly what happened in Germany, as reported by Joan Almon, then president of the Waldorf Early Childhood Association of North America:

> There is a growing body of research that supports the position of Waldorf schools that children should remain in a play-oriented preschool until the age of six. The clearest example of such research which has come to our attention is a major study undertaken in Germany comparing 100 public school classes for five-year-olds. Fifty of them had only play in their program and the other 50 had academics and play together. The children entered first grade when they were six, and the study surveyed their progress until they were 10. The first year there was little difference

to be seen. By the time the children were 10, however, those who had been allowed to play when they were five surpassed their schoolmates in every area measured. One can imagine how startling these results were to the state educators. They considered the results so conclusive that within months they had converted all of the academic programs back to play programs. They also recognized the advantage of mixed-age kindergartens in which, through play, the children help one another to grow and learn.[16]

When you find a program that you are interested in, you will want to arrange a visit to talk to the director and see what the children are doing. Talk with the director about her background, her philosophy, and the type of program she offers. Ask about staff turnover and meet the teachers. Arrange to visit and observe the program in action. Above all, make sure there is a rich oral language tradition (stories, songs, and games) and that ample time is allowed for play that is self-directed and serves no other motive than the child's own.

You will also want to consider the hours of the program. If you are working full time, you will probably be looking for a full-day program. If you are able to stay home with your child, you will probably want to consider a more gentle transition. For young children who are used to being at home, attending a half-day program two or three days a week is often the best way to start. Take your cues from your child and find a program that balances your needs and his.

When you look for child care, preschool, or kindergarten for your child, here are some things to consider:

- Is there a rhythm to the day, providing a structure within which there is time for both large movement and guided activities?
- Is there an appreciation of the importance of imaginative, self-directed play, and toys to support it?
- Do the children play outside every day? What equipment is available?
- What is the teacher's background, training, philosophy, and experience in teaching or mothering?
- What does the teacher hope the children will learn? Early reading, desk work, and workbooks don't meet the young child's needs.

- Are there artistic activities such as painting, coloring, and crafts?
- What role does music play in the program? Is all the music recorded, or are there singing and movement games?
- Do the children watch television or play with computers? Screen time is best avoided by young children.
- How many children are there? How many teachers? Does it feel calm or hectic?
- What is the environment like? Is it safe? Is it beautiful? Is it warm and homelike?
- Does the teacher love the children?

LIFEWAYS AND WALDORF EARLY CHILDHOOD PROGRAMS

Waldorf early childhood programs—whether freestanding or connected with a Waldorf school—are modeled after a good home environment and provide a nurturing program based on an understanding of the young child's special developmental needs before the age of seven. Although Waldorf schools sometimes have mixed-aged kindergartens with children from two and a half to six years old in one group, more often they have separate nursery and kindergarten classes. To ensure a more homelike, mixed-age environment for the younger children—and to meet the child care needs of parents with infants and toddlers as well—the Life-Ways approach was developed by Cynthia Aldinger out of the indications of Rudolf Steiner and contemporary educators. In LifeWays centers or in-home programs, infants through five-year-olds are together in "family groups" with the same caregiver year after year. Mixed-age, relationship-based care has the advantage of replicating the experience of a large family: the older children provide a model for the younger ones and help them, while the little ones bring a softer element to the four- and five-year-olds. And as they stay in the program for several years, those who were once the younger children in the group get to experience being the bigger children. The special needs of the older children are met at the LifeWays Early Childhood Center in Milwaukee through an onsite "preschool," which they attend three mornings each week. Here the older children from each family group come together for a Waldorf-inspired program that emphasizes stories and activities for the older children. Children in LifeWays programs typically go on to kindergarten in local public or Waldorf schools.

Interest in Waldorf education and LifeWays is expanding dramatically throughout North America, and many new school- or center-based and in-home programs are being founded each year. A list of members can be found on the website of the Waldorf Early Childhood Association (www.waldorfearlychildhood.org), and a directory is available at www.lifewaysnorthamerica.org.

The following description of a typical day in a LifeWays program may serve as a more detailed guide for things to look for in a relationship-based program, even if there is no LifeWays or Waldorf school in your area. The understanding of the young child and the activities suggested can be incorporated into home life or into existing child care or preschool programs. Some readers may even become inspired to find out more about the LifeWays training and perhaps open their own in-home program!

The Activities

Let's take a look at a child's day as it might occur in a LifeWays program. As an example, I'll describe a schedule I've used at Rainbow Bridge, an in-home program with twelve one- to five-year-olds, a lead teacher, and two assistants to help with all the cooking, snowsuits, and pottying. The morning typically consists of creative play, varied activities, a story, singing games and fingerplays, snack and lunch, and outside play. Some children go home at 12:30, while others stay for a nap and are picked up at 3:30.

Outside play. Parents and children are greeted, and most children head straight for the sandbox, where the older children are already hard at work building tunnels and "bug traps." Starting with outside play allows for the different arrival times of children. I am usually outside to receive the children, and those who are cold or want a gentler start to the day can go inside with another teacher and help her cut fruit for the morning snack.

Morning snack and songs or story. Children are gathered with a song and go inside for hand washing and lighting a candle before singing blessing songs at the table. A different child is selected each day to serve the food by taking around the bowls of fruit, and the other children are consoled by the promise that they can serve another day. We listen for "thank you's" and model how to ask for more. The art of conversation is developed, often augmented by an ongoing story about a character I have made up, such as Mauie the cat or Pirate Jack. All the children, even the littlest, learn to sit at the table until the candle is blown out with a song. Dishes are then put in the washbasins and children wipe their hands and faces and their table space with a washcloth. When everyone is finished, the children join me in singing "Red Bird, Red Bird, who will you choose today?" and eagerly wait for the red felt bird suspended from a stick to visit the nests they have made with their washcloths. As each child is chosen, the child puts his or her cloth in the bowl and may leave for free play.

Creative play and activity. Within a few moments, we might see several boys and girls in the home area, cooking and playing with the dolls. Nearby, three children are moving blanket stands to make a house covered with a sheet. A two-year-old has put on kitty ears and is meowing at the door, while a one-year-old wanders happily from area to area, taking it all in. Another boy puts on a cape and crawls under the table with two standup dolls. Two other boys have tied knitted ropes to wooden fish and are being fishermen. One of us begins to fold the towels and washcloths from the laundry and immediately has helpers with folding and "delivery drivers" to take the stacks. In a while, one of the teachers starts to chop vegetables for lunch and is joined by three children who work with their own cutting boards and table knives.

The room becomes filled with the ebb and flow of the children's play. Two children have become engaged at the workbench, and both want to use the wooden hammer. The nearest adult suggests one child ask, "Can I have it when you're done?" and agrees that it's hard to wait. "What can we find to do while you're waiting?" she asks, guiding the child to use the screwdriver to fix the truck instead. By now the cook of the day is sautéing the vegetables and mixing them into the grain from the rice cooker, all with the help of one or two children. The other teacher has finished folding the laundry and moved to the couch, where the other one-year-old climbs up for a snuggle and to look at a stiff-paged book together. The transformations are endless as the children's play unfolds over forty-five minutes to an hour.

The room could seem chaotic to a casual observer as the children experience the world through their inner-directed play. We watch attentively and help as needed by tying on a costume or helping two children take turns with a contested object. We are happy to be brought things as part of the children's imaginative play and will interact with them, but we rarely get down and play with the children or interrupt them except as necessary for safety or to resolve conflicts that they don't work out themselves. We remain aware of everyone in the room while doing household or craft work whenever possible. In this way the children not only see a model of real work, but this activity can also be transformed by them and incorporated into their play. During this time, an activity such as bread baking or coloring might be started at the table, and children join in as they are drawn to it. Also during this time children go to the bathroom and diapers are changed—it's a busy morning!

Circle time. A song tells the children it is time to put all the toys away, and a little gnome comes out of his house to see what good workers they are. When everything is in its place, another song brings the children to morning circle. With a mixed-age group, I like to start with "Ring Around the Roses," which is simple enough for the youngest and still a favorite of the five-year-olds. It is followed by a greeting song, and then fingerplays or a simple circle game, before the children are dismissed to the lunch table.

Hot lunch time. We wash hands for lunch, which consists of hot grains with organic vegetables and occurs around 11 a.m. in our program. The children sing a song of thanks for the food and then talk with one another while they eat. This is a good time to tell a fairy tale that can nourish the older children while the younger ones are occupied with their food. From the table, Red Bird again slowly dismisses the children to start getting ready to go outside.

Outside play. The children play outside for about forty-five minutes. They eagerly play on the slide, teeter-totter, and climbing dome. There is also a sandbox, crawling tubes, and a large playhouse. There is a deck, grass, and small bushy area we call the "fairy woods." Some children are picked up by their parents at 12:30, while the others come in then and gather around the table for some juice, cheese, and raisins (believe it or not, it has been an hour and a half since the start of the last meal). Then they go downstairs to brush their teeth and take their nap.

Afternoon nap. We are great believers in the health-giving powers of sleep after an active morning, and all of our children nap, including the five-year-olds! Some days we have as many as ten children napping, divided between two rooms. The teacher or assistant makes sure each child is cozy, sits and sings or plays the kinderharp in the darkened room, and then sits quietly and yawns for a while until the children are asleep.

Afternoon play. Afternoons are very sweet. The children are very different when they wake up from a nap, and it's a time to read a story together or gently brush a child's hair as he gradually reenters our shared world. Because the children wake up at different times, it is easier to give them individual attention before they start to play or are gathered for yet another snack (eating is mandated every hour and a half by our licensing requirements, which is just right for me!).

The Seasonal Rhythm

In addition to establishing a daily rhythm, which anchors the children, we change activities and stories according to the seasons of the year. These activities might include taking walks and collecting seasonal items for the nature table, baking seasonal foods, making objects for annual festivals, and participating in outdoor activities such as making leaf crowns or planting spring bulbs. Much of the preparation that the adults at the LifeWays program do relates to the rhythm of the year and the children's experience of it. This is reflected in the daily activities, the changing decorations in the room, and the special activities that are planned, such as a walk to the park to gather acorns in the fall, planting flowers in spring, or doing wet felting outdoors in summer.

With a mixed-age group, activities take place on many levels simultaneously, depending on the child's age. For example, older children will typically be drawn to watercolor painting, while the two-year-olds will come over and watch in awe, also wanting to participate (or not). The one-year-olds typically continue in their dreaminess—although some are very demanding about wanting to be at the table, too! Stories from various levels are told in mixed-age classes. Older children still love hearing a simple story like "The Three Little Pigs," while the youngest children will be carried along by the group when a more complicated story for older children is being told. The same story will be told for several weeks and then might be presented as a puppet play with table puppets or silk marionettes.

Direct intellectual teaching does not take place in a LifeWays program or Waldorf kindergarten. There are no exercises in reading readiness or doing pages from math workbooks. Nor are shapes and weights manipulated to learn concepts such as "triangle" or "heavy" and "light." The child is allowed to take in the world through his senses and to participate in it through movement, artistic activity, and play. It is recognized that one of the tasks of early childhood is the healthy mastering of bodily skills. As a result, we often do fingerplays and movement games to help the children develop coordination and the formation of speech. These activities also can form the basis for later mathematical learning, as the rhythmical counting paired with body movements forms a valuable foundation in the body for number and rhythm. Similarly, the transformation of one object into another in creative play provides a concrete basis for the more abstract manipulation of symbols involved in reading. Developmental steps are not skipped or hurried. Rather, there is a confidence in the unfolding of the young child according to the patterns of nature and the stamp of the child's own individuality.

Many times children who can already write the alphabet or even read enter a Waldorf kindergarten. However, the children are not provided time to practice such skills. Because their days are so full of creative play, stories, puppet shows, crafts, and artistic activity, they are fully engaged and often do not even notice that they aren't reading or doing mathematics. And the rich experience they receive in the Waldorf program can serve as a balancing force for the early intellectual development they have experienced.

The Setting

Because the environment is so important for the young child, a great deal of care is put into creating an environment that is nourishing and inviting to the children. When schools are built according to Steiner's indications for architecture, the early childhood rooms can feel as if they embrace and surround the children with their curves, cubbyholes, and play areas. When this is not possible, it is best to use an actual home or make an existing building as homelike and comfortable as possible, in contrast to the institutional feel of most corporate child care settings. For example, lights and right angles can be softened by hanging colored cotton gauze or silk in the corners and in front of light fixtures. A couch and a "cozy corner" created with sheepskins and pillows can also soften the feeling for the children. Beautiful items, natural materials, and pastel colors replace the chrome and plastic of many conventional programs. In addition, lofts and play areas under them can be built using wood.

Many LifeWays and Waldorf program locations are painted a light rose color that Steiner called "peach blossom." It is a color that reflects the lightness of young children, who have not yet fully arrived on earth. A special method of painting called "lazuring" uses washes of various colors on a wall to give an impression of depth on a flat surface. Using this technique, murals or images can be painted to suggest forms in a very soft, beautiful way.

The room is decorated with seasonal motifs, such as a nature table, tissue paper pictures on the windows, and decorated branches. Toys are made from natural materials and are arranged in activity areas or little scenes that invite imaginative interaction. The attention to detail and beauty will be reflected in the mood of the children and the quality of their play.

The Role of the Teachers

Waldorf nurseries and kindergartens often appear deceptively simple. Everything flows so easily and looks so effortless. The tremendous amount of work by the teacher is mostly invisible, except as it is felt by those who know children and who can sense the mood the teacher creates. Someone from another preschool program visited our preschool home in Ann Arbor, Michigan, and was surprised by how peaceful it was with twelve children in such a small space. The being of the teacher and the physical and emotional environment she or he creates are what really nourish the children.

In a LifeWays program, less of the preparation is done behind the scenes than in a Waldorf kindergarten. The teacher attempts to do most of her work while the children play and is less concerned with craft projects and other activities that would involve the teacher doing most of the work for the children. This leaves the teacher freer to be in relationship with the children, which is vital for young children.

Because the teacher is constantly an example for the children, she pays special attention to the quality of her movements and the tone of her voice. She does many things with the children, such as preparing the snack, telling a story, or leading the circle games. However, she also accomplishes a great deal just by her being, by who she is. She tries to put aside her own problems and emotional upsets so that she is as clear as possible when she is with the children. She needs to get enough sleep and to have her own meditative practices to remain centered and to keep the rest of her life in order. Her role with the children is similar to a meditative state of awareness: she is aware of everything, totally in the present moment, not thinking about other things—just there with and for the children. Being with young children often involves more being than doing. It's hard to make everything simple enough. We tend to think that we have to stimulate and provide things for the children, when our more difficult task is to provide them with the space to be themselves, to experience and grow and try on the world and its activities under the guidance and protection provided by the adults.

The teacher's attitude of warmth and love provides a calm and healthy atmosphere for the young child and is the foundation of relationship-based care. Steiner describes it as follows:

> The joy of the child in and with his environment must be reckoned among the forces that build and mould the physical organs. He needs people around him with happy looks and manners and, above all, with an honest unaffected love. A love which fills the physical environment of the child with warmth may literally be said to "hatch out" the forms of the physical organs. The child who lives in such an atmosphere of love and warmth and who has around him really good examples for his imitation is living in his right element. One should therefore strictly guard against anything being done in the child's presence that he must not imitate.[17]

Because the young child is an imitative being, the teacher simply begins each activity and the children follow along. She doesn't announce, "Now it's story time," or "Let's take hands for circle games." Instead, she simply takes two children's hands and starts singing and moving with the intention that everyone will join in, and they do. Story time may begin with the same song every day, or the teacher may light a candle or put on a special storytelling hat or apron and play a few notes on the kinderharp. Whatever she has chosen, the children soon learn what will follow.

Whenever possible during the children's free play, the teacher provides an example of work from real life—tending to the baby, sawing wood or gardening during outside play, making something for the preschool. The children can often help with the activity itself, such as by cutting fruit for snacks or winding yarn, and the activity will also appear transformed in their play. For example, if the teacher is sewing, a few children will want to get out their first sewing basket, while another might go off and pretend to sew something with her fingers.

The warmth and love of the teacher for the children involves really taking on their care as a trust, in conjunction with the parents. Thus the teacher needs as complete a picture as possible of each child before accepting him or her into the program. She will observe the child if possible and have an in-depth interview with the parents: how was her birth; how did she develop; what does she like to play; are there any health problems; has she been in other child care or preschool programs; what are the parents' hopes and expectations? The teacher needs to feel that she can really take on this child, and that she can work together with the parents for the child's growth and well-being. The parents also need to evaluate the teacher and the program and make sure that this is where they want their child to be.

Once a child has been accepted, the teacher tries to visit the family at home to get a picture of the child in his or her own surroundings, to meet any brothers and sisters or pets, and to see the child's room. In addition to helping the teacher better understand the context in which the child lives, such a visit provides a wonderful link for the child between home and school, a sense of interpenetration of the two worlds that is very supportive.

The teacher's work does not stop when the children go home. She must not only clean up and arrange things for the next day's activities, but also work with the parents through parent evenings, conferences, toy-making workshops, and so forth. At night the teacher visualizes each child and takes the image into her sleep. This practice not only supports the child and his connection with the teacher, but it can also provide the teacher with inspiration if a child is having particular difficulties.

The Training of a LifeWays or Waldorf Early Childhood Teacher

The attitude of the teacher and the understanding gained by working out of the indications that Rudolf Steiner gave about the developing human being are the most important elements of the program described above. Simply having dolls without faces or block-shaped crayons does not a LifeWays or Waldorf program make! The activities suggested in this book are appropriate for all children and are really suited for the young child. Because of this, they can be incorporated into home life and into existing child care and preschool programs with very positive results. But one needs to distinguish between "a bit of this and a bit of that" and a fully developed LifeWays or Waldorf program. The Waldorf early childhood teacher training is a two-year full-time program, or its equivalent over four summers, and qualifies the graduate to teach in a Waldorf school; the LifeWays certification combines part-time classroom experience with guided mentoring over nine to thirteen months and can lead to starting one's own LifeWays program in either a home or a center, being an assistant in a Waldorf school, or being a more satisfied and more centered, creative parent. Resources on both types of training can be found at the end of this chapter.

LIFEWAYS AND WALDORF IN THE HOME

Many parents who are trying to incorporate these ideas and recommendations about young children into their home life are faced with the dilemma of being unable to get away to take an extensive training at just the time when they could use it most! LifeWays has addressed this dilemma by meeting quarterly or over one weekend each month so the time away from the family is as little as possible. Other parents have confronted this dilemma by connecting with resources online as they work to apply these principles in their own homes. Another valuable resource can be to start a playgroup together with other parents who share the same interests and ideals. If you can find a group of interested parents, you can take turns being with the children while the other parents share resources and discuss questions they have about their children. It is also possible for group members to share craft and festival celebrations and to select a book for study and discussion. Several recommended titles—in addition to this book—are listed at the end of this chapter. If you find yourself alone in working with these ideas, you will need to keep studying and find support through networking as you attract more like-minded people.

Many parents who want to provide this kind of experience for their child often find other families attracted to what they are creating in their home. If the parent is interested, this can lead to forming an in-home program for young children, or a "Saturday club" or an after-school enrichment program to bring some of the Waldorf activities to older children who are enrolled in public schools or who are being taught at home.

Waldorf education was started for the children of the workers in a factory in Stuttgart in 1919. It embraces children of all economic and intellectual levels and welcomes children from all cultural backgrounds. This has resulted in its becoming the largest private school movement in the world. The principles of Waldorf education are neither elitist nor reserved for the relatively small number of children who live near Waldorf schools. Its principles are universal and can be applied to all children. Waldorf-oriented charter schools are arising in many areas throughout the United States, and many parents are using a Waldorf approach in homeschooling their children.

In our highly technological society, the view of child development and the principles of education initiated by Rudolf Steiner (and further developed by thousands of Waldorf teachers over the past hundred years) need to become known to more and more parents for the healthy development of young children. The quality of life in the home and the preschool environment is perhaps even more important than what kind of elementary school the child attends.

THE VALUE OF MIXED-AGE PROGRAMS

Many parents who are fortunate enough to find a mixed-age program wonder whether they should stick with it or whether their child needs "more stimulation" when he or she becomes one of the older children. We have found that giving children the gift of growth and achieving competency nourishes them as much as—or more than—always being challenged. One LifeWays parent from a program in Milwaukee, Wisconsin, described it this way:

> As Antonia grew from the suite baby to a big girl helper, I saw her complete her first journey through stages of maturity. She gently and gradually gave up her babyish ways, replacing old behaviors with new ones. There were no startling jolts so often imposed on children going from one year of schooling to the next. At LifeWays, Antonia learned to get along with other children in a confident, positive, and constructive way. She went from one who received the lion's share of attention as an infant to one who gave her attention to caring for little ones around her. She became someone who shared her toys, cleaned up willingly, worked out conflict, and gladly obeyed the rules and routines of LifeWays.
>
> And, when the time was right, she was ready to give up the comforting routines of LifeWays and take on the exciting new challenge of five-year-old kindergarten. When Antonia entered public school kindergarten, her behavior stood out from her peers. Her teacher often remarked that Antonia was a joy to have in the classroom. . . . Antonia's academic progress has remained very good. She recently received her first formal assessment as a first grader. Her highest mark was in "working cooperatively in groups." LifeWays taught her to value her peers and teachers, and to have confidence in dealing with others. I feel these lessons will be with her for a lifetime.[18]

WHEN IS YOUR CHILD READY
FOR FIRST GRADE?

Due to the downward shift of the curriculum over the past thirty years, it is even more important that children today be developmentally ready as well as chronologically ready for school. The developmental age of a child can be six months to a year or more away from his or her chronological age. Developmental age is measured by how closely the child's social, emotional, physical, and perceptual maturity corresponds to the norm for his age. Just as babies crawl, teethe, walk, and become toilet trained at different ages, older children, too, remain on their own individual timetables. There is not necessarily a correlation between developmental age and intelligence; a child with a high IQ can be developmentally delayed.[19]

In "Pupil Age at School Entrance—How Many Are Ready for Success?" James Uphoff and June Gilmore reported marked differences in school performance and emotional adjustment between children with summer and fall birthdays, who were less than five years and three months of age when they entered kindergarten, and those with birthdays the previous summer, who had been given an extra growth year and were as old as six years and three months when they entered kindergarten.

Uphoff and Gilmore summarize their research as follows:

1. The older children in a grade tend to receive many more above-average grades from teachers than do younger children in that grade.

2. Older children are much more likely to score in the above-average range on standardized achievement tests.

3. The younger children in a grade are far more likely to fail at least one grade than are older children.

4. The younger children in a grade are far more likely to be referred by teachers for learning disabilities testing and subsequently be diagnosed as being learning disabled than are older students in a grade.

5. The academic problems of younger children who were developmentally unready at school entrance often last throughout their school careers and sometimes even into adulthood.[20]

The Gesell Institute of Human Development in New Haven, Connecticut, is a leading advocate of slowing down the accelerated pace of childhood. Their studies found that only about one-third of the children they tested in kindergarten through third grade were ready for the grade in which their age had placed them. The readiness of another third was questionable, and the final third definitely were not ready. Their studies compiled from school districts across the country indicate that as many as 50 percent of students with school problems today have them because of overplacement.[21]

Regardless of a school system's cutoff dates, parents together with teachers must decide whether an individual child is really ready for kindergarten or the first grade. Giving a child who has a summer or fall birthday an extra growth year can be a lifelong gift that may put him at the head of the class instead of scrambling to keep up intellectually or socially. If a child is kept in kindergarten a second year, or needs to go into a "pre-first" program, in no way should the parents regard the child as a failure or learning disabled. Remember that developmental maturity has no correlation with IQ. If the parents feel positive about the decision and take responsibility themselves, the child can adapt well and the extra year can have lasting benefits. Parents sometimes find it hard to explain to grandparents why they are keeping their child in kindergarten for two years, but the advantages for the child are worth the effort if you are feeling pressured to keep your child going through the system when he is showing signs of not being ready.

WHAT HAPPENS AROUND AGE SEVEN?

Between the ages of five and seven you will see many dramatic changes in your child. In terms of the development of memory, your child may say something like, "I can see grandma anytime I want to now," referring to an emerging ability to call on mental images at will. He may also tell you more of his dreams.

You will notice a kind of logic appearing in speech that represents a new level of thinking and is expressed in words like "because," "so," "if," and "therefore." This new ability is expressed in creative play by the love of tying things together with string, like linking one thing to the next with logic. A growing grasp of, and interest in, time will also be apparent.

In play you may also see intention manifested as things that are built for other things. For example, a sand structure may now be built as a garage for a car rather than simply for the activity itself. An authoritative element also enters into group play at this age, with a child sometimes directing and sometimes being told who or what he will be.

In the sphere of drawing, the individualizing element expresses itself in the use of the diagonal line, such as triangular designs, a ladder leaning against a tree, the stair going up inside the house, or the appearance of the arching rainbow.

Physically you will first see the differentiation of the chest or "middle sphere" around age five. The child suddenly loses her round "Buddha belly" and acquires a waist and a neck, showing how the life forces have completed their work in the rhythmic system. As the shift of the growth forces is made to the limbs, the arms will lengthen during this time. This is why an older child will be able to reach directly over his head and touch his opposite ear, while a younger or less developed one will not. Finally, the growth shifts into the legs, and the child will also often start to eat more and will sometimes increase his awareness of digestion (expressed in the frequent stomachaches of some children at this age). At the same time the growth forces are moving into the legs, the features of the face become more individualized and the milk teeth begin to loosen.

In the area of brain development, the changes are so great that Healy says this time is commonly termed the "five- to seven-year shift." She explains, "From ages five to seven or eight the brain is in one of its most dynamic states of change as it practices combining sensory patterns from different modalities. Maturation of a small part of the parietal lobe, at the junction where all the senses come together, is one development that makes many kinds of new learning possible, but there is enormous variability in the age when it occurs. . . . Only now does it make sense to ask a youngster to look at a series of written letters and 'sound out' a word, to coordinate motor programs and visual skills such as in catching or kicking a ball, or later, reading music while playing an instrument."[22]

The child starts to have real friendships and likes to make and give surprises. He likes to play with words and create rhymes, to play riddle and guessing games, to whisper and to giggle. Meyerkort says, "He feels the future dawning, the new stage coming; he says, 'I hope. . . .'"[23]

All of the changes discussed here should be allowed to become consolidated in a play-oriented kindergarten before the child is called upon to exercise the new faculties that are used in learning to read, write, and do math in first grade.

Steiner explains the changes around the age of seven as resulting from the life forces completing their work of individualizing the child's physical body: first the head between birth and age three, then the middle sphere between ages three and five, and finally the limbs and hard, bony teeth. Once finished, the forces are freed for development of the memory and schoolwork. According to Steiner, the way to teach the elementary-school child between the change of teeth and puberty is with images and pictures, through which the child is allowed to take guidance from the inner meaning she discovers for herself in the pictures and allegories. What the child sees and perceives with the eye of the mind is a more appropriate means of education than abstract conceptions for the elementary-school child.

It is upon this ground of imagination that the later powers of intellect, judgment, and critical thinking will be based. Therefore, all of the subjects—from reading to mathematics to physics—are taught in an imaginative and artistic way in the Waldorf elementary school, providing a rich and nourishing foundation for the faculty of analytical thinking that arises and can be developed in puberty.

BEGINNING ACADEMIC WORK: THE WALDORF APPROACH

In the Waldorf approach, reading, writing, and math aren't started until the first grade. Children who start these academic tasks when they are developmentally more mature do not fall behind peers who start earlier in other school systems. In fact, there are definite advantages in delaying instruction in the "three R's" until around the age of seven.

Writing is taught in the Waldorf first grade through stories and pictures, and then the children learn to read from what they have written themselves. Just as humans first wrote using picture glyphs before developing the alphabet, so the young child develops the forms and the sounds of the letters through stories and pictures provided by the teacher. In this way the letters and their sounds "live within the child" as vibrant pictures. One morning when she was in first grade, my daughter said, "I dreamed about the letter A. There were all these A's. . . ." The children progress to writing from verses that they know and then "reading" from what they have written themselves. Thus the more abstract work of reading begins toward the end of first grade, and the transition to printed books is generally not made until the second grade.

Children who are first taught to read at a later age miss out on years of "I can read" books, but what are they really missing? Bruno Bettelheim, in his article "Why Children Don't Like to Read," lambastes most of the early readers and texts used in elementary schools as being totally devoid of meaning, content, and interest for young children. He points out the constant reduction in the number of words taught to children, so that books become a series of repeated words that lack any relationship to spoken communication and lack a meaning or story line that the child would want to learn to read in order to discover. He states, "Although in the 1920s few children went to kindergarten and little preschool reading instruction was given, by the 1970s, when many children were attending kindergarten and reading was consistently taught there, the first-grade primers contained only a quarter of the vocabulary presented to first-graders fifty years ago."[24]

Some people have the mistaken idea that there are no books in a Waldorf school. This is far from true! Although there aren't readers in the kindergarten, and in the first grade children learn to read from what they have written themselves, books with real literary content are introduced from second grade on, and students are never given anything that is condescending in tone or that has been predigested especially for children. Real literature is always used in the classroom, selected according to the reading level and inner maturity level of the children. Waldorf schools have libraries for children's reading pleasure and for doing research in the upper grades.

Although reading is taught more slowly in the Waldorf curriculum, math is not. Nothing is done until first grade, but then all four processes—addition, subtraction, multiplication, and division—are introduced. This is possible because the concepts are introduced imaginatively. For example, there might be a story about four gnome brothers: Mr. Plus is fat and jolly with stuffed pockets; Mr. Minus is thin and sad, and all of his jewels keep falling out of a hole in his sack; and so forth. The children work from the whole to the part, first using chestnuts or shells to see that eight is one plus seven, eight is two plus six, and so on. In third grade they walk and clap various rhythms and verses that help make the multiplication tables much easier to learn. When mathematics is made concrete and imaginative, children take to it with delight.

A complete listing of the Waldorf curriculum for grades one through eight can be found in the appendix.

WHAT ABOUT THE ADVANCED OR GIFTED CHILD?

Waiting until a child is in the first grade before starting academic work has obvious advantages for an average or a slow child, who needs the extra neurophysiological maturity before beginning tasks such as reading and mathematics. However, what about the bright child, who wants to start writing letters or learning to read at age three or four, or certainly by kindergarten age? As children become more aware of the world around them, they want to imitate and learn, and many children will show interest in these activities by age five. Reading and writing are the way of the future for children, so you will want to share their enthusiasm and can harness anticipation by saying, "You will learn more about how to do that when you are in the first grade!" Teaching the first letter or how to write their name will often satisfy this interest for the time being. But it is still too soon to exercise the memory or the intellect directly with sit-down lessons. There is no critical window when you have to teach a child to read or risk his not being interested later on. On the contrary, telling a child "That's what you'll learn when you go to the big school" develops eagerness and anticipation and keeps the young child learning through imitation rather than through direct lessons.

By not being taught to read in kindergarten or before, children miss several years of early readers (which isn't missing much), and they are given the gift of the final year or more of early childhood. Direct cognitive work wakes the child up and brings her out of the magical world of early childhood. Children grow out of these years soon enough on their own. Allowing your child to stay in the magical realm of early childhood without pushing cognitive development provides a sound basis for later health and creativity.

Especially with bright children, it is important to emphasize balance. It is possible to teach them intellectual skills at a young age and to put them into academically advanced programs from preschool or kindergarten on. The result, however, is often the creation of a forty-year-old in a five-year-old body. Advanced intellectual development in childhood is usually at the expense of the artistic and emotional spheres or the healthy development of the body. Elementary-school education should appeal so much to the child's imagination that the gifted child still feels fully interested and engaged. If that kind of creative education isn't available for the very bright child, you may face some hard choices.

You will need to investigate different educational approaches and make your own decisions for your child. I felt it was important to work toward a balanced development of the heart forces, the head forces, and the body/will forces, so that there would emerge a whole human being who would be able to lead a fruitful life and act in service to humanity. The danger of education that emphasizes only intellectual development is that we might turn out thinkers and scientists who are emotionally divorced from humanity and from the consequences of their work for the world. For this reason, I chose for my children an approach to education that emphasized balance rather than a program designed specifically for gifted children.

In most communities there are an increasing number of schooling options, including regular public schools, charter and magnet schools, independent private schools, and religious schools. Many parents are also turning to homeschooling as a viable alternative, or pursuing some combination of school and enrichment at home. Making decisions about your child's education is an ongoing adventure, but one that is well worth the research and effort.

RECOMMENDED RESOURCES

Brain Development and Academics

Endangered Minds: Why Children Don't Think and What We Can Do About It, by Jane M. Healy, Ph.D. (Simon & Schuster).

Failure to Connect: How Computers Affect Our Children's Minds— for Better and Worse, by Jane M. Healy, Ph.D. (Simon & Schuster).

The Hurried Child, by David Elkind (Knopf).

Miseducation: Preschoolers at Risk, by David Elkind (Knopf).

Your Child's Growing Mind: A Practical Guide to Brain Development and Learning from Birth to Adolescence, by Jane M. Healy, Ph.D. (Doubleday).

School Readiness

Better Late Than Early, by Raymond and Dorothy Moore (Reader's Digest Press).

First Grade Readiness: Resources, Insights and Tools for Waldorf Teachers, edited by Nancy Blanning. Available from www.waldorfearly childhood.org.

The Hurried Child, by David Elkind (Knopf).

"Readiness for First Grade," by Daena Ross. CD available from www.waldorfinthehome.org.

You're Not the Boss of Me! Understanding the Six/Seven Year Old Transformation, edited by Ruth Ker. Available from www.waldorf earlychildhood.org.

Waldorf Education

Understanding Waldorf Education: Teaching from the Inside Out, by Jack Petrash (Nova Institute).

Various videos on Waldorf education, including "The Waldorf Experience" and "Waldorf Education: The Best Kept Secret in America," available from www.waldorfinthehome.org.

"The Wisdom of Waldorf: Education for the Future," by Rahima Baldwin Dancy. CD and article reprint in full color, available from www.waldorfinthehome.org.

Journals on Waldorf Education

Gateways, newsletter of the Waldorf Early Childhood Association of North America, published twice a year. More information at www.waldorfearlychildhood.org.

LifeWays North America. Offers a quarterly e-newsletter. See www.lifewaysnorthamerica.org.

Renewal: A Journal of Waldorf Education, published twice a year by the Association of Waldorf Schools of North America. Available from www.awsna.org.

Books for Beginning Study Groups

Beyond the Rainbow Bridge, by Barbara Patterson and Pamela Bradley (Michaelmas Press). Discusses nurturing our children from birth to age seven, creating balance in family life, and how Waldorf education supports the development of the whole child.

Heaven on Earth, by Sharifa Oppenheimer (SteinerBooks). An excellent book that helps parents understand child development and strengthen home life.

Lifeways: Working with Family Questions, edited by Gudrun Davy and Bons Voors (Hawthorn Press). Chapters deal with issues of family life. Excellent for a mother's group.

Waldorf Education: A Family Guide, by Pamela Fenner and Karen Rivers (Michaelmas Press). Deepens understanding and enriches family life.

Waldorf Parenting Handbook, by Lois Cusick (Rudolf Steiner College Press). An introduction to some of the ideas behind Waldorf education from birth through high school.

You Are Your Child's First Teacher. Share it with friends and subscribe to my blog at www.waldorfinthehome.org.

Courses and Training Programs for Parents and Teachers

"Joyful Days with Toddlers and Preschoolers," by Faith Baldwin Collins. Telecourse and other resources from www.joyfultoddlers.com.

LifeWays certification in early childhood and human development. Offers part-time classes throughout the country that occur four times a year over nine to thirteen months, plus directed study at home with a mentor. See www.lifewaysnorthamerica.org.

Sophia's Hearth Family Center (in Wilton, NH). Offers workshops and programs for parents and teachers in the field of birth to three. At www.sophiashearth.org.

Waldorf Teacher Training Programs for early childhood, the grades, or high school. At various locations throughout North America; see www.aswna.org.

Resources for Waldorf Homeschooling and Enrichment

Kindergarten at Home with Your Three- to Six-Year-Old, by Donna Simmons. Book and many other homeschooling resources for the grades from www.christopherushomeschool.org.

Live Education! Offers a Waldorf-inspired homeschooling curriculum and advising for grades K–8. At www.live-education.com.

Online Waldorf Library. A valuable resource site for teachers and homeschoolers. At www.waldorflibrary.org.

"Starting a Waldorf Enrichment Program." DVD of a workshop given by Kristie Burns. Available from the online store at www.waldorfinthehome.org.

Various videos on Waldorf homeschooling and curriculum topics such as "Teaching Reading and Writing the Waldorf Way," "Form Drawing," and "Math by Hand" are available from the online store at www.waldorfinthehome.org.

Waldorf Without Walls. Consulting and resources for homeschoolers from Barbara Dewey. At www.waldorfwithoutwalls.com.

CHAPTER 12

Common Parenting Questions: From Television to Immunizations

When I speak with parents around the country, similar issues come up again and again as parents consider the approach to the young child suggested in this book. By sharing some of these questions and the reasoning behind my answers, I hope this chapter will spark your own questions and your search for the answers that are most nurturing to you and your family.

Even if I wanted to provide an idyllic world for my young child, I don't think I could do it. Modern life is just too fast-paced and stressful. Besides, don't children need to adjust to the realities of today's world?

The best way to prepare your children for the stresses of today's world is not to expose them to problems early in their life, but to provide them with an environment that is warm and nurturing and that shelters them from as many of the problems of the adult world as possible. Child psychologist David Elkind has discussed at length the difficulties children encounter when they are hurried to grow up and face adult choices too soon, or when they are subjected to miseducation in academic subjects, swimming, gymnastics, ballet, and so forth.[1] Kim John Payne has found similar effects in his counseling practice with children and families and has outlined many practical suggestions in his book *Simplicity Parenting*.

The rushed lives that most of us live make it difficult to provide children with an ideal world for their early childhood years. We tend to move frequently or travel a lot, to work too much and be too busy, and to move too fast for the tempo of our children. Divorce, single parenting, and blended families all add to the stresses of a child. And, with the best intentions, many parents push their children to achieve at an early age or to be grown-up emotional companions for them.

Yet there is a great deal that parents can do for their children by providing an environment filled with love and warmth. By understanding a young child's development and his complete openness to his surroundings, we can do our best to provide a stable and nurturing environment within our current living situation. Fortunately, children are very giving and forgiving—and fairly resilient.

Now that we have recognized some of the ways in which children differ from adults, how can we let them be children in a society in which changing family, social, and academic pressures make them deal with the adult world earlier than they are ready? Most of us can't radically change our life situations, even if we wanted to. For the most part we are members of our highly technological, urban, material-minded society. Yet no matter where we find ourselves, many ways to meet the real needs of the young child have been suggested in this book. In summary:

- Attend to your own life and emotions. The emotional environment you create for your child is far more important than the material environment.
- Honor the spiritual element in life, especially as it is brought to you by your children.
- Work toward rhythm in family life that can support you and your children.
- Remember that imitation and repetition, not reasoning and punishment, are the keys to discipline with the young child.
- Set limits and enforce them consistently; accept that you are the parent.

- Allow plenty of time for your child's creative free play as well as musical and artistic play. Allow time for just being home and "doing nothing."
- Buy or make childlike toys that encourage imaginative play. Simplify and phase out other toys.
- Avoid pressuring your child to be an early achiever in academics, sports, or the arts. Keep it unstructured and fun!
- Continue to pay attention to what your child experiences, limiting overstimulation from loud music, movies, and television.
- Avoid concerning your child with adult problems through news broadcasts, conversations, and so forth. Even third graders don't yet need to be taught about AIDS or substance abuse, as they have no way of comprehending such things!
- Read *Simplicity Parenting* and see whether there is a support group in your area.

Your description of a play-oriented kindergarten leaves me wondering whether it really prepares children for the high-tech world in which we live. What about computer literacy? I want my child to have a competitive edge, not be behind the times.

Every parent should read Jane Healy's extensively researched book *Failure to Connect: How Computers Affect Our Children's Minds—for Better and Worse.* She reviews numerous studies about what is and isn't working with educational software, both at home and in the schools. She also provides recommendations for evaluating games and educational programs before purchasing them and gives vital guidelines for parents in starting and guiding their child's computer use at home. She also shares her understanding, as a learning specialist and developmental neuropsychologist, of the effects that video games and extensive computer use may be having in actually changing children's "wiring" through hours of rapidly changing visual images. And she makes recommendations for protecting children's health, pointing out that if employers let people use computers under the conditions found in most schools, they would be cited by OSHA. In fact, the American Academy of Pediatrics has expressed concern about how much time children spend in front of various types of screens and recommends that a "media history," including the amount and type of computer, television, and video use, be taken by physicians as a routine part of a child's media record for diagnosis of media-related problems—physical, academic, and emotional.[2]

Precisely because computers are changing our world so rapidly, what children will need most in the future is the ability to think creatively. Most of the jobs that your children will be entering don't even exist today! The qualities that children will need in the future are not technical skills, but mental habits such as analytical thinking and problem solving, the ability to communicate, imagination, values, persistence, creativity, kindness, and tolerance. Todd Oppenheimer reported in his *Atlantic Monthly* article, "The Computer Delusion," that even high-tech corporations that are seeking creative employees rarely hire people who are primarily computer experts. Rather, they look for innovation, teamwork, flexibility, and innovative thinking, qualities they often find lacking in many "technology nerds."[3]

Children who start to use computers in preschool show no demonstrable advantage over those who start using them at age twelve or fourteen. Computers, as word processors and vehicles for logical thinking through programming, are suited to the adolescent, not the preschool-age child! Computers as toys are inappropriate, because they present a two-dimensional abstraction of the world to the young child, who should be moving and playing and acquiring a broad base of experiences of the physical world and the world of imaginative play. The visual image on the computer screen is especially hard on the developing eyes of the young child.

Because children's senses and brains are developing throughout childhood, Healy says that "age-appropriate computer use may help establish some forms of connections, but inappropriate use may also build resistant habits that interfere with academic learning. Once set into the brain's connectivity, such patterns are hard to break."[4] Parents, like educators in the nation's schools, are jumping on the bandwagon that every child should be computer literate and be on the Internet without sufficiently investigating the nature of brain development, how children learn, and what is necessary for healthy development at various ages.

Most of the educational programs for young children try to teach concepts at too young an age. Remember that the young child needs to be addressed through movement and imitation. Steiner says, "Have we the right to believe that with our intellectual mode of knowledge we can ever participate in the experience of the outer world which a child has, the child who is all sense-organ? This we cannot do. . . . It is immensely important that we do not consciously or unconsciously call upon the child's intellect prematurely, as people are so prone to do today."[5]

We need to remember how the fantasy and play of the young child transform into the artistic imagination of the elementary-school child, the questioning of the teenager, and the rational thinking of the young adult. Then we will have confidence that fantasy and imagination, which are so natural for the young child, form a better foundation for later creative thinking than early learning. Creative thinking is more needed in our highly technological world than four-year-olds who can tap the screen of an iPad or manipulate the mouse of a computer.

My five-year-old has always been precocious and already reads. And he can outreason me in getting what he wants. If we want to try to encourage balanced development, what can we do now? He can't go back to early childhood!

In working toward balanced development, it is necessary to have a picture of your child that includes more than intellectual achievements. What is he like emotionally? Is he happy being a child? Does he relate well with other children, or almost exclusively with adults? What is he like physically? Is he at home in his body and well coordinated? Does he have frequent illnesses and require antibiotics?

Many times early intellectual awakening can result in a weakening of the child's vital forces, manifesting in frequent colds or other illnesses. The dreamy state of early childhood is an essential element in the healthy formation of the physical body during the first seven years. The intellect is crystalline and hardening in its effect. When it is engaged prematurely, it can inhibit the proper development of the physical organs and the unfolding of the fluid emotions. Steiner even relates some illnesses in later life to influences in the first seven years:

> Whoever studies the whole course of a man's life from
> birth to death, bearing in mind the requirements of which
> I have spoken, will see that a child who has been exposed

to things suitable only to grown-up people and who imitates these things will in his later years, from the age of
about 50, suffer from sclerosis. . . . Illnesses that appear
in later life are often only the result of educational errors
made in the very earliest years of childhood.[6]

Because the job of the intellect is to analyze and exercise critical judgment, very bright children tend to have difficulty relating emotionally with
other children, a problem that can intensify as the child becomes older.

While an awakened child cannot go back to the dreamy world of
early childhood, imaginative play and the arts can have a healing influence on the child's life forces, helping to "reweave the web" that protects
the child during the first seven years. Images from fairy tales are also
nurturing to the unconscious elements of the young child.

Although you can't go back in time and do things differently with
your child, it is also important not to feel guilty about choices you have
already made. You were just as good a parent then as you are now. You
made the best decisions you could then, based on your knowledge
and perceptions of your choices. Guilt only takes us out of the present
moment and makes us less able to see what is needed now, thus per-
petuating problems rather than leading to meeting the present creatively.
If there is going to be the possibility of healing, it must take place in
the present. We make the best choices we can for our children in each
moment, just as our parents did for us.

Why do you suggest eliminating television for young children? We only let Jessica watch educational programs and she loves them!

Probably anyone who is reading this book is concerned enough about
their children's development that they think seriously about television
watching and have probably limited it in some ways, to only certain
programs, a certain amount of time, or watching programs together
and talking about them, for example. However, the problem is two-
fold. First, television watching, including DVDs, is very seductive, and
the time children spend doing it expands the moment your awareness
drops. This is because it entertains the child and buys time for you as
a parent. Creative play does the same thing, but television watching

tends to squelch imagination and free play, leaving only bored children and more need for TV or another movie!

Second, any amount and any kind of screen time—TV, DVD, video game, or computer—is not healthy for the young child, regardless of the content of the program. In 1999 the American Academy of Pediatrics recommended that children under the age of two not watch any television for healthy development. That was done in the face of statistics that show two-year-olds spend an average of twenty-seven hours a week watching television. There has also been recent heavy marketing of television programs designed for toddlers under the age of two. The doctors also recommended that older children not have televisions in their bedrooms.

I was delighted that the pediatricians finally took the most rudimentary stand for child health, developmentally appropriate activities, and brain development with regard to the media. And I was astounded that they took so much criticism for it, from editorials in the *New York Times* to the *Sacramento Bee*. The primary criticisms were that their recommendations were dogmatic, unrealistic, and unscientific, because studies of the effects of TV viewing on infants and toddlers haven't been done yet. When the "experts" finally recommend something sensible, society discredits them as "unscientific."

Television is an important source of information and diversion for most adults. But children are not in the same stage of development as adults. The lack of physical movement and the rapidly changing sensory stimulation on the screen make television watching problematic for all children. In an article titled "Children and Television," John Rosemond suggests that you look at your child next time he is watching television and ask yourself what he is doing—or, better yet, what he is not doing. He states:

> In answer, the child is not:
>
> • scanning
> • practicing motor skills, gross or fine
> • practicing eye-hand coordination
> • using more than two senses

- asking questions
- exploring
- exercising initiative or motivation
- being challenged
- solving problems
- thinking analytically
- exercising imagination
- practicing communication skills
- being either creative or constructive

Also, because of television's insidious "flicker," television does not promote long-term attention.

Lastly, because the action shifts constantly and capriciously backward, forward and laterally in time, not to mention from subject to subject, television does not promote logical, sequential thinking.[7]

Rosemond notes that the deficiencies listed above are characteristic of learning disabled children, "children who don't seem to 'get it all together' when it comes to learning how to read and write." Although television is not the only cause of the learning problems plaguing our schools, we need to look at the fact that learning disabilities have become epidemic, and functional illiteracy among seventeen-year-olds has steadily risen since television became a mainstay of our culture in 1955.

In her article "Movement or Television," special education expert Audrey McAllen also reports that kindergarten teachers of long experience observe that children show less initiative than formerly and expect grown-ups to start something. They wait passively for something to stimulate them when indoors, and their play lacks the imaginative inventiveness children once had.[8] Rosemond reports the same phenomena: "Veteran teachers consistently report that today's children are less resourceful, imaginative, creative and motivated than pre-television generations. They also comment that the average child's attention span seems to have shortened mysteriously since 1950."[9]

Jane Healy found the same phenomena in interviewing teachers and in her own work with children over the past twenty-five years as a learning specialist. She found through her research in brain development that "fast-paced, nonlinguistic, and visually distracting television may literally have changed children's minds, making sustaining attention to verbal input, such as reading or listening, far less appealing than faster-paced visual stimuli. (This thesis is explored in depth in my book *Endangered Minds*.)"[10] Healy also reported that optometrists and other specialists have found an increase in vision problems among children due to the two-dimensional nature of the images, the flicker, and the lack of eye movement involved in watching TV and videos.[11] And in 1997 more than 650 viewers aged three to twenty fell ill in Japan with nausea or seizures from the flashing lights in a Pokémon cartoon; 150 were still hospitalized the following day.

Healthy development for the young child must engage all the senses. The young child wants to run and jump in space, touch and grasp with his hands, hold his breath for the fun of it, jump with joy, experience the world for himself with all his senses. "Can I see it?" means "Can I touch it?" The child is hungry to experience everything as fully as possible. Dr. Ann Barber, a developmental optometrist in Santa Ana, California, explains:

> When the child is born the wiring is all there, the light hits the retina but he makes no sense of it. He needs to learn by touching, putting things in his mouth, moving around, and then he has to integrate all this with vision and the other senses to make an intelligent child that's ready for school. There are about eight or ten perceptual processes developing in the preschool years that go beyond the eyeball, and so much . . . is done with the body, manipulating objects, dropping toys to learn about distance and develop visual convergence, practicing how to catch or kick a ball, hit a target. The child also must learn to focus on what's important and make sense out of the world. How can you understand "above, below, inside, outside" if you're not crawling into the cardboard box and seeing and feeling it? But today we see so many kids are delayed in these skills—six-, seven-, eight-year-olds who are more at a four-year-old level.[12]

And yet *Sesame Street* makes parents wonder whether their preschooler will learn "above" and "below" or will somehow be behind if she doesn't watch Grover and company teach it.

Marie Winn, in her book *The Plug-In Drug*, again emphasizes, "It isn't what your children watch on TV but the act of watching that harms them." She states that with heavy television viewing, the right hemisphere of the brain is developed at the expense of the left. The left hemisphere controls the verbal, rational thought—the ability to read and write, to reason, to organize ideas and express them in speech and writing. Television viewers are bombarded with images that don't require them to think, or even give them time to do so.[13]

With the popularity of children's programming on cable stations, children's viewing is steadily increasing. More than 40 percent of children aged six to eleven have televisions in their bedrooms to watch on their own, and nearly a quarter of toddlers aged two to five also have their own TVs.[14] By the time most children graduate from high school they will typically have spent 35,000 hours in front of a television set—enough for a bachelor's degree in television watching—compared with having spent only 11,000 hours in the classroom. If you subtract hours for sleeping and doing homework, children are left with relatively few hours spent in reading, playing, and doing the other creative activities of childhood. Radically limiting your child's screen time before the age of ten or eleven is probably one of the most far-reaching gifts you can possibly give him or her developmentally. This may mean putting the television set in your bedroom, if there are shows that you or your partner watch regularly while the children are up, or finding another way to keep it covered or inaccessible if your child is a button pusher. You will probably need to put more time into family activities when you first get rid of the television, but then you will find that the children become self-motivating and that you, as well as they, will have more time to do things alone as well as together. The world without television is very different and very much more in keeping with the developmental needs of the young child.

I want to change the kind of toys my child plays with, but she always pesters me to buy her the other ones when we go to the store. I can't just throw everything out. Where can I start?

At first it may be difficult to step outside of the chrome and plastic world of high-tech toys, but as you and your daughter begin to experience more alternatives, it will become easier. Certainly you won't want to take away favorite toys and create lots of strife! Possibly you can make a start by eliminating toys she doesn't play with now. That will clear out some of the clutter and make some space. Then make something, or buy an imaginative toy, and have a special place in her room where it lives or is played with. Invest some energy into the imaginative aspect of it, and make sure that it is put away each day in an attractive manner, ready for the new day. Gradually add toys that encourage imagination while you phase out old ones that are no longer played with. You will find that costumes and toys that invite imaginative play in little scenes will easily become favorites.

Decrease the number of toys of the type you don't want your child to have by requesting that appropriate catalogs be sent to grandparents and others who send gifts. Some parents have a "rainy day box" for gifts and toys that don't match their values for daily play but that can be a fine adventure for a rainy day.

Sometimes it is necessary to go cold turkey, as when we decided to get rid of our television set. We did it at a time when we were moving anyway, so it didn't become associated with patterns in the new home. And, though I had been braced for a loud wail, I was amazed that the children didn't even complain. At first we replaced television time with activities the children were doing at school—knitting, singing, playing recorder, and reading stories out loud—so they wouldn't go around asking what to do now that they couldn't watch television. We also tried to keep television from becoming forbidden fruit by telling the oldest child that he could watch certain events, like special football games, at the neighbor's house if invited. With the younger children, we told the neighbors that we didn't have a television, so they should tell our girls their daughter couldn't play if she wanted to watch television instead. I found being tolerant and avoiding being "holier than thou" helped things go smoothly, without a lot of emotional upset.

Sometimes parents are discouraged by their children playing with neighbors who have different values. You can't continually police your child when he is out of the house, so have faith that your values make the strongest impression on your child. What you can do most effectively is to make your own rules at your house, and then make your house sufficiently attractive that your children and their friends will play there much of the time.

The issue of play with guns, for example, is one that parents need to discuss together and decide for themselves. I still don't have any clear philosophical or psychological answers as to what parents should do on this issue and why; I just knew that I wouldn't buy guns and my children learned that no gun play was allowed in our house. That limited their access without bringing up long discussions or making our neighbors wrong. Children can accept that there are different rules in different places. "This is the way we do it at our house" is enough of an answer to many a "why?" from a young child. Similarly, I told children in my kindergarten that certain play was all right at home but not at school. They didn't have any problem with that.

Ryan loves his video games so much that he'd play through meals if we let him. I'm thinking about some of the things you've said about passive screen time, but video games are more active and encourage eye-hand coordination, don't they?

Video games have become a huge business in this country. Professor Dale Mann of Teacher's College of Columbia University points out that the entertainment industry has now replaced the defense industry as the main developer of technology in the United States, and at least half as much again is spent on entertainment as on education in this country.[15] Although it is true that video games improve the kind of coordination needed by airplane pilots (hence the value of flight simulators in training), they were also used by the military to desensitize recruits to actually firing and killing another person in training during the Vietnam War (this was reported by a high-ranking former Army officer in an article in *Time* after the killings at Columbine High School in May 1999). As the analysts have said, all television, videos, and video games are educational; the question is, what are they teaching? Consider this development:

Setting the stage for an unprecedented collaboration between the Pentagon and Hollywood, the U.S. Army will announce the formation of a major research center today at the University of Southern California to develop core technologies that are critical to both the military and to the entertainment industry.

The primary goal of the new Institute for Creative Technologies is to allow the Army to create highly realistic training simulations that rely on advances in virtual reality, artificial intelligence and other cutting-edge technologies. The entertainment industry is expected to use the technology to improve its motion picture special effects, make video games more realistic and create new simulation attractions for virtual reality arcades.[16]

Jane Healy found in her research that because video games strongly engage the player, they have more profound effects (good or bad) than viewing TV. They also "decrease the psychological distance" between the child and the medium, especially as games become increasingly sophisticated and realistic. Healy asks that we consider what behaviors and worldviews certain games might be conveying (for example, "this is a violent place where I can't trust anyone"). She also found that the hyperactivation of the adrenaline response that accompanies most video games and even some "educational" computer games may, with repeated experience, become an ingrained physical habit. Measurements of blood pressure, heart rate, and even brain waves during virtual interactions mirror those that would be present in a real-life situation—all without conscious control or being discharged through movement.[17]

Video games prior to the age of seven, while the child is so open in the realm of the senses, simply can't be considered healthy for children. Although video-game-related seizures (called VGRS by neurologists) are rare, a recent study indicated they can occur in youngsters without previous seizure difficulties. Nintendo now attaches a warning of epilepsy-like symptoms triggered by the games' optical stimuli after a handful of teenagers suffered seizures while playing Nintendo video games several years ago. Symptoms include stiffening, shaking, or even losing consciousness for a few seconds, or they may be less dramatic and involve merely staring for a few seconds and then "coming back" with a start. Less dramatic symptoms may also occur as a result of such overstimulation. Robert W. Kubey of Rutgers University reported, "I have many parents report to me that, short of seizures, their children have become nauseated, tired, or listless, or experienced headaches during and after playing a video game."[18]

The later you can postpone the world of video games for your children, the better. If you already have them, or you plan to introduce them into your home, Healy provides valuable guidelines for their use in *Failure to Connect*.[19]

What about immunizations? I've heard some people say that childhood illnesses could be beneficial. How could this be?

While no one wants his or her child to become ill, many parents today question whether it is necessary to immunize their children with the standard array of more than fifty injections, and at what age the immunizations should be given. There are many opposing views on the subject, and parents need to do their own research and make responsible decisions.

The medical doctors in Germany who are working out of the indications of Rudolf Steiner will not immunize infants until they are one year old, and then they will only immunize for the more serious illnesses, such as polio, diphtheria, and tetanus. They feel that the childhood illnesses such as measles, mumps, chicken pox, and even whooping cough can have beneficial effects. They feel that by activating the immune system in a natural way, childhood illnesses can strengthen it and help prevent susceptibility to other illnesses in later life.[20] Most childhood illnesses are characterized by fevers, which not only activate the immune system but can have developmental benefits as well. Pediatrician Uwe Stave reports:

> Fever attacks can affect children in quite a positive way.
> Even though his physical strength is reduced, the child
> may disclose a wealth of new interests and skills. He may
> find new and advanced ways to communicate, think, and
> handle situations, or display a refinement of his motor
> skills. In short, after a fever, the child reveals a spurt of

development and maturation. Parents, frequently surprised, fail to mention their observation of such development to their physicians.[21]

Dr. Stave explains this observation by referring to the effect of warmth
on the process of incarnation:

> Fever acts by shaking and loosening up the physical body.
> Activation by heat can help the Ego form and reshape the
> physical organization of the young child. In addition, the
> physiological and biochemical functions of organs and
> systems are assisted in the maturation process through
> febrile illness, and inner forces gain strength and become
> more differentiated. Although the pediatrician often shares
> parental concern that repeated feverous infections over-
> stress the young child's fragile organism, fever most often
> supports development and individualization, although it
> is sometimes a warning signal, indicating weakness in the
> child's defense against his environment. As children grow
> older and learn how to control the will, gradually an "inner
> fire" replaces the "developmental fever" of a young child.[22]

Many of the childhood illnesses that involve fever, such as measles,
chicken pox, and mumps, have nearly become anachronisms through the
routine immunization of infants. Parents who choose not to have their
children vaccinated for some or all illnesses need to appreciate the seri-
ousness of the diseases and the child's special need for strict home care
and medical help in mustering his or her forces to overcome the illness.
Measles can't be treated like a common cold or flu; it can develop into
pneumonia, encephalitis, or worse. Whooping cough requires weeks of
convalescence and may require medicine or other remedies to help fight
the illness successfully.[23]

On the other hand, if you do immunize your child, you need to recognize that introducing the illness through the vaccine is a powerful shock
to the body. Dr. Wilhelm zur Linden states that the reason vaccinations
are given to babies and infants is because older children can react with
cramps, fever, vomiting, and confusion. He states, "It is now known that

small children react so mildly because they do not yet possess sufficient strength with which to counteract the vaccination."[24] He suggests that the homeopathic remedy Thuja 30X given morning and evening starting on the day of vaccination can help protect the child when vaccinations are given. Whether or not to immunize a child, for which illnesses, and at what age are individual decisions that parents must make, as they weigh the pros and cons as best they can.

In order to make informed decisions for your children, you need to gather information on all sides of the issues. The "pro" side is readily available from your pediatrician or health department. However, you need to realize that in public health there are other forces at work than wanting what is best for your individual child. Many of these issues are discussed in detail in the books listed at the end of this chapter.

You have the ultimate responsibility for your child's health and well-being. You—not your doctor or state or federal health officials—will live with and be responsible for the consequences of your decisions. Obtain a copy of your state's mandatory vaccination laws and your rights and legal exemptions to vaccination. Work in conjunction with your health care provider to assess what is best for your individual child. Don't be intimidated by medical personnel and forced into a vaccination decision before you are comfortable with your decision. On the other hand, don't let your child come down with whooping cough because you haven't gotten around to figuring out whether or not you're immunizing! It's a lot of work to take responsibility for your child's birth, health, and education, but somebody's got to do it.

How should I care for my child when he is sick?

Before talking about *how* to care for a sick child, it is necessary to emphasize how important it is that you *do* care for a sick child. A child needs time and rest to fight off an illness and to consolidate the physical and developmental changes that may be occurring. If given insufficient time to recuperate, the child's system will become weaker and more prone to complications or future infections. Many parents are so harried that they don't think to call everything to a halt and get help (for example, with taking another child to school or going shopping) so they can keep the sick child at home and really attend to his needs. Parents who have to work are often tempted to give antibiotics immediately to suppress the child's symptoms so that he can be back in preschool within twenty-four hours, not realizing that he needs quiet time to regather his inner forces and to heal. And some working parents must take their children to unfamiliar day care centers for sick children if they can't use their own sick days to stay home with a child. Clearly our culture is not set up to meet the needs of children and working parents!

When a child is sick with any illness, certain principles need to be kept in mind. The most important is that the child needs less stimulation so that the forces of the body and of the ego can fight off the illness and go through whatever changes are necessary. This means quiet play, staying in bed, if necessary, and eating lighter foods (which usually means less meat or fewer eggs, which most sick children know naturally). Television is especially to be avoided when the child is sick. It is amazing how most hospitals not only pay so little attention to the environment but also expect patients to get well while watching something like *General Hospital* on the television!

Once you recognize the importance of home care for a sick child, what should you do? One important thing is to observe your child, both physically and intuitively. With an infant, note how he holds his body when he cries; observe the breathing and the nature of the cough; and note the child's eyes and facial expression. Try to feel what is happening and whether the child is getting better or worse. All good pediatricians will ask the mother for her observations and intuitions about a sick child and will take them seriously. It is important to try to find a doctor with whom you can develop a trusting relationship and feel that you are both working toward the healing of the whole child.

Maintaining the health and vitality of your children is a responsibility that is shared by you and your children in conjunction with their health care providers when they are ill. We are a nation prone to the "quick fix." But, if we can take the time for real healing when our children (or we) are ill, we will have gained a great deal. As parents, there is a great deal we can do to help members of our family when they are ill. Compresses and poultices, herbal teas, and therapeutic touch are all home measures that can be learned to comfort a sick person and aid in healing.

**My children are so different from one another that it's
as if they're hardly related at all! How can that be?**

Parents who have an "easy" child are often silently critical of other parents and think, "If they only would do what I did." Then when their next child comes along and is totally different and a real handful, they are amazed by how different children can be with the same parents. There's nothing like children to keep us humble! Similarly, parents with a "difficult" child may feel like a failure until they have another child who is sweetness and light.

What we need is perspective on how different children can be and why. For one thing, they are unique individuals even if they come from the same genetic pool. In addition, each person has a characteristic way of being and interacting with the world. T. Berry Brazelton, pediatrician and author of *Infants and Mothers: Differences in Development*, states, "Just as adults have different personalities, so do babies, and these personalities are distinctive almost from birth." He develops the idea of three basic personalities in infants—quiet, average, and active—and each is quite normal.[25]

Rudolf Steiner recognized four basic "temperaments," or groups of traits. Although everyone is a mixture of several of the temperaments, one tends to dominate. By gaining insight into your child's and your own temperament, you can understand how people can be so different and will be able to try different ways of parenting and teaching children with different temperaments.

The first type of person Steiner described is one who has an abundance of energy and likes to do things. As adults they are quick to see the future and want to manifest things. Such children are very powerful, with tremendous force of will and action. They tend to dominate in play, using images of power such as eagles, tornadoes, or bears. Their emotions tend to be hard to control—especially anger, aggression, and annoyance—and they become frustrated if not given enough opportunity to engage their abilities. They can be overbearing, but they also have positive leadership abilities and can be characterized as the "movers and shakers" who make things happen. They tend to be compactly and powerfully built, and walk with their heels dug into the ground. Well-known historical examples of this choleric or fiery temperament are Napoleon and Teddy Roosevelt.

Contrast that child with one who is dreamy and likes to sit. Sometimes movement seems like too much effort for this type of child. These children are very concerned with the comfort of their bodies, and their favorite part of the day is often snack time or mealtime. When they interact with other children, they usually have a harmonizing effect; often they are content to just sit and watch. These children are very comforted by routine and rhythm; they are hard to get started, but they are equally hard to change, so loyalty is one of their virtues. Transitions and any kind of change are hard for these children, and they can have as many temper tantrums as the choleric child. Such a child will become engrossed in anything he starts and will keep at something like a painting until the paper has a hole in it! Such a phlegmatic temperament is related to the element of water, with its rhythmical wave action that goes on and on without tiring.

A third type of temperament appears in the child who is almost always bright and happy. He or she is usually very cheerful, with tears changing to laughter as quickly as they appear. This child seems to barely touch the ground, and in fact can be observed to walk on the toes much of the time. These children can be very easy to parent; the difficulty in the elementary grades is in getting them to finish their work. Their interest is so ephemeral that they're like butterflies flitting from one thing to the next. They are quick and observant and enthusiastically rush into things, but tend to lack follow-through. They are so aware of sense impressions that they are easily distracted by each new thing. This sanguine temperament is related to the quality of air, which is light and always changing.

To round out our description of the four temperaments, picture a child who is often very inward, more involved in his or her own emotional world than in external action. This kind of child is not so easy to spot in early childhood, because most young children seem to be happy much of the time, but as they grow older, such children seem to take everything personally and experience a great deal of personal suffering (for example, because someone doesn't like him, or because one child didn't give her a valentine). Crying at his or her birthday party is often typical of this child. The positive side of this temperament is a very compassionate and caring nature, but the negative side is extreme sensitivity, as they are more caught up in their own reactions than in what is actually happening. They tend to live in the past, to contemplate their thoughts, memories, and emotional reactions, and they never forget or let go of something. This melancholic temperament is related to the element of the earth, offering resistance to what is happening; but, like geode stones with shining crystals inside, such people have a rich inner life of thoughts and feelings and can be very caring.

Knowledge of the temperaments is an invaluable tool for parents and teachers because it can increase our understanding and compassion for someone who is different from ourselves. A person's temperament changes from childhood to adulthood in characteristic ways, and anyone interested in this fascinating area is encouraged to read Steiner's *The Four Temperaments*.[26]

My husband and I don't go to church, but we want to do something with our child in terms of religious instruction or upbringing. We don't just want to send her off to Sunday school, but what can we do that is meaningful and appropriate?

Having children usually brings up questions about your own experiences with religion as a child, your current spiritual orientation, and what you (both) want for the children. Many times children lead parents back into a relationship with the religion of their childhood, which they rediscover with new depth and meaning. Because the expression of spiritual beliefs is so individual, I encourage you and your partner to discuss them together and work toward finding or creating an appropriate expression of your beliefs that is suitable for your children as they grow.

It is our job as parents to acclimatize the child to this new land, this new condition of life on earth, but to do this in such a way that the child is not driven into forgetfulness of his or her true origin and ultimate goal. How can we help our children develop their innate religious sense? How can we feed their spiritual hunger? How can we assist them in developing their spiritual nature? These questions are addressed in *The Spiritual Hunger of the Modern Child*, a compilation of ten lectures by notable speakers representing a variety of religious perspectives, including Judaism, Christianity, Subud, and Buddhism.[27] In great depth the writers discuss the nature of children, the effect of the home environment, the use of prayer, the power of attraction, heredity, and conscience.

All of the writers agree that who you are and what you do around young children are more important than religious dogmas or indoctrination. Reviewer René Knight-Weiler summarized the book's common theme thus: "Religion must be caught, not taught, and indeed it cannot be caught from someone who doesn't truly have it. It will be caught through practice, feeling, symbolism, image and spirit in the home."[28]

In one of the essays, the Reverend Adam Littleton of the Christian Community speaks on the ideas of Rudolf Steiner and echoes the theme that the real work of early childhood is work on oneself: "That is really the fundamental thing to satisfy the spiritual hunger of the child—that the grown-up does not stop working upon himself, that no day does he stop working on himself."[29]

Joseph Chilton Pearce, in *Magical Child Matures*,[30] emphasizes this same theme: in order for the child to be whole, he must have a model who is whole. While none of us qualifies as a fully realized human being (and our children must know this!), our striving, efforts, awareness, and yearning communicate to the child and are far more valuable than either complete materialism or sanctimonious piety, both of which children can see through and reject as false.

Sanctuaries of Childhood, by Shea Darian, and her book *Living Passages for the Whole Family* together provide a rich foundation for developing ways to honor and celebrate the spiritual in family life.[31] Principles to keep in mind include not calling on the intellect or giving moral exhortations but instead providing stories and images that awaken in the child a feeling for the holidays or the qualities one is trying to convey.

Because of the imitative nature of the young child, the child's experiences during any kind of Sunday school will have a deeper effect than the words that are spoken, just as who you are and what you do speak more clearly than your words. Thus it is important to give attention to the quality of this experience in your church, temple, or mosque. Is there an atmosphere of calm and warmth in the early childhood classes? Do the activities and methods fit the nature of the young child? You may find that you have to become a teacher yourself!

According to Steiner, the imitative nature of the young child has a spiritual basis. In speaking of the young child, he says:

> He is still filled with the devotion that one develops in the spiritual world. It is for this reason that he gives himself up to his environment by imitating the people around him. What then is the fundamental impulse, the completely unconscious mood of the child before the change of teeth? This fundamental mood is a very beautiful one, and it must be fostered in the child. It proceeds from the assumption, from the unconscious assumption, that the whole world is of a moral nature.[32]

The child gives himself over to the people and objects of the world with the assumption that they are good and then imitates them. Steiner states:

> The child is completely given up to his environment. In adult life the only parallel to this devotion is in religion, expressed in the soul and spirit of man. . . . [The adult's] own soul and spirit are given up to the divine spirit of the world. The child gives up his whole being to his environment. In the adult the activities of breathing, digestion and circulation are within himself, cut off from the outside world. In the child all these activities are given up to his environment and are therefore by nature religious. This is the essential feature of the life of the children between birth and the change of teeth; his whole being is permeated by a kind of "natural-religious" element, and even the physical body is in a religious mood.[33]

In another lecture, Steiner clarifies:

> It is not the soul of the child that is given up to the environment, but its blood circulation, its breathing activities and processes of nourishment through the food it takes in. All these things are given up to the environment. The blood circulation, the breathing and the nourishment processes are praying to the environment. Naturally, such

expressions seem paradoxical, but in their very paradox they present the truth. [34]

If we observe such a thing with our whole being and not with the theoretical intellect, then we will develop an attitude or mood in being with young children that Steiner calls "priestly." Thus parents, child care providers, and early childhood teachers are like "caretakers of the divine" as they recognize divinity in the child and introduce him or her to earthly life through the sacred qualities of rhythm, beauty, and love.Although I feel it is beneficial to recognize the importance of our role with young children, I am the first to admit the shortcomings in my attitudes and actions in bringing up my own children and in being with young children in many given moments. However, we not only try to do the best we can, but we can also strive to do better, for the most important work of the parent with young children is inner work on oneself. The young child trustingly accepts us as perfect and good; once he becomes older and sees our imperfections, the most important thing is that the child sees we are striving to do better. Our desire for inner growth (or our complacency) is perceived by the child and has a very deep effect on him.

How can we help the child's natural development of religious feeling? Because the child is so given over to the environment, we help the child by furthering an attitude of gratitude in ourselves and hence in the child for all that the world gives us. Steiner explains:

> If he sees that everyone who stands in some kind of relationship to him in the outer world shows gratitude for what he receives from this world; if, in confronting the outer world and wanting to imitate it, the child sees the kind of gestures that express gratitude, then a great deal is done towards establishing in him the right moral human attitude. Gratitude is what belongs to the first seven years of life.[35]

Reverence is another attitude important to foster in early childhood. Steiner explains how this quality transforms:

> If one observes children who, by a right upbringing, have developed a natural reverence for the grownups in their surroundings, and if one follows them through their

various stages of life, one can discover that their feelings of reverence and devotion in childhood are gradually being transformed during the years leading to old age. As adults such persons may have a healing effect upon their fellow-men so that by their mere presence, or through the tone of their voice, or perhaps by a single glance they can spread inner peace to others. Their presence can be a blessing because as children they have learned to venerate and to pray in the right way. No hands can bless in old age, unless in childhood they have been folded in prayer.[36]

However, qualities such as reverence and prayer cannot be taught to a young child through doctrine or exhortation. They must live within the parents. If prayer is a living reality for the mother or father, then he or she can communicate that to the child and teach him, through example, about prayer. Think about your own childhood. What experiences brought you closer to the Divine? Which people seemed to have a special quality? Looking at spiritual questions can be another great gift that your children bring to you.

RECOMMENDED RESOURCES

Health and Illness

The practice of medicine directly inspired by Steiner's work has developed more extensively in continental Europe, with fewer practitioners in North America. These doctors and nurses work out of an inner effort to understand the entire human being and the meaning of illness, utilizing many things in addition to standard techniques: nutrition, massage, painting, eurythmy, sculpture, music, baths, herbal oils, and so forth. Further reading about this approach can be found in:

A Guide to Child Health, by Dr. Michaela Glöckler and Wolfgang Goebel (Floris Books).

An Introduction to Anthroposophical Medicine: Extending the Art of Healing, by Victor Bott, M.D. (SteinerBooks).

Lilipoh. A quarterly journal providing a forum for many different kinds of healing therapies, including anthroposophical medicine. See www.lilipoh.org.

Physicians' Association for Anthroposophical Medicine (PAAM). Provides information and a directory of physicians. See www.paam.net.

When a Child Is Born, by Wilhelm zur Linden, M.D. (Thorsons). Information on dealing with childhood illnesses.

Immunizing Your Children

"Childhood Illnesses, Vaccination, and Child Health," and other articles by Philip Incao, M.D., an anthroposophical doctor. See www.philip incao.com.

A Guide to Child Health, by Michaela Glöckler and Wolfgang Goebel (Floris Books). Considers childhood illnesses and immunizations from the view of anthroposophical medicine.

The Immunization Resource Guide, by Diane Rozario (Patter). An annotated listing of nearly everything in print concerning "where to find answers for all your questions about childhood immunizations." Available from Amazon.

The National Vaccine Information Center. A national nonprofit organization dedicated to public education. Numerous publications and legislative alerts. At www.nvic.org.

Vaccination: The Issue of Our Times. Articles, research, references, and resources by physicians, public health workers, and parents from *Mothering* magazine. See www.mothering.com.

The Vaccination Dilemma, edited by Christine Murphy (SteinerBooks).

Your County Health Department. Start here and proceed to the state health department, if necessary, to receive the official information on immunizations, risks, and legal requirements. Be sure to ask about exemptions and immunization registries as well.

Media and Children

Amusing Ourselves to Death, by Neil Postman (Viking).

The Child and the Machine: How Computers Put Our Children's Education at Risk, by Alison Armstrong and Charles Casement (Key Porter Books).

Endangered Minds: Why Children Can't Think and What We Can Do About It, by Jane M. Healy, Ph.D. (Simon & Schuster).

Failure to Connect: How Computers Affect Our Children's Minds—for Better and Worse, by Jane M. Healy, Ph.D. (Simon & Schuster).

Four Arguments for the Elimination of Television, by Jerry Mander (Harper Collins).

The Plug-In Drug, by Marie Winn (Penguin).

Unplugging the Plug-In Drug, by Marie Winn (Penguin).

Who's Bringing Them Up? by Martin Large (Hawthorn Press).

Religious Life

In the Light of a Child, by Michael Burton (SteinerBooks). Fifty-two verses for children inspired by Rudolf Steiner's *Calendar of the Soul*.

Living Passages for the Whole Family: Celebrating Rites of Passage from Birth to Adulthood, by Shea Darian (Gilead Press).

Prayers for Parents and Children, by Rudolf Steiner (SteinerBooks).

The Radiant Child, by Thomas Armstrong (Theosophical Publishing House).

Sanctuaries of Childhood: Nurturing a Child's Spiritual Life, by Shea Darian (Gilead Press).

The Spiritual Hunger of the Modern Child: A Series of Ten Lectures, by John G. Bennett et al. (Claymont Communications).

CHAPTER 13

Help for the Journey

CONSCIOUS PARENTING IS A PROCESS

Conscious parenting requires keeping perspective and not letting our-selves become so bogged down in the day-to-day task of raising our chil-dren that we neglect to focus on the larger picture. Part of our task is to see the spiritual in the mundane, to recognize the inner light in a child, or to see the ways in which a child's drawing, for instance, might give us a picture of his emerging consciousness. Another part of our task is to let the events or experiences of the everyday world lead us to questions and experiences of the divine. As we come to see the relationship of micro-cosm to macrocosm, to "see a world in a grain of sand . . . and eternity in an hour," we will find ourselves transformed in the process.

Conscious parenting also means using the events of everyday life—including our reactions to them—as grist for the mill of inner trans-formation. In this sense our children are our best teachers, for they provide endless opportunities for us to grow. We all have shortcomings and failings; there wouldn't be any growth if we didn't. But we need to have patience and kindness toward our own development and not be self-critical. Practicing kindness toward one's own shortcomings is as important as developing patience with others.

Parenting takes a tremendous amount of energy. If you don't keep your energy replenished, you become frazzled, harried, short-tempered, and otherwise hard to be around. Especially while your children are young, you need to make sure that you get adequate sleep. It helps to have some kind of meditation or prayer practice, even if it is only five minutes a day, which can help keep you centered. Creative activities such as art, music, sculpture, or dance are also unique in actually replenishing the kind of energy that children demand. Being in nature does this, too. When you're taking the baby out for a walk or taking your two-year-old to the park, cherish this time as something that can renew your energy as well.

Taking parenting seriously can remind you that what you are doing is important and worthwhile. Because nurturing work is undervalued and underpaid by our society, we can fall into the same trap of undervaluing it unless we put intentionality into what we are doing. Peggy O'Mara McMahon, editor of *Mothering*, states very clearly:

> I believe, however, that women will never be satisfied with a life that is an economic imitation of men's lives. Women must find a new way, a way of the spirit, and they must insist on an economic reality that acknowledges the concerns of the heart. If women are satisfied only to find success as men have found it, in the traditional market-place separate from the home, we will never create a better world. When women polarize over daycare and at-home mommies, they polarize over a male model of the separation of work and family that has not worked for men and is not now working for women. It doesn't work not because we need more daycare centers, but because the current social reality we emulate has no heart.
>
> We must seek broader solutions to the economics of family life, and we must be very careful not to fall into the trap of defining ourselves solely by the values of a society in transition.[1]

Viewing parenting as part of the path of love and service can help get you through the rough spots. Having children certainly opens your heart and makes you stretch, through constantly having to consider the needs of another person who is dependent on you—and whom you must gradually release. Parenting can be a rich source of life experiences in the course of one's development as a human being, if you use what is given to you for self-knowledge and transformation. In her article "An Ethic of Parenting," O'Mara McMahon describes the inner work of parenting as follows:

> In our society, we are not accustomed to the surrender and service required by the human infant. In order to sustain an ethic of parenting that honors the necessity of surrender and service, we will have to surround ourselves with the kind of support and information that will enable us to overcome the limitations. . . .
>
> Serve your child—for in serving your child, in trusting your child, you serve yourself and give yourself an opportunity to be reparented and reloved. The greatest kept secret of the world is the personal transformation inherent in developing an ethic of parenting that is truly in keeping with the nature of the child. Parenting with this type of ethic releases the full potential of the human being, a force greater than anything we have yet to see on this planet.[2]

IN CONCLUSION

All parents want what is best for their child, but most first-time parents know very little about children or parenting (I certainly didn't!). Learning as you go is often uncomfortable, but it can provide many opportunities for growth for parents as well as for our children. As our children's first teachers, we can and must provide the love and warmth, calm and rhythm, interest and enthusiasm vital to their growth. They also provide us with new areas of study, work, and self-examination as we come up against our shortcomings and the new dilemmas our children present to us.

What is needed today is not another expert, some new authority to follow or to reject, but a new way of seeing the human being that takes into account all aspects of development—physical, emotional, intellectual, and spiritual—so we and our children can meet the challenges of our changing world and fulfill the purposes of our time on earth.

We are living in a time of transition, a time in which the old patterns of society no longer hold us. We are being called upon to approach all aspects of our lives with new awareness. Life in our families, cities, churches, and schools is changing at an ever-increasing rate as we struggle to find our balance and then create something new.

We can't go back to a milk-and-cookies mentality that denies the changes that have led to the present. However, we need to recognize that the world of the young child is critically endangered today, as more and more children are placed in child care beginning in infancy and academics are pushed onto younger and younger children. It has become even more urgent that we understand that children are not little adults. They do not think, reason, feel, or experience the world as an adult does. Instead, they are centered in their bodies and in the will, which manifests in such powerful growth and the need for movement in the first seven years. They learn primarily and more appropriately through example and imitation. Repetition and rhythm are also vital elements in the healthy world of the young child and need to be emphasized by parents and others responsible for the care of young children.

The young child takes in everything without blocks or filters, and for this reason we must put special attention into the quality of his or her environment and experiences. There needs to be a balance between stimulating and protecting the baby's and young child's senses. Stimulation from artificial sources (movies, recordings, synthetic fabrics) has a different impact on the young child than stimulation from your own voice or objects from nature. Because the young child is all sense organ, we need to be selective in what we let our children experience and help guard against violating the young child's natural dreamy state.

Everything in life is taken in deeply by the young child, to be transformed and expressed later in creative play. Providing the time and appropriate materials for this kind of play helps the child work his way into earthly life by imitating, through his play, everything that he experiences. Allowing this natural impulse of creative imagination to flourish is one of the greatest gifts parents can give their child between birth and first grade.

The young child also has a natural artistic and musical ability, which can be furthered by allowing its free expression without lessons or pressure to produce something in a certain way. Songs, rhythmical move-ment, and circle games all speak to the magical world of early childhood.

Just as it is important that children crawl before they walk (and that they do not skip other developmental steps), it is equally important that children not be prematurely awakened from the dreamy, imaginative world of early childhood before the natural time for this, around the age of six or seven. Lessons, workbooks, and academic tasks not only take the child away from movement and valuable play, but they also acceler-ate the child's change of consciousness and rob him of the last valuable years of early childhood—years that are vital to a person's later physical health as well as mental and creative development. Trying to speed up development in young children places them at risk, with no apparent gain to justify such risks.

As our children's first teachers, there is a lot we can do, as well as many things that are better if we don't do! It is my hope that this book will contribute to parents' understanding of the special nature of the young child and his or her unique needs. If we can take both knowledge and practical experience into our hearts, we will have increased confi-dence as we develop our own ethic of parenting and make our own best choices for our children. The challenges are great, but so are the rewards!

APPENDIX:
RUDOLF STEINER AND
WALDORF EDUCATION

Rudolf Steiner (1861–1925) spent his early adult years preparing the scientific writings of Goethe for republication. A. P. Shepherd, a canon of the Anglican Church, says of him, "Steiner thought, spoke and wrote as a scientist. . . . Although his own investigations carried him into fields far beyond the range of physical science, he always carried into these investigations, and into the application of them to physical phenomena, the concepts and methods of scientific thought."[1]

In the early 1900s, Steiner began to lecture and write extensively, imparting knowledge about the realms beyond the physical and our connection with them. During the last six years of his life, he was active in applying his spiritual scientific knowledge in various fields such as education, agriculture, arts, medicine, theology, and so forth. To help carry on his work as a force for personal and cultural renewal, he founded the Anthroposophical Society ("anthroposophy" comes from the roots "anthro," meaning "man," and "sophia," meaning "wisdom"). The society now has working groups and branches all over the world.

Steiner turned his attention to education after the First World War at the request of Emil Molt, who helped him found a school for the children of the factory workers at the Waldorf-Astoria cigarette factory in Stuttgart, Germany, in 1919. The impulse for "Waldorf education," as it came to be called, spread throughout Europe, with the first school in America being founded in New York City in 1928.

Steiner was a pioneer in the area of developmentally based, age-appropriate learning, and many of his indications were later borne out by the work of Gesell and Piaget and by later brain research in the 1990s. In addition, he sought to develop a balanced education for the "whole child," one that would engage the child's feeling and willing as well as thinking and would leave his or her spiritual nature acknowledged but free. From preschool through high school, the goal of Waldorf education is the same, but the means differ according to the changing inner development of the child. According to Steiner, "Our highest endeavor must be to develop free human beings, who are able of themselves to impart purpose and direction to their lives."

Because of this emphasis, the Waldorf schools were closed by the Nazis during World War II, but they soon reopened, and they have spread in the past several decades to such troubled areas as South Africa, the Middle East, Eastern Europe, and Russia. Waldorf has become the largest private school movement in the world. In 2011 there were 1,003 schools, 2,000 kindergartens, and 629 curative (special education) centers in 60 countries based on Rudolf Steiner's pedagogical impulse. Growth of the movement in America has been very rapid since 1980.

During the early childhood years, the child is surrounded by a homelike environment that encourages imaginative free play and artistic activity. Steiner recognized that the young child learns primarily through example and imitation, with an emphasis on the importance of movement, rhythm, fairy tales, and oral language. Steiner felt that it is not healthy for children to concentrate on cognitive skills such as reading, writing, and math until the body has reached a certain level of maturity, freeing the forces of growth for cognitive work. Typical daily activities in preschool and kindergarten include free play, movement games, story circles, and craft or artistic activities (watercolor painting, beeswax modeling, coloring with beeswax crayons, baking, and so forth). Puppet plays, nature walks, and celebrating festivals are frequent events throughout the year. The work of LifeWays North America took the indications of Rudolf Steiner as its foundation in supporting parents and professionals in caring for children from birth through age six.

In Waldorf elementary schools (grades one through eight), all of the subjects are presented in a lively and pictorial way, because Steiner

THE WALDORF CURRICULUM

1ST GRADE	2ND GRADE	3RD GRADE	4TH GRADE

Language Arts
• writing
• phonics
• reading
• fairy tales
Mathematics
• add./subtr.
• mult./div.
German*
French*
Beeswax
  Modeling
Painting
Knitting
Recorder
Phys. Ed.
	Language Arts
	• extended skills
	• legends and
	  fables
	Mathematics
	• +, -, x, ÷
	• telling time
	• money
	German*
	French*
	Beeswax
	  Modeling
	Painting
	Crochet
	Recorder
	Phys. Ed.
		Language Arts
		• extended skills
		• grammar
		• letter writing
		• Old Testament
		  stories
		Mathematics
		• extended skills
		• measurement
		German*
		French*
		Farming
		Painting
		Crafts
		Recorder
		String Instr.
		Phys. Ed.
			Language Arts
			• grammar
			• drama
			• Norse myths
			Mathematics
			• adv. skills
			• fractions
			German*
			French*
			Zoology
			Local History
			State History and
			  Geography
			Embroidery
			Recorder
			String or Wind
			  Instr.
			Phys. Ed.

5TH GRADE	6TH GRADE	7TH GRADE	8TH GRADE

Language Arts
• extended skills
• stories of
  ancient
  cultures and
  Greece
Mathematics
• adv. skills
• decimals
• fractions
German*
French*
Botany
Greek History
U.S. Geography
Crafts
Recorder
Orchestra
Phys. Ed.
	Language Arts
	• biography
	Pre-algebra
	Geometry
	German*
	French *
	Greek and Latin
	Physics
	Roman History
	World Geography
	Woodworking
	Recorder
	Orchestra
	Choral Singing
	Gardening
	Phys. Ed.
		Language Arts
		• biography
		• drama
		Algebra
		Geometry
		German*
		French*
		Greek and Latin
		Physics
		Chemistry
		Astronomy
		Med./Ren. Hist.
		World Geography
		Woodworking
		Sewing
		Recorder
		Orchestra
		Choral Singing
		Gardening
		Phys. Ed.
			Language Arts
			• biography
			• drama
			Algebra
			Geometry
			German*
			French*
			Greek and Latin
			Physics
			Chemistry
			Physiology
			U.S. and Modern
			  History
			World Geography
			Woodworking
			Sewing
			Recorder
			Orchestra
			Choral Singing
			Gardening
			Phys. Ed.

*Languages vary by schoool, including Spanish, Russian, Chinese, etc.

found that children of this age learn best when information is artistically and imaginatively presented. The same teacher stays with the children from the first through eighth grade, teaching the "main lesson" subjects, which include language arts, mathematics, history, and the sciences. The main lesson is taught during the first two hours of the morning in blocks of three to six weeks per topic. Students create their own "main lesson books" as artistic records of their learning rather than using textbooks or worksheets. During the rest of the day special subject teachers fill out the curriculum with two foreign languages, orchestra, singing, arts, crafts, gardening, eurythmy (a movement art developed by Steiner), and physical education (see the chart on page 288).

The adolescent's emerging powers of analytical thinking are met and developed in the Waldorf high school, where subjects are taught by specialists in their fields. The role of the teacher is seen as helping the students develop their own thinking powers. A key to this process is presenting students with an immediate experience of phenomena, such as hands-on experiments or primary sources in literature and history, instead of presenting them with predigested work from textbooks or anthologies. The rapidly changing psychological nature of the adolescent is addressed through each year's studies being tailored to the central "questions" that typically live in the hearts of students of that grade level.

A complete list of Waldorf schools can be obtained from the Association of Waldorf Schools of North America at www.awsna.org.

NOTES

Chapter 1
You Are Your Child's First Teacher

1. Barbara Kantrowitz, "Off to a Good Start," in "Your Child from Birth to Three," *Newsweek* Special Edition, Spring/Summer 1997, p. 8.

2. Burton L. White, *The First Three Years of Life* (New York: Prentice-Hall, 1985), p. 4.

3. Ibid., p. 5.

4. Ibid., p. 90.

5. Rudolf Steiner, "The Child Before the Seventh Year," lecture delivered in Dornach, Switzerland, December 23, 1921, reported by Albert Steffen in *Lectures to Teachers* (London: The Library of the Anthroposophical Society in Great Britain, 1948), p. 39.

6. Kantrowitz, "Off to a Good Start."

7. Rudolf Steiner, quoted by Werner Glas in lectures at the Waldorf Institute, October 1980.

8. Betty Friedan, *The Second Stage* (Cambridge, MA: Harvard University Press, 1998 [1981]).

9. Fern Schumer Chapman, "Executive Guilt: Who's Taking Care of the Children?" *Fortune*, February 16, 1987.

10. David Elkind, *Miseducation: Preschoolers at Risk* (New York: Alfred A. Kopf, 1987), p. 120.

11. Rudolf Steiner, *Philosophy of Freedom* (Spring Valley, NY: Anthroposophic Press, 1964).

12. For accounts of the spiritual aspects of conception and pregnancy, see Jeannine Parvati Baker et al., *Conscious Conception* (Monroe, UT: Freestone,

1986), and Murshida Vera Justin Corda, *Cradle of Heaven* (Lebanon Springs, NY: Omega Press, 1987).

13. Quoted in Sharon Begley, "How to Build a Baby's Brain," in *Newsweek* Special Edition, Spring/Summer 1997, p. 30.

14. Ibid., p. 31.

15. Quoted in Jerry Adler, "It's a Wise Father Who Knows . . . ," *Newsweek* Special Edition, Spring/Summer 1997, p. 73.

Chapter 2
Home Life as the Basis for All Learning

1. Betty Friedan, *The Feminine Mystique* (New York: Norton & Co., 1997 [1963]).

2. Friedan, *The Second Stage*.

3. Jean Liedloff, *The Continuum Concept* (Boston, MA: Addison-Wesley, 1993 [1975]).

4. Barbara Dewey, "Play with Your Child?" *Herb 'n Home Newsletter*, July 1998, p. 8.

5. Ibid.

6. Gudrun Davy and Bons Voors, eds., *Lifeways* (Gloucestershire, UK: Hawthorn Press, 1983).

7. Kim John Payne, *Simplicity Parenting* (New York: Ballantine Books, 2009).

8. Kathryn Black, *Mothering without a Map* (New York: Penguin Books, 2004).

9. Cynthia Aldinger and Mary O'Connell, *Home Away from Home: LifeWays Care of Children and Families* (Norman, OK: LifeWays North America, 2010).

Chapter 3
Birth to Three: Growing Down and Waking Up

1. Jane Healy, *Your Child's Growing Mind*, rev. ed. (New York: Doubleday, 1994), p. 30.

2. Jean Ayers, *Sensory Integration and Learning Disorders* (Los Angeles: Western Psychological Services, 1973).

3. White, *The First Three Years of Life*, p. 60.

4. "Pediatric Notes," March 26, 1987, p. 46, summarized in *Pediatrics for Parents* 8, no. 6 (June 1987).

5. *Canadian Medical Association Journal*, January 1, 1987, p. 57, summarized in *Pediatrics for Parents* 8, no. 6 (June 1987).

6. "Pediatric Notes."

7. White, *The First Three Years of Life*, p. 80.

8. Rudolf Steiner, lectures delivered in Dornach, Switzerland, April 15–22, 1923, reported by Albert Steffen in *Swiss Teachers' Course* (London: The Library of the Anthroposophical Society in Great Britain, n.d.).

9. Rudolf Steiner, "Pneumatosophy: The Riddles of the Inner Human Being," lecture delivered in Berlin, Germany, May 23, 1923 (Spring Valley, NY: Anthroposophic Press), p. 2.

10. Steiner, "The Child Before the Seventh Year."

11. Shea Darian, *Seven Times the Sun: Guiding Your Child Through the Rhythms of the Day* (Phoenix, AZ: Gilead Press, 2001 [1994]).

12. Geoffrey Cowley, "The Language Explosion," *Newsweek* Special Edition, Spring/Summer 1997, p. 20.

13. Begley, "How to Build a Baby's Brain," p. 31.

14. Cowley, "The Language Explosion," p. 21.

15. Karl König, *The First Three Years of the Child* (Spring Valley, NY: Anthroposophic Press, 1969), p. 24.

16. Daniel Udo de Haes, *The Young Child* (Spring Valley, NY: Anthroposophic Press, 1986), p. 24.

17. Ibid.

18. Steiner, "Pneumatosophy," p. 3.

19. "A Baby's 'Ga-ga' Speaks Volumes," *Los Angeles Times*, republished in the *Sacramento Bee*, January 1, 1999, p. A8.

20. Cowley, "The Language Explosion," p. 21.

21. Reprinted from p. 19 of Lois Cusick, *Waldorf Parenting Handbook*, by permission of the publishers, St. George Publications, Spring Valley, New York, 1984.

22. Rudolf Steiner, lectures delivered in Torquay, England, Summer 1924, quoted in Elizabeth Grunelius, *Early Childhood Education and the Waldorf School Plan* (Englewood, NJ: Waldorf School Monographs, 1974), p. 42.

23. Rainer Patzlaff et al., *The Child from Birth to Three in Waldorf Education and Child Care* (Spring Valley, NY: Waldorf Early Childhood Association of North America, 2011), p. 20.

24. Payne, *Simplicity Parenting*.

25. White, *The First Three Years of Life*, p. 157.

Chapter 4
Helping Your Baby's Development

1. Sister MorningStar, "Welcoming Sophie," *Midwifery Today* 99 (Autumn 2011).

2. Karl Konig, *Eternal Childhood* (N. Yorkshire, UK: Camphill Press, 1994), p. 33.

3. Frederick Leboyer, *Birth without Violence* (New York: Alfred Knopf, 2009 [1975]).

4. Begley, "How to Build a Baby's Brain," pp. 30–31.

5. Debra Rosenberg and Larry Reibstein, "Pots, Blocks & Socks," *Newsweek* Special Edition, Spring/Summer 1997, p. 34.

6. Rudolf Steiner, *The Spiritual Ground of Education* (London: Rudolf Steiner Press, 1947), p. 38.

7. See www.mothering.com for the topic "babywearing" and reprints of "Babywearing 101" and other articles.

8. Reported in *Lancet* 2 (1983), p. 1014.

9. White, *The First Three Years of Life*, p. 19.

10. Rudolf Steiner, *The Education of the Child* (London: Rudolf Steiner Press, 1965), p. 24.

11. Rudolf Steiner in a lecture delivered January 30, 1913, and quoted in *The Waldorf Kindergarten Newsletter*, Winter 1987, p. 15. For an inspiring description of one mother's work with this picture, see Joan Salter, *Mothering with Soul* (Gloucestershire, UK: Hawthorn Press, 1998), pp. 17–21.

12. Helle Heckmann, *Nøkken: A Garden for Children* (Silver Spring, MD: Waldorf Early Childhood Association, 1998), p. 4.

13. Ibid., p. 16.

14. References quoted in Robert B. McCall, "Support Thy Wife," *Parents*, July 1987, pp. 168–69.

15. See work by Audrey McAllen, available through the Remedial Research Group, 9200 Fair Oaks Blvd., Fair Oaks, California 95628.

16. Joseph Chilton Pearce, *Magical Child* (New York: E. P. Dutton, 1977).

17. White, *The First Three Years of Life*, p. 102.

18. Healy, *Your Child's Growing Mind*, pp. 47–48.

19. Ibid., pp. 29, 39.

20. White, *The First Three Years of Life*, p. 106.

21. Ibid., 91.

22. Ibid.

23. Healy, *Your Child's Growing Mind*, p. 33.

24. Heckmann, *Nøkken*, p. 18.

Chapter 5
Helping Your Toddler's Development

1. Elkind, *Miseducation*.

2. Begley, "How to Build a Baby's Brain," p. 31.

3. White, *The First Three Years of Life*, p. 176.

4. Ibid., p. 151.

5. Ibid., p. 181.

6. Udo de Haes, *The Young Child*.

7. Ibid., p. 61.

8. Ibid.

9. Ibid., p. 65.

10. Ibid., p. 72.

11. Steiner, *The Education of the Child*, p. 26.

12. Heidi Britz-Crecelius, *Children at Play: Preparation for Life* (New York: Inner Traditions International, 1986), pp. 94–96.

13. Steiner, *The Education of the Child*, pp. 25–26.

14. For detailed directions on making knot dolls, see Susan Smith, *Echoes of a Dream* (London, Ontario: Waldorf School Association of London, 1982); or Freya Jaffke, *Toymaking with Children* (Edinburgh, UK: Floris, 1988).

Chapter 6
Rhythm in Home Life

1. Grunelius, *Early Childhood Education*, p. 28.

2. Rudolf Steiner, *Signs and Symbols of the Christmas Festival* (Spring Valley, NY: Anthroposophic Press, 1969).

3. Grunelius, *Early Childhood Education*, p. 27.

4. Ibid.

5. Andrea Gambardella, "Rhythm in Home Life," *Waldorf Kindergarten Newsletter*, Fall 1984, p. 10.

6. Bons Voors, "Family Meals," in Davy and Voors, eds., *Lifeways*, pp. 154–60.

7. Darian, *Seven Times the Sun*, pp. 41–58.

8. Margret Meyerkort, "Sleeping and Waking," in Davy and Voors, eds., *Lifeways*, pp. 142–53.

9. Darian, *Seven Times the Sun*, pp. 133–48.

10. Meyerkort, "Sleeping and Waking," p. 150.

11. Rudolf Steiner, *Prayers for Mothers and Children* (London: Rudolf Steiner Press, 1983), p. 50.

12. Friedel Lenz, *Celebrating the Festivals with Children* (Spring Valley, NY: Anthroposophic Press, 1986).

13. Diana Carey and Judy Large, *Festivals, Family and Food* (Gloucestershire, UK: Hawthorn Press, 1982).

14. Margret Meyerkort, ed., *Spring* (West Midlands, UK: Wynstones Press, 1983). Available from Rudolf Steiner College, 9200 Fair Oaks Blvd., Fair Oaks, California 95628.

Chapter 7
Discipline and Other Parenting Issues

1. Marshall Rosenberg, Ph.D., *Nonviolent Communication: A Language of Life* (Encinitas, CA: PuddleDancer Press, 2003).

2. Harvey Karp, MD, *The Happiest Toddler on the Block* (New York: Bantam Dell, 2003).

3. Margret Meyerkort, "Creative Discipline," in Davy and Voors, eds., *Lifeways*, pp. 214–23.

4. Rudolf Steiner, *Soul Economy and Waldorf Education* (Spring Valley, NY: Anthroposophic Press, 1986), p. 121.

5. Ibid., p. 115.

6. Grunelius, *Early Childhood Education*, p. 29.

7. Regina Sara Ryan, *The Woman Awake* (Prescott, AZ: Hohm Press, 1998).

8. Tine Thevenin, *The Family Bed* (Garden City, NY: Avery, 1987).

9. Norbert Glas, *Conception, Birth and Early Childhood* (Spring Valley, NY: Anthroposophic Press, 1972).

10. Salter, *Mothering with Soul*, pp. 49–52.

11. Wilhelm zur Linden, *When a Child Is Born* (New York: Thorsons Publishers, 1984).

12. Michaela Glöcker and Wolfgang Goebel, *A Guide to Child Health* (Hudson, NY: Anthroposophic Press, 1984).

13. Aletha Jauch Solter, *Exercises in Self-Awareness for New Parents* (Goleta, CA: Shining Star Press, 1984).

14. Aletha Jauch Solter, *The Aware Baby* (Goleta, CA: Shining Star Press, 1984).

15. Vimala Schneider, "Crying," *Mothering*, Spring 1987, p. 23.

16. David Sobel, *Waldorf Teacher Training Newsletter*, Spring 1987, p. 5.

17. Heckmann, *Nøkken,* pp. 10–12.

18. Melissa Healy, "Study Links Good Daycare, Success in Early Grades," *Sacramento Bee*, June 9, 1999, p. A5.

19. T. Berry Brazelton, *Working and Caring* (Reading, MA: Addison-Wesley, 1985).

20. White, *The First Three Years of Life*, p. 272.

21. Kim Boatman, "Parenting Guru's Push for Bigger Diapers Embraced by Consumers," *Sacramento Bee*, January 2, 1999.

22. Ibid.

Chapter 8
Nourishing Your Child's Imagination and Creative Play

1. Caroline von Heydebrand, *Childhood: A Study of the Growing Soul* (London: Anthroposophic Publishing Co., 1946), p. 60.

2. Britz-Crecelius, *Children at Play*, p. 7.

3. Caroline von Heydebrand, "The Child at Play," in *Education as an Art: Rudolf Steiner and Other Writers*, ed. Paul M. Allen (Blauvelt, NY: SteinerBooks/Multimedia Publishing, 1970), p. 89.

4. Britz-Crecelius, *Children at Play*, p. 32.

5. Richard Louv, *Last Child in the Woods* (Chapel Hill, NC: Algonquin Books, 2008).

6. Bruno Bettelheim, *The Uses of Enchantment: The Meaning and Importance of Fairy Tales* (New York: Alfred A. Knopf, 1975), p. 46.

7. Britz-Crecelius, *Children at Play*, pp. 79–101.

8. Ibid., p. 92.

9. Bruno Bettelheim, "The Importance of Play," *Atlantic Monthly*, March 1987, p. 40.

10. Britz-Crecelius, *Children at Play*, p. 97.

11. Ibid.

12. Bettelheim, *The Uses of Enchantment*, p. 37.

13. Ibid., p. 36.

14. See www.allianceforchildhood.org and their report, *Crisis in the Kindergarten: Why Children Need to Play in School* (College Park, MD: Alliance for Childhood, 2009).

15. Helle Heckmann, "Imagination Surpasses Reality—Also When It Comes to Toys," unpublished handout at her lecture, Ann Arbor, Michigan, April 1998.

16. Dr. Gilbert Childs and Sylvia Childs, *Your Reincarnating Child* (London: Rudolf Steiner Press, 1995), p. 89.

17. Ibid., p. 107.

18. Quoted in Britz-Crecelius, *Children at Play*, p. 81.

19. Heckmann, "Imagination Surpasses Reality."

20. Dr. Karen N. Olness, "Little People, Images and Child Health," *American Journal of Clinical Hypnosis* 27, no. 3 (January 1985).

21. Barry Sanders, *A Is for Ox: The Collapse of Literacy and the Rise of Violence in an Electronic Age* (New York: Pantheon Books, 1994), p. 243.

22. Joan Almon, "Choosing Fairy Tales for Young Children," *Waldorf Kindergarten Newsletter*, Fall 1985, p. 7.

23. See Helmut von Kügelgen, "Fairy Tale Language and the Image of Man," *Waldorf Kindergarten Newsletter*, Fall 1986, and Rudolf Steiner, *The Interpretation of Fairy Tales* (Spring Valley, NY: Anthroposophic Press, 1943).

24. Diana Hughes, "Fairy Tales: A Basis for Moral Education," *Ethics in Education* 6, no. 4 (March 1987): 11.

25. Ibid., p. 12.

26. Bettelheim, *The Uses of Enchantment*, p. 9.

27. Hughes, "Fairy Tales," p. 11.

28. Bettelheim, *The Uses of Enchantment*.

29. Neil Postman, *The Disappearance of Childhood* (New York: Dell Publishing, 1982), pp. 93–94.

30. Almon, "Choosing Fairy Tales for Young Children."

31. Udo de Haes, *The Young Child*, p. 52.

Chapter 9
Developing Your Child's Artistic Ability

1. Michaela Strauss, *Understanding Children's Drawings* (London: Rudolf Steiner Press, 1978).

2. Ibid., pp. 22, 29.

3. Ibid., p. 47.

4. Ibid., p. 62.

5. Isabel Wyatt, *Seven-Year-Old Wonder-Book* (San Rafael, CA: Dawn-Leigh Publications, 1978).

6. Rauld Russell, "Wet-on-Wet Watercolor Painting," *Mothering*, Summer 1987, p. 89.

7. Steiner, *The Education of the Child*, p . 27.

8. Johann Wolfgang von Goethe, *Theory of Colours* (Totowa, NJ: Biblio Distribution Center, 1967).

9. Rudolf Steiner, *Practical Advice for Teachers* (London: Rudolf Steiner Press, 1970), p. 11.

10. Brunhild Müller, *Painting with Children* (Edinburgh, UK: Floris Books, 1987), p. 11.

11. Russell, "Wet-on-Wet Watercolor Painting," p. 90.

12. Ibid., p. 89.

13. Caroline von Heydebrand, "The Child When He Paints," in *Education as an Art: Rudolf Steiner and Other Writers*, ed. Paul M. Allen (Blauvelt, NY: SteinerBooks/Multimedia Publishing, 1970), p. 86.

14. Freya Jaffke, "About Painting and Human Development through Art," translated from *Plan und Praxis des Waldorfkindergartens* and printed in the *Waldorf Kindergarten Newsletter*, Fall 1984.

15. Ibid.

16. Ibid.

17. Julia Cameron, *The Artist's Way: A Spiritual Path to Higher Creativity* (New York: Tarcher/Putnam, 1992), p. 35.

Chapter 10
Encouraging Your Child's Musical Ability

1. Julius Knierim, *Quintenlieder: Music for Young Children in the Mood of the Fifth,* trans. Karen and Peter Klaveness (Fair Oaks, CA: Rudolf Steiner College Press, 2002).

2. Rudolf Steiner, *Practical Course for Teachers* (London: Rudolf Steiner Press, 1937), pp. 18–19.

3. Vadim Prokhorov, "Will Piano Lessons Make My Child Smarter?" *Parade Magazine,* June 14, 1999, p. 15.

4. Quoted in Pamela G. Kripke, "Get the Beat, Baby," *American Baby,* February 1998, p. 51.

5. Rudolf Steiner, *The Kingdom of Childhood* (London: Rudolf Steiner Press, 1974), p. 110.

6. Knierim, *Quintenlieder.*

7. Eileen Hutchins, "The Value of Fairy Tales and Nursery Rhymes," in *Child and Man Extracts* (Sussex, UK: Steiner Schools Fellowship, n.d.), p. 44.

8. Rosemary Gebert, in a lecture delivered at the Waldorf Institute, Southfield, MI, October 1981.

9. Jane Winslow Eliot, *From Ring Around the Roses to London Bridge Is Falling Down: Some Incarnating Games* (New York: Rudolf Steiner School Press, 1982), p. 1.

10. Steiner, *The Education of the Child,* p. 29.

11. Music in the "mood of the fifth" is a special kind of pentatonic music that is discussed in Julius Knierim's *Quintenlieder.* Readers interested in the healing and other esoteric aspects of music are referred to Rudolf Steiner's work *The Inner Nature of Music and the Experience of Tone* (Spring Valley, NY: Anthroposophic Press, 1983).

12. Rudolf Steiner, course of lectures delivered at the foundation of the Waldorf school in Stuttgart, Germany, August 21 to September 5, 1919, and quoted in Grunelius, *Early Childhood Education,* p. 45.

13. "Head Trauma Questions," *USA Weekend,* January 3, 1999.

Chapter 11
Cognitive Development and Early Childhood Education

1. Elkind, *Miseducation*, pp. 119–22.

2. Grunelius, *Early Childhood Education*, p. 26.

3. Jodie Morse, "Preschool for Everyone," *Time*, November 9, 1998, p. 98.

4. "Kids Need Time to Be Kids," *Newsweek*, February 22, 1987, p. 57.

5. Steiner, *The Education of the Child*, p. 21.

6. Healy, *Your Child's Growing Mind*, pp. 49–50.

7. Ibid., p. 238.

8. Ibid., p. 240.

9. Ibid., p. 265.

10. Healy, *Failure to Connect* (New York: Simon & Schuster, 1998), p. 241.

11. Healy, *Your Child's Growing Mind*, p. 63.

12. S. W. Haughland, "The Effects of Computer Software on Preschool Children's Developmental Gains," *Journal of Computing in Childhood Education* 3, no. 1 (1992): 15–30.

13. "Kids Need Time to Be Kids," p. 58.

14. Ibid., p. 56.

15. Ibid., pp. 57–58.

16. Joan Almon, "What Are the Needs of the Five-Year-Olds?" *Leading Forth, Journal of the Waldorf School of Baltimore* 4 (Spring 1988): 5–6.

17. Steiner, *The Education of the Child*, pp. 28–29.

18. Aldinger and O'Connell, *Home Away from Home*.

19. Diana Loercher Pazicky, "Just Because a Child Is the Right Age Doesn't Mean He's Ready for School," *Philadelphia Inquirer*, April 22, 1984.

20. James K. Uphoff and June Gilmore, "Pupil Age at School Entrance—How Many Are Ready for Success?" *Educational Leadership*, September 1985, pp. 86–90.

21. Pazicky, "Just Because a Child Is the Right Age."

22. Healy, *Your Child's Growing Mind*, p. 55.

23. Audrey McAllen, "On First Grade Readiness: An Interview with Margret Meyerkort," *Bulletin of the Remedial Research Group* No. 5, August 1986 (Fair Oaks, CA: Remedial Research Group at Rudolf Steiner College), pp. 12–15.

24. Bruno Bettelheim and Karen Zelan, "Why Children Don't Like to Read," *Atlantic Monthly*, November 1981.

Chapter 12
Common Parenting Questions:
From Television to Immunizations

1. Elkind, *The Hurried Child*, and Elkind, *Miseducation*.

2. Healy, *Failure to Connect*, p. 110.

3. Todd Oppenheimer, "The Computer Delusion," *Atlantic Monthly*, July 1997, pp. 45–62.

4. Healy, *Failure to Connect*, p. 133.

5. Rudolf Steiner, from a course of lectures delivered in Oxford, England, in the summer of 1922, quoted in Grunelius, *Early Childhood Education*, p. 43.

6. Rudolf Steiner, *Human Values in Education*, lectures delivered in Arnheim, Switzerland, July 17–24, 1924 (London: Rudolf Steiner Press, 1971), p. 55.

7. John Rosemond, "Children and Television," *Boston Globe*, January 3, 1984.

8. Audrey McAllen, "Movement or Television," *Bulletin of the Remedial Research Group* (Fair Oaks, CA: Rudolf Steiner College, n.d.).

9. Rosemond, "Children and Television."

10. Healy, *Failure to Connect*, p. 32.

11. Ibid., pp. 112–15.

12. Ibid., pp. 114–15.

13. Marie Winn, *The Plug-In Drug* (New York: Viking, 1985).

14. Study by BJK&E Media Group of Manhattan, reported in David Bauder, "Children Today Watching More and More TV, Study Shows," *Ann Arbor News*, December 30, 1997.

15. *Education Week*, February 14, 1996, p. 32; quoted in Healy, *Failure to Connect*, p. 104.

16. Karen Kaplan, "Army, Hollywood to Co-star in Research," *Sacramento Bee*, August 18, 1999, p. A4.

17. Healy, *Failure to Connect*, p. 180.

18. Robert W. Kubey, letter to the editor, *New York Times*, December 25, 1997, p. A14.

19. Healy, *Failure to Connect*, pp. 158–59.

20. See Otto Wolff, "Childhood Diseases as a Source of Development," *Weleda News* 4 (1983): 14–15.

21. Dr. Uwe Stave, "Reflections on Fever in Childhood," *Journal for Anthroposophy* 42 (Autumn 1985): 9.

22. Ibid., p. 10.

23. In addition to Western allopathic medicine, other systems such as home-opathy, naturopathy, and anthroposophical or ayurvedic medicine also can provide helpful approaches.

24. zur Linden, *When a Child Is Born*, pp. 163–64.

25. T. Berry Brazelton, *Infants and Mothers: Differences in Development* (New York: Dell, 1986).

26. Rudolf Steiner, *The Four Temperaments* (London: Rudolf Steiner Press, 2008).

27. John. G. Bennett et al., *The Spiritual Hunger of the Modern Child: A Series of Ten Lectures* (Charles Town, WV: Claymont Communications, 1984).

28. René Knight-Weiler, *Spiritual Mothering Journal*, Summer 1986, pp. 28–29.

29. Ibid.

30. Joseph Chilton Pearce, *Magical Child Matures* (New York: Bantam, 1986).

31. Shea Darian, *Sanctuaries of Childhood* (Phoenix, AZ: Gilead Press, 2011) and *Living Passages for the Whole Family* (Phoenix, AZ: Gilead Press, 2008).

32. Rudolf Steiner, *Study of Man* (London: Anthroposophic Press, 1947), p. 138.

33. Rudolf Steiner, *The Roots of Education* (London: Rudolf Steiner Press, 1968), pp. 37–38.

34. Rudolf Steiner, *The Essentials of Education* (London: Rudolf Steiner Press, 1948), p. 29.

35. Steiner, *Human Values in Education*, p. 125.

36. Rudolf Steiner, *The Renewal of Education* (Forest Row, UK: Steiner Schools Fellowship Publications, 1981), p. 65.

Chapter 13
Help for the Journey

1. Peggy O'Mara McMahon, "An Ethic of Parenting," *Mothering* 47, Spring 1988, p. 6.

2. Ibid., p. 7.

Appendix
Rudolf Steiner and Waldorf Education

1. Quoted in Joan Salter, *The Incarnating Child* (Gloucestershire, UK: Hawthorn Press, 1987), p. 146.

BIBLIOGRAPHY

Aldinger, Cynthia, and Mary O'Connell. *Home Away from Home: LifeWays Care of Children and Families.* Norman, OK: LifeWays North America, 2010.

Al-Gailani, Noorah, and Chris Smith. *The Islamic Year: Surahs, Stories and Celebrations.* Gloucestershire, UK: Hawthorn Press, 2003.

Alliance for Childhood. *Tech Tonic: Towards a New Literacy of Technology.* College Park, MD: Alliance for Childhood, 2004.

Almon, Joan. "Choosing Fairy Tales for Young Children." *Waldorf Kindergarten Newsletter*, Fall 1985.

Almon, Joan, and Edward Miller. *Crisis in the Kindergarten.* College Park, MD: Alliance for Childhood, 2009.

Baker, Jeannine Parvati, et al. *Conscious Conception.* Monroe, UT: Freestone, 1986.

Baldwin Dancy, Rahima. *Special Delivery.* Berkeley, CA: Celestial Arts, 1986.

Baldwin Dancy, Rahima, and Terra Palmarini Richardson. *Pregnant Feelings.* Berkeley, CA: Celestial Arts, 1986.

Bennett, John G., et al. *The Spiritual Hunger of the Modern Child: A Series of Ten Lectures.* Charles Town, WV: Claymont Communications, 1984.

Bettelheim, Bruno. "The Importance of Play." *Atlantic Monthly*, March 1987.

___. *The Uses of Enchantment: The Meaning and Importance of Fairy Tales.* New York: Alfred A. Knopf, 1975.

Bettelheim, Bruno, and Karen Zeland. "Why Children Don't Like to Read." *Atlantic Monthly*, November 1981.

Black, Kathryn. *Mothering without a Map.* New York: Penguin Books, 2004.

Brazelton, T. Berry. *Infants and Mothers: Differences in Development.* New York: Dell, 1986.

___. *Working and Caring.* Reading, MA: Addison-Wesley, 1985.

Britz-Crecelius, Heidi. *Children at Play: Preparation for Life.* New York: Inner Traditions International, 1986. (A revised edition of this title is available. Please see the Recommended Resources on page 108.)

Cameron, Julia. *The Artist's Way: A Spiritual Path to Higher Creativity.* New York: Tarcher/Putnam, 1992.

Caplan, Mariana. *Untouched.* Prescott, AZ: Hohm Press, 1998.

Carey, Diana, and Judy Large. *Festivals, Family and Food.* Gloucestershire, UK: Hawthorn Press, 1982.

Carlgren, Frans. *Education Towards Freedom.* East Grinstead, UK: Lanthorn Press, 1976.

Carter, Robert. *The Tao and Mother Goose.* Wheaton, IL: Theosophical Publishing House, 1988.

Childs, Dr. Gilbert, and Sylvia Childs. *Your Reincarnating Child.* London: Rudolf Steiner Press, 1995.

Chukovsky, Kornei. *From Two to Five.* Berkeley: University of California Press, 1963.

Cooper, Stephanie, et al. *The Children's Year.* Gloucestershire, UK: Hawthorn Press, 1987.

Corda, Murshida Vera Justin. *Cradle of Heaven.* Lebanon Springs, NY: Omega Press, 1987.

Cordes, Colleen, and Edward Miller, eds. *Fool's Gold. A Critical Look at Computers in Childhood.* College Park, MD: Alliance for Childhood, 2003.

Cusick, Lois. *Waldorf Parenting Handbook.* Spring Valley, NY: St. George Publications, 1984. (A revised edition of this title is available. Please see the Recommended Resources on page 62.)

Darian, Shea. *Living Passages for the Whole Family: Celebrating Rites of Passage from Birth to Adulthood.* Phoenix, AZ: Gilead Press, 2008.

___. *Sanctuaries of Childhood: Nurturing a Child's Spiritual Life.* Phoenix, AZ: Gilead Press, 2011.

___. *Seven Times the Sun: Guiding Your Child Through the Rhythms of the Day.* Phoenix, AZ: Gilead Press, 2001 [1994].

Davy, Gudrun, and Bons Voors, eds. *Lifeways: Working with Family Questions.* Gloucestershire, UK: Hawthorn Press, 1983.

Eliot, Jane Winslow. *From Ring Around the Roses to London Bridge Is Falling Down.* New York: Rudolf Steiner School Press, 1982.

Elkind, David. *The Hurried Child.* New York: Alfred A. Knopf, 1984.

___. *Miseducation: Preschoolers at Risk.* New York: Alfred A. Knopf, 1987.

___. *The Power of Play.* Philadelphia: DaCapo Press, 2007.

Flinders, Carol Lee. *At the Root of This Longing: Reconciling a Spiritual Hunger and a Feminist Thirst.* San Francisco: HarperCollins, 1998.

Friedan, Betty. *The Feminine Mystique.* New York: Norton & Co., 1997 [1963].

___. *The Second Stage.* Cambridge, MA: Harvard University Press, 1998 [1981].

Gabert, Erich. *Punishment in Self-Education and the Education of the Child.* Forest Row, UK: Steiner Schools Fellowship Publications, 1972.

Glas, Norbert. *Conception, Birth, and Early Childhood.* Spring Valley, NY: Anthroposophic Press, 1972.

Glöckler, Michaela, and Wolfgang Goebel. *A Guide to Child Health.* Hudson, NY: Anthroposophic Press, 1984. (A revised edition of this title is available. Please see the Recommended Resources on page 279.)

Grunelius, Elizabeth. *Early Childhood Education and the Waldorf School Plan.* Englewood, NJ: Waldorf School Monographs, 1974.

Hahn, Herbert. *From the Well-Springs of the Soul.* Forest Row, UK: Rudolf Steiner Schools Fellowship, 1966.

Harwood, A. C. *The Recovery of Man in Childhood.* Spring Valley, NY: Anthroposophic Press, 1958.

Hassauer, Werner. *Die Geburt der Individualität.* Stuttgart, Germany: Verlag Urachhaus Johannes M. Mayer GmbH, 1984.

Hayda, Dzvinka. *Little Angel's Journey.* Warren, MI: Trillium Forest Press, 2008.

Hayes, Shannon. *Radical Homemakers.* Richmondville, NY: Left to Write Press, 2010.

Healy, Jane. *Endangered Minds: Why Children Can't Think and What We Can Do About It.* New York: Simon & Schuster, 1990.

___. *Failure to Connect: How Computers Affect Our Children's Minds—for Better and Worse.* New York: Simon & Schuster, 1998.

___. *Your Child's Growing Mind,* rev. ed. New York: Doubleday, 1994.

Heckmann, Helle. *Nøkken: A Garden for Children.* Silver Spring, MD: Waldorf Early Childhood Association, 1998.

Honeybloom, Shannon. *Making a Family Home.* Great Barrington, MA: Steiner-Books, 2010.

Hughes, Diana. "Fairy Tales: A Basis for Moral Education." *Ethics in Education* 6, no. 4 (March 1987): 10–14.

Hutchins, Eileen. "The Value of Fairy Tales and Nursery Rhymes." *Child and Man Extracts.* Sussex, UK: Steiner Schools Fellowship, n.d.

Jaffke, Freya. "About Painting and Human Development through Art." *Waldorf Kindergarten Newsletter,* Fall 1984.

___. *Toymaking with Children.* Edinburgh, UK: Floris, 1988.

___. *Work and Play in Early Childhood.* Hudson, NY: Anthroposophic Press, 1996. (A revised edition of this title is available. Please see the Recommended Resources on page 128.)

Karp, Harvey, MD. *The Happiest Toddler on the Block.* New York: Bantam Dell, 2003.

Knierim, Julius. *Quintenlieder: Music for Young Children in the Mood of the Fifth,* trans. Karen and Peter Klaveness. Fair Oaks, CA: Rudolf Steiner College Press, 2002.

König, Karl. *Eternal Childhood.* North Yorkshire, UK: Camphill Books, 1994.

___. *The First Three Years of the Child.* Spring Valley, NY: Anthroposophic Press, 1969.

Leboyer, Frederick, MD. *Birth without Violence.* New York: Alfred A. Knopf, 2009 [1975].

Lebret, Elisabeth. *Pentatonic Songs.* Toronto, Ontario: Waldorf School Association of Toronto, 1985.

Lenz, Freidel. *Celebrating the Festivals with Children.* Hudson, NY: Anthroposophic Press, 1986.

Liedloff, Jean. *The Continuum Concept.* Boston, MA: Addison-Wesley, 1993 [1975].

Long-Breipohl, Renate. *Supporting Self-directed Play in Steiner/Waldorf Early Childhood Education.* Spring Valley, NY: Waldorf Early Childhood Association of North America, 2010.

Louv, Richard. *Last Child in the Woods.* Chapel Hill, NC: Algonquin Books, 2008.

___. *The Nature Principle.* Chapel Hill, NC: Algonquin Books, 2011.

Masters, Brien, ed. *Rudolf Steiner Waldorf Education.* Spring Valley, NY: Steiner Schools Fellowship, 1986.

Meyer, Rudolf. *The Wisdom of Fairy Tales.* Edinburgh, UK: Floris Books, 1987.

Montagu, Ashley. *Touching.* New York: Columbia University Press, 1971.

Moore, Raymond, and Dorothy Moore. *Better Late Than Early.* New York: Reader's Digest Press, 1975.

___. *School Can Wait.* Provo, UT: Brigham Young University Press, 1979.

Müller, Brunhild. *Painting with Children.* Edinburgh, UK: Floris Books, 1987.

Neuschütz, Karin. *The Doll Book.* Burdett, NY: Larson Publications, 1982.

Olness, Karen N. "Little People, Images and Child Health." *American Journal of Clinical Hypnosis* 27, no. 3 (January 1985): 169–74.

O'Mara McMahon, Peggy. "An Ethic of Parenting." *Mothering,* Spring 1988.

Oppenheimer, Sharifa. *Heaven on Earth: A Handbook for Parents of Young Children.* Great Barrington, MA: SteinerBooks, 2006.

Patzlaff, Rainer, et al. *The Child from Birth to Three in Waldorf Education and Child Care.* Spring Valley, NY: Waldorf Early Childhood Association of North America, 2011.

Payne, Kim John. *Simplicity Parenting: Using the Extraordinary Power of Less to Raise Calmer, Happier, and More Secure Kids.* New York: Ballantine Books, 2009.

Pearce, Joseph Chilton. *Magical Child.* New York: E. P. Dutton, 1977.

___. *Magical Child Matures.* New York: Bantam, 1986.

Pritzker, Linda. *The Princess Who Wept Pearls: The Feminine Journey in Fairy Tales.* Boulder, CO: Self-published, 1998.

Querido, René. *Creativity in Education: The Waldorf Approach.* San Francisco: H.S. Dakin Company, 1985.

Rabuzzi, Kathryn Allen. *Motherself: A Mythic Analysis of Motherhood.* Bloomington: Indiana University Press, 1988.

Rosenberg, Marshall, PhD. *Nonviolent Communication: A Language of Life.* Encinitas, CA: PuddleDancer Press, 2003.

Russ, Johanne. *Clump-a-Dump and Snickle-Snack.* Spring Valley, NY: Mercury Press, n.d.

Russell, Rauld. *How to Do Wet-on-Wet Watercolor Painting and Teach Your Children.* Coos Bay, OR: The Iris, 1987.

___. "Wet-on-Wet Watercolor Painting." *Mothering,* Summer 1987.

Ryan, Regina Sara. *The Woman Awake.* Prescott, AZ: Hohm Press, 1998.

Salter, Joan. *The Incarnating Child.* Gloucestershire, UK: Hawthorn Press, 1987.

___. *Mothering with Soul.* Gloucestershire, UK: Hawthorn Press, 1998.

Sanders, Barry. *A Is for Ox: The Collapse of Literacy and the Rise of Violence in an Electronic Age.* New York: Pantheon Books, 1994.

Schmidt-Brabant, Manfred. *The Spiritual Tasks of the Homemaker.* London: Temple Lodge, 1996.

Scott, Anne. *The Laughing Baby.* South Hadley, MA: Bergin & Garvey, 1987.

Siegel, Richard. *The First Jewish Catalog.* Philadelphia, PA: Jewish Publication Society of America, n.d.

Smith, Susan. *Echoes of a Dream.* London, Ontario: Waldorf School Association of London, 1982.

Solter, Aletha Jauch. *The Aware Baby.* Goleta, CA: Shining Star Press, 1984.

___. *Exercises in Self-Awareness for New Parents.* Goleta, CA: Shining Star Press, 1984.

Stave, Uwe. "Reflections on Fever in Childhood." *Journal for Anthroposophy* 42 (Autumn 1985): 9–11.

Steiner, Rudolf. *The Arts and Their Mission.* Spring Valley, NY: Anthroposophic Press, 1964.

___. *The Cycle of the Year.* Spring Valley, NY: Anthroposophic Press, 1984.

___. *The Education of the Child.* London: Rudolf Steiner Press, 1965.

___. *The Essentials of Education.* London: Rudolf Steiner Press, 1948.

___. *The Four Temperaments.* Hudson, NY: Anthroposophic Press, 1987.

___. *Human Values in Education.* London: Rudolf Steiner Press, 1971.

___. *The Interpretation of Fairy Tales.* London: Rudolf Steiner Press, 1971.

___. *An Introduction to Waldorf Education.* Spring Valley, NY: Anthroposophic Press, 1985.

___. *The Kingdom of Childhood.* London: Rudolf Steiner Press, 1974.

___. *Lectures to Teachers.* London: Rudolf Steiner Press, 1974.

___. *Pneumatosophy.* New York: Anthroposophic Press, n.d.

___. *Practical Advice for Teachers.* London: Rudolf Steiner Press, 1970.

___. *Practical Course for Teachers.* London: Rudolf Steiner Press, 1937.

___. *Prayers for Mothers and Children.* London: Rudolf Steiner Press, 1983.

___. *The Renewal of Education.* Forest Row, UK: Steiner Schools Fellowship Publications, 1981.

___. *The Roots of Education.* London: Rudolf Steiner Press, 1968.

___. *Signs and Symbols of the Christmas Festival.* Spring Valley, NY: Anthroposophic Press, 1969.

___. *Soul Economy and Waldorf Education.* Spring Valley, NY: Anthroposophic Press, 1986.

___. *The Spiritual Ground of Education.* London: Rudolf Steiner Press, 1947.

___. *Study of Man.* London: Anthroposophic Press, 1947.

___. *Swiss Teachers' Course.* London: The Library of the Anthroposophical Society in Great Britain, n.d.

Strauss, Michaela. *Understanding Children's Drawings.* London: Rudolf Steiner Press, 1978.

Stressor, Michael. *The Jewish Holidays.* New York: Harper & Row, 1985.

Thevenin, Tine. *Mothering and Fathering: The Gender Differences in Child Rearing.* Garden City Park, NY: Avery Publishing, 1993.

Thoman, Evelyn, and Sue Browder. *Born Dancing.* New York: Harper and Row, 1987.

Udo de Haes, Daniel. *The Young Child.* Spring Valley, NY: Anthroposophic Press, 1986.

Uphoff, James, and June Gilmore. "Pupil Age at School Entrance—How Many Are Ready for Success?" *Educational Leadership* (September 1985), pp. 86–90.

van Bentheim, Tineke, et al. *Caring for the Sick at Home.* Edinburgh, UK: Floris Books, 1987.

von Heydebrand, Caroline. "The Child at Play." In *Education as an Art: Rudolf Steiner and Other Writers*, ed. Paul Allen. Blauvelt, NY: SteinerBooks/Multimedia Publishing, 1970.

___. "The Child When He Paints." In *Education as an Art: Rudolf Steiner and Other Writers*, ed. Paul Allen. Blauvelt, NY: SteinerBooks/Multimedia Publishing, 1970.

___. *Childhood: A Study of the Growing Soul*. London: Anthroposophic Publishing Co., 1946.

von Kügelgen, Helmut. "Fairy Tale Language and the Image of Man." *Waldorf Kindergarten Newsletter*, Fall 1986.

Watson, Clyde. *Catch Me & Kiss Me & Say It Again*. New York: Philomel Books, 1978.

White, Burton L. *Educating the Infant and Toddler*. Lexington, MA: D.C. Heath and Co., 1988.

___. *The First Three Years of Life*. New York: Prentice Hall, 1985.

Whitfield, Miriam. *Fairy Stories . . . Why, When, How*. Boulder, CO: The Juniper Tree, 1986.

Wiboltt, Anne-Marie Fryer. *Cooking for the Love of the World*. Benson, NC: Goldenstone Press, 2009.

Winn, Marie. *The Plug-In Drug*. New York: Viking, 1985. (A revised edition of this title is available. Please see the Recommended Resources on page 280.)

Zahlingen, Bronja. "The Pedagogical Value of Marionette and Table Puppet Shows for the Small Child." *Waldorf Kindergarten Newsletter*, Fall 1982.

___. *Plays for Puppets and Marionettes*. Silver Spring, MD: Acorn Hill Children's Center, 1983.

zur Linden, Wilhelm. *When a Child Is Born*. New York: Thorsons Publishers, 1984. (A revised edition of this title is available. Please see the Recommended Resources on page 279.)

INDEX

on premature
    development, 258–60
on Raphael, 72
on relationship-based
    care, 240
on religion, 276–77
on reverence, 277–78
on rhythm, 111, 216
on right and wrong,
    135–36
on the senses, 59
on sleep, 66
on soccer, 219–20
on sound quality, 70
on temperaments,
    272–74
on thinking, 56, 57
on toys, 105
waking-up verse by,
    122–23
on walking, 48–49
Stories
    animals in, 182–83
    curative, 188
    imagination and,
        178–79
    importance of, 180–83
    from parents'
        childhood, 182
    resources for, 187,
        188, 189
    See also Fairy tales
Stranger anxiety, 47
Strauss, Michaela and
    Hans, 191–95, 207
Structure. See Rhythm
Sudden infant death
    syndrome (SIDS),
    67–68
Sugar, avoiding, 118
Summer (Meyerkort), 127
"Super baby syndrome,"
    221, 225
Suzuki method, 220
Swimming classes, 89, 94
Swings, 104

T
Talking
    ability of, 52–53
    to children, 51–52, 57
Tantrums, 98–99
The Tao and Mother
    Goose (Carter), 188
Teachers
    children as, 281
    parents as first, 18
    role of, 239–42
    training for, 242, 254
Teething, 46
Television
    average hours viewing,
        261, 264
    effects of, on child
        development, 95,
        179–80, 260–64
    language development
        and, 52–53
    limiting, 260–61, 264,
        265
    media history for,
        257–58
    pediatricians'
        recommendations
        on, 261
    resources for, 280
Temperaments, 161,
    272–74
Tetanus, 268
Theory of Colours
    (Goethe), 197
Thevenin, Tine, 20, 90, 161
Thinking
    creative, 258, 259
    emergence of, 56–57
    See also Cognitive
        development
This Is the Way We Work-
    a-Day (Schunemann),
    109, 128
Tickling, 46–47
Time, children's orientation
    to, 13

Toddlers
    activities with, 107–8
    change and, 97
    classes for, 94
    cognitive development
        of, 56–57
    encouraging balanced
        development of,
        92–96
    environment for, 103–6
    equipment for, 107
    imagination and, 102
    inner life of, 54–55
    inquisitiveness of, 92–93
    language development
        of, 99–101
    movements of, 104,
        164, 165
    negative behavior by,
        60–61, 96–99
    physical development of,
        93–94
    play and, 102
    sense of self in, 60–62
    social development
        of, 93
    television and, 95,
        179–80, 260–64
    toilet training, 155–56
    toys for, 104–7, 109
    warmth and, 71
Toilet training, 155–56
Torso, control of, 44–45
Touch, sense of, 66–67
A Toy Garden, 109,
    190, 208
Toymaking with Children
    (Jaffke), 109, 188,
    189, 208
Toys
    appraising, 173
    arranging, 174
    for babies, 78, 79,
        87–89, 91
    changing, 265
    computers as, 258
    excessive number of,
        172–73